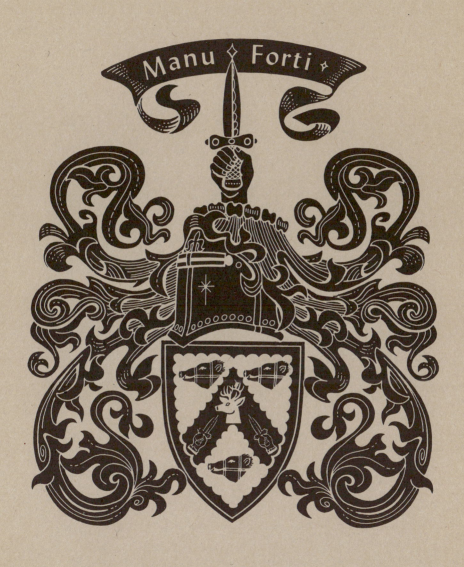

Manu ✦ Forti ✦

Highlights in the Life of President David O. McKay

Carolyn Hunt

Highlights
in the Life of
President David O. McKay

by
Jeanette McKay Morrell

Published by Deseret Book Company
Salt Lake City, Utah 1971

Library of Congress No. 66-30512

SBN No. 87747-108-8

Copyright
1966
Deseret Book Company

Revised and Enlarged Edition 1971

Printed by

DESERET NEWS PRESS

in the United States of America

The handsome portrait of President David O. McKay was painted by Alvin L. Gittins, professor of art at the University of Utah. It hangs in the central foyer of the Pioneer Memorial Theatre on the University of Utah campus in Salt Lake City.

Foreword

In these days of self-searching, it is significant to know what goes into the making of a man, and from what kind of home and family came one of this generation's most beloved men—a prophet of God and a revered leader of his people.

Here in *Highlights in the Life of President David O. McKay,* Jeanette McKay (Mrs. Joseph R.) Morrell has intimately told some of the family life, the love and loyalty, the sorrows, the trials, the teachings, the reverence and respect, the fun-loving recreation, the happiness of the home from which came President McKay. And then she has recounted but a few of the outstanding accomplishments of this most remarkable man, who was spiritual leader of nearly three million people, and President of The Church of Jesus Christ of Latter-day Saints.

Of President McKay it cannot be said that "a prophet hath no honour in his own country." (John 4:44) Loved, trusted, admired, and looked to for leadership by men and women of his own faith, and by many others, worldwide, he was also loved and revered by his family, his closest associates and lifelong friends, and by those who know him nearest to his beloved Huntsville home.

As a measurement for our own times, as a perspective of other times, and as a source of counsel and comparison, and as a personal picture and appraisal, this book by a beloved sister shares childhood memories, and highlights of the later years, with an insight into the life of the man who said: "No other success can compensate for failure in the home."

Richard L. Evans

Acknowledgments

To my dear husband, Dr. Joseph R. Morrell, for encouragement and valuable assistance during the compiling of this biography.

To Miss Clare Middlemiss for her generosity in making available her collection of more than two hundred volumes of diaries, recorded during her thirty-one years as President McKay's secretary.

To Alva H. Parry and Wm. James Mortimer of Deseret Book Company for their helpful suggestions in editing and arranging the material in this volume.

To all who have contributed in any way to the material used in this brief history of one whose life and accomplishments could fill many volumes, I express deep appreciation.

Jeanette McKay Morrell

Preface

Few men in this dispensation have had so profound an effect on the growth and progress of The Church of Jesus Christ of Latter-day Saints as has President David O. McKay.

After becoming President of the Church in 1951, President McKay effectively led the dynamic growth of the Kingdom of God on earth. Through increased missionary efforts directed by him the membership of the Church more than doubled. There was rapid increase in wards, stakes, branches, and missions. Thousands of new chapels and five new temples were erected. Great programs of home teaching and family home evenings were instituted, and correlated Priesthood programs were taught wherever units of the Church are established.

President McKay was always concerned with the growth and development of the members of the Church, and in preparing them for the responsibilities and challenges which he saw ahead for the Church and the world. His vision extended far beyond today's needs, though he daily gave guidance and direction for the Church's immediate problems. His counsel, his concern, and his desire were for continued growth through effective development of the individual testimonies of all members of the Church.

As his sister, I witnessed this great man grow to the full stature of a Prophet of God. I was close to him in family problems. I attended the University of Utah while he was also a student there. I taught at the Weber Stake Academy while he was its principal. I also served on the Weber Stake Sunday School board while he was in the superintendency. I saw him overcome worldly things to fulfill the full measure of his creation. I shared many of his joys and sorrows, and knew part of the weight that he bore so well as a leader among his people.

Because I know he was a powerful witness of the divinity of Jesus Christ and a true emissary of the Living God, it has been my desire to share with others some highlights in my brother's life as I viewed it.

This book, *Highlights in the Life of President David O. McKay,* is by no means a complete biography. Such a presentation would require many volumes, and is yet to be written. This is just as the title says—some of the highlights in the life of a great man.

I offer it to the world as my own testimony that the Spirit of God moved upon President McKay and enabled him to lead the only true and living Church upon the face of the earth.

Throughout his ministry, President McKay testified to all men everywhere that only through obedience to the teachings of the Lord Jesus Christ can this world know peace and happiness. It is my profound desire that this sketch of his life and testimony may be an inspiration to all who read it to forsake the things of the world and seek first the Kingdom of God.

Jeanette McKay Morrell

Ogden, Utah
1970

Contents

This striking portrait of President David O. McKay
taken by Salt Lake photographer Ida Wilcox reveals
the strength of character and the depth
of soul which have always characterized the life of
this great man.

Chapter I

Ancestry

Pride in their clan is a feature which has marked all who share in the ancient traditions of great Scottish names. Though they are now scattered throughout the world there is still a brotherhood within the clan or name, and this links all Scots together, particularly because this pride of name has never depended on wealth or rank.

The Clan McKay or MacKay developed in the northern highlands of Scotland early in the Fourteenth Century and had its roots in the old royal houses of McEth and Moray.

The first historic chief of the clan was Angus Dubh, who lived from 1380 to 1429. Early in the 1400's, Donald, Lord of the Isles, claimed the Earldom of Ross and invaded Sutherland, the territory of the MacKays. He was opposed by Angus and those of the Clan MacKay, but he succeeded in defeating them and taking Angus captive. Later they became reconciled and Angus married Elizabeth, daughter of his captor, with whom he received many lands. Angus was killed in 1429 at the time of the Battle of Drumnacoub.

In 1626 Sir Donald MacKay, then chief of the clan, raised an army of 3,000 men for service in Bohemia, and afterwards in Denmark. Because of his distinguished service, Donald was created Lord Reay in 1628, with the remainder of his male heirs continuing to claim the name and arms of MacKay. The major portion of the MacKay lands were sold during this period to pay the cost of maintaining and transporting the men whom Lord Reay had recruited for foreign service. The remainder of the MacKay country was sold in 1829 to the house of Sutherland.

One of the fascinating traditions of the clans was the claiming of coats of arms as identifying symbols. These symbols always included a crest, and early clan chiefs began taking this crest and forming it on a metal plate. The metal plates were given by the chiefs to their followers to wear as badges, and this became a symbol of kinship with the clan. The badge was affixed to the clansman's clothing by a strap and buckle and when not in use the strap and buckle were coiled around the crest badge.

The modern conventional representation of the old metal plate crest badge takes the form of the chief's crest encircled by a metal strap and buckle and the chief's motto cut or engraved on the strap. This is the only form in which a clansman is permitted to display his chief's crest. Its use, in the correct and approved manner, indicates that the wearer is a kinsman of the chief whose crest is thus shown.

The McKay crest badge is a dexter cubit arm holding erect a dagger in pale. The motto inscribed is "manu forti" literally meaning "with a strong hand."

Though this motto was claimed for the clan by its historic chieftain, no more appropriate description could be found today to portray the life and works of a modern kinsman, David O. McKay, the President of The Church of

The McKay Crest

Jesus Christ of Latter-day Saints. Throughout his life he has exhibited the "strong hand" of leadership, and for more than half a century as a general authority of the Church his has been a strong and valiant hand in carrying out the work of the Lord.

President McKay has always been proud of his name, and of the ancient traditions in which it is steeped. His trips to Scotland, his frequent mention of this land of his ancestry, and the love he has exhibited for the people and their culture are evidences of this pride.

Indicative of the ancient nature of the McKay name is this excerpt from a poem, *The True-Born Englishman,* written by Daniel Defoe, who lived from 1661 to 1731. He wrote:

> Even Scotland, too, her elder glory shows
> Her Gordon's, Hamiltons, and her Monroes,
> Douglases, MacKays, and Grahams, names well known,
> Long before ancient England knew her own.

On his mother's side, President McKay's ancestry includes the names of Evans and Powell, which date back into the ancient history of Wales, and are as prominent there as are the McKays in Scotland. Both his paternal and maternal ancestry were known for their deep religious convictions.

Ellen Oman McKay, grandmother of President McKay, was one of ten children—seven girls and three boys. Her father, David Oman, for whom President McKay was named, was the manager of the estate of the Earl of Caithness at Thurso. He was a widower with two small sons when he married Isabella Sutherland, and they became the parents of one son and seven daughters.

When the two older sons were grown, they went to India to live. They later sent for their younger brother, and the three became successful owners of a large tea plantation. Their families were reared in India, but were sent to London for their education.

The seven daughters remaining in Scotland were given the best education available. They all sang in the Presbyterian Church choir, and were popular among the young people of the church and in Thurso.

A word picture of their home and the town of Thurso was given some years ago by Isabella McKay Edward, a grand niece of Ellen Oman McKay. Mrs. Edward visited the area before leaving Scotland to make her home in Ogden, Utah.

She wrote:

> As I walked toward Thurso, I was looking for the cottage in which Ellen Oman McKay lived at one time. I soon located it some distance off the highway, with a background of lovely shrubs hanging with red berries. The path leading to the house was flagstone, and the surrounding country was beautiful. There were yellow corn fields, green turnip fields, and, most striking of all, were the moorelands covered with gleaming purple heather. Hawthorne hedges divided the small farm, and grew along the roadsides.
>
> Thurso is a picturesque town with its Castle and Lodge, an academy, grade schools, and several churches. One walks down the main street, unaware of the beautiful view that lies just ahead. There is a high wall with an arch, and on stepping through this, the scenery takes one's breath; the shining white sand, the waves rolling in with their white caps, and the Victoria Walk leading around east to the Port of Thurso, which is the safest and most sheltered port of the north for all kinds of shipping.
>
> It was from here that the British hero, Lord Kitchner, sailed on that fateful night in June, 1916, when his ship, the Hampshire, was blown up by a submarine a few miles out. A spot not for from here marks the German cemetery, Scappa Flow, where the German fleet was sunk.

This part of Scotland, with its wild scenery, is a favorite one for tourists, and especially for artists who never tire of the stormy Pentland Firth. The castle and lodge are open to visitors now, since the airport has been completed.

It was in this picturesque setting that Ellen Oman met and married William McKay, a contractor from Strathnaver, Sutherlandshire. They built their home in Thurso, and it was here that their family, three daughters and two sons, were born to them. Their children were Isabella, Williamena, Katherine, Isaac, and David.

The year 1850 was a momentous one for the William McKay family, for it was in this year that they learned of the restored gospel of Jesus Christ from missionaries of The Church of Jesus Christ of Latter-day Saints. William and Ellen embraced the new faith with great enthusiasm, and on November 3, 1850, they, and their three oldest children entered the waters of baptism. The whole family became enthusiastic workers in their new faith.

Ellen was greatly surprised and grievously disappointed when her parents and sisters refused to accept the gospel as she explained it to them. Though they never destroyed the books and tracts which she gave them to read, they refused to accept any of the doctrine which she tried to teach them. However, this rebuff from her family failed to cool Ellen's ardor, and when her husband was ordained an elder in 1852 and became the branch president in Thurso, she was right beside him in proclaiming the tenets of the Church.

Along with many other saints, William and Ellen felt the urge to emigrate to the headquarters of the Church in Utah, and so began making their preparations. When the time came for them to leave Scotland, Ellen's family pleaded with her to desist from what they termed "this mad adventure." The Presbyterian minister visited her, at the request of her family, and spent many hours arguing against her leaving. He left her home saying, "I am sorry to lose such a strong Christian member." The Earl and Countess of Caithness added their pleas for her to remain, but Ellen Oman McKay knew she was right, and nothing could change her conviction.

After William had disposed of the property and made the arrangements to leave Scotland, the children developed measles and their departure had to be postponed. A friend of the family took advantage of the delay and asked William to lend him sufficient money to take his family to the United States, promising to return the amount when the McKays arrived in New York with a later company.

The McKay family finally left Liverpool on Sunday, May 4, 1856 on the sailing vessel Thornton, commanded by a Captain Collins. They reached New York on June 4, and to their great disappointment could find no trace of the friend to whom they had loaned their money. They found themselves in a new country with no means to continue the journey to Utah.

Undaunted, William and Ellen called the children together and held a family council. With the advice of the president of the New York branch of the Church, William and the two boys, Isaac, sixteen, and David, twelve, found work, the father going to Connecticut, Isaac to New Jersey, and David to upstate New York. Ellen and her three small daughters rented an unfurnished upstairs apartment with only their bedding and the few household articles they had been able to carry on the ship.

Since the family observed the word of wisdom, there was an accumulation of tea which had been issued to them on the ship. Ellen used this to exchange for bread and groceries which lasted them until they had earned their first money.

After living two years in the east, the McKays were ready for the journey west. They traveled as far as Iowa, where they remained for another year to prepare for the long journey across the plains. They moved from Iowa City with a company of ten wagons to Florence, where they joined the company of Captain James Brown, which headed westward on June 13, 1859.

As the family was leaving, word reached Ellen that the company included a lame woman and her daughter who had no means of travel. Ellen immediately offered the woman her own place in the wagon, and walked the entire distance to Salt Lake City, where they arrived on Monday, August 29, 1859.

It would seem to be more than coincidence that the experiences of President McKay's mother's family in Wales paralleled those of the McKays in Scotland.

His maternal grandfather, Thomas Evans, was born in Glamorganshire, South Wales, in October of 1812, a son of Edward and Jennette Powell Evans. His forebears included many professional people, among whom were lawyers, ministers, and teachers.

President McKay's maternal grandmother, Margaret (Peggy) Powell, daughter of Thomas and Ann Lewis Powell, was born July 2, 1813, in Brecknockshire, South Wales. The family members were devout adherents to the Methodist faith.

Margaret Powell and Thomas Evans were married March 27, 1837, and established their home in Cofen Coed, near Merthyr Tydfil, Glamorganshire, where their eleven children were born to them.

In 1850, the same year as the McKays embraced the gospel in Scotland, missionaries contacted the Evans family in South Wales. They responded to the gospel message, and were baptized in May, 1850. Because of his baptism, Thomas was disinherited by his family and had no further contact with family members before his death in Ogden, Utah, May 25, 1877. Since that time some descendants who came to the the United States, but remained in the east, have exchanged visits with those in Utah.

Thomas Evans was ordained an elder by William Richards, and later became president of the branch in which he lived. With his wife and children he made plans to emigrate to Utah, and on May 25, 1856 the family sailed for America on the packet ship *Horizon*, arriving in Boston harbor, June 30. They immediately boarded a train for Iowa City, arriving there July 8, 1856.

The Evans family remained in Iowa three years, and after securing wagons, teams, and an extra cow to supply them with milk, they left Florence, June 7, 1859 in the private company of Philip H. Buzzard, arriving in Salt Lake City, August 24, 1859.

Thus, these two families, living in different parts of the British Isles, were baptized in the same year, sailed for the United States during the month of May, 1856, and reached America about the same time. The McKays remained in New York two years and Iowa one year, while the Evans family spent three years in Iowa. Both families arrived in Utah during August, 1859, but neither was conscious of the other until they met in Ogden.

The Evans family remained in Salt Lake City only about two weeks before they decided to settle in Ogden. They purchased property that is now between Adams and Madison Avenues and 28th and 30th Streets. Here they built a temporary log cabin and later a four-room rock house. This was a comfortable and quite elaborate house for the time, and was occupied by family members continuously until 1951 when it was replaced by an apartment house built by a grandson, Thomas Edward Gibbons.

David McKay, a lad of fifteen, saw Jennette Evans as she sat on the tongue of the Evans' wagon shortly after the family arrived in Ogden. He said he could not forget the large, brown eyes under her pink sunbonnet. She became one of the most beautiful and popular young women in Ogden, and a girl in whom David McKay showed much interest. The two fell deeply in love, and David succeeded in convincing her parents that they should be married, even though she was not yet eighteen. The marriage was performed by Apostle Wilford Woodruff on April 9, 1867 in the Endowment House in Salt Lake City.

Prior to his marriage David had lived with his family in Huntsville, Weber County, where his father had taken up farming. Father William, David and his brother all had their own farms by the time of David's marriage. The father had large herds of cattle and sheep from which he supplied his meat market in Ogden. The family lived in a log cabin, with David's sister Williamena keeping house for the family. Even as a young man David was active in the religious affairs of the community. Indicative of his diligence was the discovery of his name on a list of builders who erected the old Huntsville school and chapel in 1866. When the old rock structure was torn down in 1934, the cornerstone was removed and a sealed jar was found which contained the following:

"Huntsville, Weber County, Utah Territory, United States of America, July 4, 1866. The following named persons, members of The Church of Jesus Christ of Latter-day Saints, agree to assist in building a house in Huntsville, wherein to worship God and educate their children." Then followed a list of names, including that of David McKay. This was nearly a year before his marriage.

The parents of President David O. McKay
David McKay and Jennette Evans McKay

11

After claiming Jennette Evans as his bride, David settled in a log cabin in Huntsville where he and his wife commenced life as pioneers. Indians came frequently to the village, and David and Jennette tried to follow Brigham Young's counsel to feed them rather than fight with them. They were always welcomed as friends at the McKay cabin.

At one time a large group of Indians visited the Huntsville area, bringing some concern to the townspeople. The *Deseret News* indicated that the party included seven chiefs of the Shoshones, accompanied by about 1,000 of their men, women, and children. They arrived on a Thursday, and made their camp one mile west of the settlement. On Sunday the chiefs attended the meetings of the Church. President Francis A. Hammond asked for a donation of food to be brought the next day to the public square, and the Indians were invited as an entire party to come and receive the gifts from the townspeople. The Indians came, singing and dancing, and concluded their performance with a sham battle. They were given four beeves, nine sheep, several sacks of flour, and from fifty to seventy-five bushels of potatoes, carrots, beets, and turnips. Such visits were not uncommon in Huntsville, but the Indians generally came in smaller groups.

On one occasion a young Indian brave decided that pretty Jennette Evans McKay would make a good bride for him. He came to the cabin one morning while she was washing clothes, and startled her with the exclamation, "You be my squaw!" She grabbed a wet towel from the washtub, struck the surprised Indian in the face, and ran to the room where Grandfather McKay was sleeping. As soon as the Indian realized that she was not alone in the cabin he hurried to his horse and disappeared.

During the months that followed Jennette was always a little nervous when Indians approached the cabin. Although she fed a great many of them she always said she was relieved when they were on their way back to camp.

Life continued happily for the newly-weds in their log cabin, and two daughters were born there before the front part of the rock house, now known as "The Old Home," was completed. Margaret was born January 22, 1869, and Ellena, May 22, 1870. It was a happy day for the young family when they moved into the larger and more comfortable rock home. It was in this home that President David O. McKay was born on September 8, 1873.

Chapter 2

President McKay's Home Town

*H*untsville, where President McKay was born in 1873, is situated in beautiful Ogden Valley about thirteen miles east of Ogden City. The Huntsville of President McKay's youth was an industrious, growing community with homes clustered around the church, school, post office, general store, and park. From this hub of community life extended out in every direction the farms that sustained the lives of the people.

The community was an independent commonwealth, for each family owned its own home, with ample acreage for a good sized vegetable garden, fruit trees, and attractive shrubbery. Each lot also had its barnyard with horses, cows, pigs, sheep, chickens, and frequently ducks and turkeys. Hay stacks were in evidence, along with graneries for wheat and feed grains. There were also dirt cellars for storage of potatoes and other vegetables during the winter months, along with basements where butter, eggs, and canned fruits were kept.

Each family was expected to provide the greater part

of its daily living requirements, including milk, butter, eggs, vegetables, wheat for grinding into flour, and meat. Each autumn the community butcher would make his rounds and the family would slaughter a pig to furnish ham, bacon, chops, and sausage. Often two or three families would combine in raising and slaughtering a beef for winter needs, each taking a half or their own portion. Lamb and veal were also popular meat dishes. Each home usually was equipped with a large meat grinder, fastened to a wooden bench, for the making of sausage, head cheese, and fagots.

Scraps of fat not used on the table were carefully saved for use in manufacturing soap. Waste tallow was used to make candles, and every kitchen included several molds for making candles. Many homes also boasted cheese presses, and an excellent quality cheese was made and properly aged to add to the food supply. The wooden churn, also a common household item, was the source of fresh butter and delicious buttermilk, always flecked with tiny pieces of golden butter.

As President McKay grew up in Huntsville the town's services included a blacksmith shop, tin shop, a shoemaker, a wooden shoe or clog maker, two dress makers, a tailor, a milliner, a cloth weaver, a carpet weaver, a printer, butcher, basket weaver, an artificial flower maker, a flour mill, and a saw mill. In addition there was a caterer who served wedding suppers and a man who had a special formula for smoking and curing hams and bacon.

Entertainment was usually simple and often combined with the necessities of family life. There were sewing bees at which a group of neighbors and friends were invited to tear or cut rags into strips, then sew and wind them into balls for the carpet weaver. At quilting parties, the quilt, having been pieced into a lovely design, was stretched on frames around which the women sat to use their skill in making tiny stitches back and forth through the lining and padding of wool, which required patience and dexterity. At the end of the day the quilt was bound and added to the store of bedding used during the cold, winter weather. At these parties the hostess always served luncheon and often "tea" during the afternoon, the latter usually consisting of a barley coffee, mint tea, or chocolate, with cookies or thin buttered slices of currant cake. There was usually some harmless gossip, but more often the conversation consisted of pioneer experiences, latest news from a husband or son away from home doing missionary work, or items of interest from the semi-weekly *Deseret News,* which was always more eagerly awaited than our daily newspapers of today.

A familiar man-about-town was the cow herder who came every morning on his trusty steed to drive the cows to the foothills to graze until the evening milking time when they were returned to their several barnyards.

Families also depended on their personal flocks of sheep for wool. At shearing time the wool would be washed thoroughly, and then carded into pads for quilts, or into rolls to be made into yarn at the spinning wheel for knitting socks, gloves, mittens, or sweaters.

One of the most difficult times of the year for mothers and older girls, and yet one of the most delightful occasions for youngsters, was threshing season. Each autumn, after the harvest was gathered, the old-fashioned threshing machines operated by horsepower would go from farm to farm to thresh the grain.

The threshing machines required from six to twelve men to keep them going, in addition to regular farm help. The crews spent from two days to a week at each farm, depending on the amount of grain. As neighbors pooled their efforts to help one another, the womenfolk did their part also. They were expected to provide three hearty meals a day, and only these women knew just how heartily the threshers could eat. But doing this for their husbands, brothers, and neighbors gave them a satisfaction in knowing that they had made their contribution toward the year's harvest and a winter's supply of wheat for flour and oats to feed the horses and other farm animals.

Young David grew up with all of the blessings of farm life. He learned how to work hard and how to enjoy the fruits of honest toil. As he grew into the responsibilities of the Aaronic Priesthood he learned how to keep busy with useful projects in the service of others. The Aaronic Priesthood boys were organized each winter, in addition to their regular meetings and Church duties, to go into the canyons and secure firewood.

The older boys would go into the canyons and bring the logs into town, and the younger boys assumed the responsibility of sawing, splitting, and piling the wood in the sheds until the supply was sufficient to carry the family through the coldest months. They also saw to it that plenty of wood was available for the widows and the wives of those away on missions.

After these mountain excursions, and days of strenuous work in the wood sheds, the Relief Society sisters would prepare banquets to which all the willing workers were invited.

Sundays in Huntsville were special days, and meetings and family visits provided a restful change from the hard work of the rest of the week. On Sunday mornings at 9:30, the bell in the old church tower would be rung, telling everyone that they had one-half hour to get ready for Sunday School. Then, just a few minutes before ten it would be rung again so that everyone could be seated in time for the opening exercises promptly at ten o'clock.

When illness came to any home the neighbors were soon

The historic Huntsville Ward Chapel, scene of President David O. McKay's early Church experiences. The building was dedicated July 8, 1883.

18

aware of it, and if it became serious the news spread through the entire town. A death in any family was mourned by all the townspeople, for they were all friends and many of them relatives. There were no florists in the town, but around every home there were flower gardens and from these could be made many bouquets to be placed on or around the casket by loving, sympathetic hands. During the winter months the blossoms came from window boxes and flower pots. David's mother always had one window box of carnations, and these, added to the more common garden flowers, made unusually lovely bouquets. On Memorial Day there were wild roses, larkspur, and other flowers in the fields and meadows to make appropriate wreaths or arrangements.

Like so many other pioneer farming communities, Huntsville's civic center was its old rock school house. In addition to serving its school functions five days a week, it was also the dance hall, theater, and concert hall. The stage was in the center of the building's west wing, with rooms on each side for storage of scenery and stage properties.

On every holiday the school was the scene of afternoon dancing parties for the children, and in the evening for adults. Dances were also held frequently on Friday evenings between holidays. During the winter months at least three plays were produced by the Home Dramatic Association, and more often than not David O. McKay was found in one of the leading roles.

Concerts gave local talent the opportunity to perform, and many excellent programs were produced by those in the community.

A fond remembrance of all who grew up in Huntsville were the ward sleighing parties. Many farmers owned bobsleds and teams of spirited horses, and these were sufficient to allow everyone in town to participate. These were gay, winter parties with sleigh bells ringing, and red-cheeked youngsters singing at the tops of their voices. After riding and singing, the groups would gather in different homes for hot suppers and evenings of games, unless a dancing party was scheduled at the school house.

Summers were times for strenuous work, but there was still opportunity for fun and recreation. When young David's father was made bishop in Huntsville he suggested that the farmers set aside Saturday afternoons for baseball, and after the noon meal all the youngsters in town hurried to the public square for this activity.

Frequently the time on Saturday afternoons was used for picnic excursions to the canyons or to the grove south of town. These activities usually ended with a huge bonfire around which there was singing and story telling.

Two special holidays in Huntsville were the Fourth and Twenty-Fourth of July. For these July celebrations a bowery was constructed in the southeast quarter of the public square. The townsfolk were awakened at daybreak by the firing of a cannon, and then serenaded by the town's brass band. After breakfast everyone witnessed a parade, which was always a credit to those in the community.

The meetings held in the bowery were always inspiring. On the Fourth of July they consisted of the reading of the Declaration of Independence, a patriotic oration, introduction of the individuals chosen to be the Goddess of Liberty and Uncle Sam, interspersed with band music and vocal selections. In the afternoons there were races with numerous prizes for the children, baseball games, and fireworks in the evening, followed by a dancing party in which both old and young took part.

Celebrations on the Twenty-Fourth of July were a repetition of this schedule, except the theme was always the pioneer heritage of the area.

As young David O. McKay grew to manhood in this town of the mountains he found peace, love, and neighborliness. Everyone knew everyone else, and friendships were formed which will always continue among those who were fortunate enough to participate in the joys and sorrows of this little village commonwealth.

Chapter 3

Early Experiences

*H*untsville, President McKay's birthplace, has always been an ideal spot for the rearing of families. Nestled at the foot of majestic mountains, it is near beautiful canyons with excellent fishing streams and camping grounds. Its farm lands yield bounteous crops, and its people are humble in their endeavors. Pine View Lake is nearby, and Ogden City, with its urban advantages, is only a short distance away.

David's birth was a momentous event in the McKay family, for he was the first son. He was ushered into the world by Mary Heathman Smith, lovingly known to those in the area as Grandma Smith. She was more than the ordinary midwife of her time, for she had received medical training in England and was prepared to go beyond the practice of obstetrics if her skill was required.

Young David's childhood was a happy one, and his pleasures were those which any child seeks. He owned a dog, a pony, pigeons, rabbits, and a magpie that he taught to talk. He was active in all the games known to youngsters of his day, and most important of all, he grew up in a home full of love, discipline and yet sympathetic understanding.

His first great sorrow came in 1880 when he was seven. It was in that year that his two older sisters became ill and died. Margaret the eldest, had contracted rheumatic fever and when school opened in the fall of 1879 she was too ill to attend classes. Since little was known about rheumatic fever at that time she grew steadily worse through the winter until death came on March 28, 1880. The grief of the family became more severe, however, when Ellena, the second daughter, developed pneumonia and died on April 1, the date of her sister's funeral. The grave, prepared for Margaret, was enlarged and the two were placed side by side, just as they had been during their brief lives of eleven and nine years.

It was just one year later that father David McKay received a call from the Church to do missionary work in Scotland. When the call came it brought much concern, for Jennette was expecting a child soon, and David was reluctant to leave her alone with the family, as well as the responsibilities of the farm. They had just recently made the last payment on the farm, and seemed to have within their grasp the fulfillment of their dreams and hopes to enlarge the house and furnish it. But now the acceptance of the mission call would mean postponement of everything.

There was really only one decision, and Jennette insisted that her husband accept the call and join the group of missionaries going to Scotland. Remembering the courage of her own mother, Jennette knew she was equal to any sacrifice, and bade her husband farewell on his long journey to the British Isles on April 19, 1881. On that day, David O. McKay's childhood came to an end, for his father had instructed him to "take care of Mama," and the responsibilities he assumed at that time were far beyond his eight years.

The new baby, a daughter, and the sixth child of the family, was born ten days after her father's departure, but the news of her birth did not reach him until he was settled in Scotland. Then, as always during his mission, the letter said ". . . everything at home is going smoothly and we are all well, and you must not worry about us." Many times during his absence there were serious problems to be solved, but their existence never reached him in the mission field. He received only encouraging reports of the baby's development, the wonderful help the two boys, David, and Thomas E., were giving, and of the great kindnesses of relatives, neighbors, and friends.

Before he left, Father McKay had arranged for a man to take the responsibility for the cattle and other heavy outside work. He came, bringing with him a yoke of oxen, which only became an additional barnyard worry. He had not been there long when he went away to visit distant relatives, leaving the oxen for young David to attend. One evening when David and his mother were feeding the animals in the barnyard, they came to the discouraging task of carrying sufficient hay to satisfy the huge bovines, who always seemed to eat faster than they could be supplied. With tears in his eyes, David hefted the heavy hay, and said to his mother, "Now, let's give them two large armfuls of hay and run to the house before they eat it."

In spite of the difficulties, Jennette kept her two sons, David O. and Thomas E. in school, and also taught them to assume part of the household duties, which they did willingly because it was "helping mama."

Family prayer was an established procedure in the McKay home, and when Jennette was left alone with her small family it seemed an ever more important part of the day's events. David was taught to take his turn at morning and evening prayers and learned the importance of the blessings of heaven in the home.

Brethren of the priesthood assisted in planting the spring crops, and the season proved to be a bounteous one for the McKay farm. Hay brought a good price, but grain prices dropped, and so the family was advised to keep that part of the harvest until prices were better. Jennette, at some sacrifice, stored the grain until spring when prices were higher than ever and she realized a generous return. She took comfort in an ample bank account at the end of the season.

Encouraged by their success, Jennette and her sons worked harder the next season and again enjoyed a profitable year. Their bank account increased until they felt justified in making the additions to the house which had previously been planned. The home in which they were living had been built by William Christy, and the missionary who had converted the McKay family in Scotland. By coincidence his name was William McKay, though he was not a relative. Unfortunately these brethren had moved from Huntsville, and so Jennette had to locate other builders to do the work. She found good help in the community, and the addition to the house was built without disclosing the work to David in Scotland. It was truly a joyous reunion when he returned in 1883 to find not only a fine young daughter but also the new home for which he had dreamed and planned so long.

Only a few months after he returned home, David McKay was called by the Church to be bishop of the Eden Ward. He assumed that calling on November 20, 1883, and served until March 29, 1885, when he was called to succeed Bishop Francis A. Hammond in the Huntsville Ward.

Bishop McKay's home was always welcome to visitors in Huntsville, and since the town had no hotel or restaurant, many travelers took advantage of the McKay hospitality. The table in the large dining room was always kept out at full length, and guest rooms were usually always occupied, especially on weekends. Young David met many general authorities and other Church leaders as they visited in his father's home. Patriarch John Smith was a frequent visitor, coming often to spend several weeks giving patriarchal blessings to members of the three wards in the valley. On one of these occasions, July 17, 1887, just a few weeks before his fourteenth birthday, David received his patriarchal blessing. After pronouncing the blessing, Patriarch Smith placed his hands on David's shoulders, and looking into his eyes said "My boy, you have something to do besides playing marbles." David went to the kitchen where his mother was preparing dinner and said, "If he thinks I'm going to stop playing marbles, he is mistaken." His wise mother set aside her meal preparation long enough to sit down with her son and explain what the white-haired patriarch really meant, though even she could not realize the full impact of the words that had been spoken, for among other things, the patriarch had said to young David:

> Brother David Oman McKay, thou art in thy youth and need instruction, therefore I say unto thee, be taught of thy parents the way of life and salvation, that at an early day you may be prepared for a responsible position, for the eye of the Lord is upon thee. . . . The Lord has a work for thee to do, in which thou shalt see much of the world, assist in gathering scattered Israel and also labor in the ministry. It shall be thy lot to sit in council with thy brethren and preside among the people and exhort the Saints to faithfulness.

It was a McKay family custom that the children were baptized on the day of their eighth birthday anniversary. When David's sister Ann was baptized in 1889, there were also three cousins and a friend who were baptized at the same time. As the group came from the swimming hole toward the house, they met Elders Richard Ballantyne, George Goddard, and William Willis, the general superintendency of the Church Sunday Schools. They had come to attend a Sunday School conference the following day, but were invited to assist with the confirmations of the young people who had just been baptized. That evening at family prayer in the McKay home Elder Goddard offered a prayer of gratitude that he had been permitted to witness these young people become members of the Church. The McKay children had often taken baptism as a matter of course, but as David and the others knelt in prayer with these brethren they were more impressed by its sacredness than they had ever been before.

Members of the Weber Stake presidency, Lewis W. Shurtliff, Charles F. Middleton, and Nels C. Flygare, were as well known in the McKay home as if they were relatives because of their regular visits to the ward. Stake officers of the auxiliary organizations also came regularly, and were always honored guests. Some of these included Jane S. Richards, Emily Shurtliff, Harriet Brown, Josephine West, Elizabeth Stanford, Aunt Rose Canfield, Harriet Woodmansee, and many others. Jennette McKay often wearied from so much entertaining, but she would always say to her family, "They always leave a blessing in our home, so we are happy to have them."

One of the happiest days in the McKay home was a visit from the First Presidency of the Church, President Wilford Woodruff and his counselors George Q. Cannon and Joseph F. Smith. As they sat around the table enjoying a fine meal, Ann was tending the young McKay baby, Morgan, in another room. After the meal she brought the baby into the living room. President Woodruff took the child in his arms and gave him a beautiful blessing. The experience was an in-

27

spiration to all present, and President Cannon remarked that it should be recorded and given to the boy when he was old enough to appreciate it.

An occasional visitor in the home was Elder Orson F. Whitney of the Council of the Twelve. On one of these visits Apostle Whitney composed one of his longest poems. In the evenings, around the large fireplace, he would entertain the family by reading his own poems and those of his favorite authors. After one of his visits to Huntsville he sent the McKays an autographed copy of his poems, which is still among the treasures of the Old Home.

It was in this environment that President McKay spent his boyhood years, though his life was far from being consistently serious. He enjoyed swimming, horseback riding, reading, baseball, dancing, and singing in the glee club in addition to his Church duties. In all of these activities he was known as an enthusiastic leader.

At the age of fifteen he was called as secretary of the Sunday School in the Huntsville Ward, and served from January 27, 1889 until August 20, 1893 when he was called to serve as a Sunday School teacher. Prior to that time he had served in the presidency of the deacons quorum when the duties of the deacons included keeping the chapel clean, seeing that chopped wood was always available for the chapel's stoves, and also going two by two to chop wood for the widows of the ward.

On one occasion as a youngster David accompanied his father to the canyon to get a load of timber to build a large barn. As his father would chop the large trees, David would hitch them to the single-trees and snake them down the mountainside to the wagon. Finding it necessary to spend the night in the mountains, David and his father made a bed of pine boughs and settled down for a well-earned sleep. During the darkness of the night David was awakened by the howls of coyotes and the crashing of bears through the brush near the camp. He was so frightened he nearly cried out, but hearing his father's even breathing he nestled up to him and knew instinctively that there was protection and security as long as he was near. So, under the stars, young David slept peacefully next to his father for the rest of the night. Such was the influence of loving security and understanding sympathy that David McKay gave to his family.

Christmas experiences in the Old Home were always joyous occasions. Perhaps the finest description of these days is contained in a letter written in 1938 by President McKay to his brother, Thomas E., who was at that time presiding in the Swiss-German Mission of the Church.

> Salt Lake City, Utah
> December 12, 1938
>
> My Dear Brother and Playmate, Thomas E.,
>
> I went to Huntsville the other day and visited the Old Home. It was a typical wintery day, so you can easily imagine how cold the rooms were in which no fires were burning, and in which none had been for weeks. The house was just like a large refrigerator.
>
> There were a few things which I wanted to do so I threw your old coonskin coat over my shoulders, and soon felt warm and comfortable. For a few moments I strolled leisurely from room to room, and, being in a reminiscent mood, I let my mind wander at will down the lanes of memory. I saw "Tommy" and "Dadie" go up stairs to bed, and felt the tender touch of the dearest, sweetest mother that ever lived as she tenderly tucked the bed-clothes around her two roguish boys and gave them good-night kisses.
>
> Again it was Christmas Eve. Our stockings having been hung where Santa couldn't help but see them, we lay half expecting to hear the jingle of the sleigh bells announcing the approach of good old St. Nick to the chimney top—sleep came tardily, but finally the sandman succeeded in closing our eyes.

Christmas morning. I can see those boys creeping down the stairs before daybreak—no electric switch to press and flood the room with light; no flashlight at hand. They didn't even light the old kerosene lamp. Step by step they groped their way in the dark, and sought the nail (or chair) on which each had hung respectively his empty stocking. Who can ever forget the thrill of that first touch of the stocking filled with Santa's treasures! Apple in the toe, sticks of red and white candy protruding from the top, and trinkets and presents hidden in between! Perhaps a trumpet stuck out with the candies; but the drum and sled were standing near by.

The air in the room was cold even though the last embers in the kitchen were still smouldering—evidence, if the boys had stopped to think, that father and mother had sat up late enough to welcome St. Nick to our house.

Soon the girls were awake also, and the lamp was lit—then the "oh's" and the "ah's," and the medley of sounds of drums, jewsharp, harmonica, and music box!

As the sun came smiling over those snow-capped mountains, he turned the frost into diamonds that sparkled from the leafless trees and seemed to dance on the twelve-inch blanket of pure white snow.

Then came the playmates with their merry cry "Christmas Gift."

In the afternoon the children's dance! (One of those boys danced with a sweet little girl eleven successive times!) Oh the romance of childhood!

Chores—evening shadows, supper and bed, and another Christmas was gone. Why, to childhood, is Christmas day so short, and the next far away?

Christmas again, anticipated by the trip up South Fork to get our own Christmas tree from the hillside. They were older then, those boys, but their stockings still were hung, and good old Santa never failed to fill them.

Summer time and the swimming hole in Spring Creek; baseball on the "square." Boys and girls strolling "across the Creek," over on the knoll plucking flowers—daisies, blue bells, and the modest forget-me-nots, then leisurely back to town where we played croquet—parlor games in the evening where we had to redeem the forfeits!

Later came school and missions, yet still the tender ties that radiated from a devoted father and loving mother ever pulled us back to the Old Home, the dearest, sweetest spot on earth.

It is only an old country home, but no palace was ever filled with truer love and devotion on the part of parents, brothers, and sisters, than those which pervaded the hearts of the loved ones in that family circle.

Hanging your coat in its accustomed place, I walked out of the front door; as the night-latch clicked, I thought it might have been the click of the lid of a treasure chest that held the wealth of memories that no money could buy.

Well, my brother and pal of youthful days, I just wanted you to share with me this glimpse of happy memories, and to say as the Yuletide now approaches, my heart is full of loving wishes to you, that you and yours may enjoy the happiest Christmas ever, and that the New Year may come laden with happiness and joy supreme.

After completing the eighth grade in the Huntsville school David attended Weber Stake Academy in Ogden. During this time he lived at the home of his Grandmother Evans, and her old rock home on Twenty-eighth Street became a second home to him. He remained at the Academy two years and then returned to Huntsville as a teacher in his own boyhood school.

By this time, David, Thomas E., and two of the sisters, Jeanette and Ann, were ready for advanced schooling at the University of Utah, but the limited farm income of father McKay was too little to meet the demand. Fortunately, around that time Grandmother Evans made a gift to each of her three living children of $2,500 each. This seemed like a small fortune at the time. David's mother, recipient of this gift, was urged by her brother and sister to invest her money in stocks or bonds for future security. In her own tender way she replied to them, "Every cent of this goes into the education of our children." Even though they economized in every possible way, the four years these young people spent at the University would have been impossible without their mother's willingness to sacrifice for them.

David was graduated as president of his class at the University in 1897. He also played as a member of the first football team to win high honors for the U.

The University days were important ones to David for it was during this time that he met Emma Ray Riggs, who later became his beloved wife. When they first met, David was dating a beautiful classmate, and Ray was engaged to a fine, young man in the business world. Their real romance did not begin until several years later when David became principal of the Weber Stake Academy and she was teaching at the Madison School in Ogden.

While at the University David also became acquainted with Stephen L Richards, a man with whom he enjoyed a life-long companionship, including service together in the General Superintendency of the Sunday Schools, the Council of the Twelve, and the First Presidency of the Church. The young McKays attending the University spent many pleasant evenings together in the beautiful Richards home in Salt Lake.

Following his graduation from the University, David made plans for a teaching career and had his work all planned when he received a letter calling him to do missionary work in Great Britain. At first he was concerned about the call because it meant changing all his well-made plans. But in his family he realized that no one had ever refused a call to work in any capacity in the Church, and even though the decision meant his own plans had to be set aside, he accepted the call and prepared for his two years as a missionary.

When the call came to David, the McKay household consisted of four brothers and four sisters, and his leaving was the first break in the family circle. While all the family

The David McKay family in 1897 prior to David O. McKay's first mission.
Seated, left to right, are Bishop David McKay, Wm. Monroe McKay,
Katherine McKay, Morgan Powell McKay, Elizabeth McKay, Jennette Evans
McKay. Standing, left to right, are Jeanette McKay, David Oman McKay,
Thomas Evans McKay and Ann McKay. This historic photo was taken by
C. R. Savage of Salt Lake City when the four children standing in the
rear were students at the University of Utah.

was proud of his worthiness and willingness to go, there was
some sadness at his parting. The distance from the British
Isles seemed great, but he had received a blessing and setting
apart for his new work, and he knew that he would have
the prayers of his parents, brothers, and sisters, and so he
bade them farewell knowing that all would be well with
those at home as well as with him.

President McKay's tribute to his mother, entitled "Mother's Influence," was printed in a booklet presented by the Downey (Idaho) Ward Sunday School on Mother's Day, 1929.

MOTHER'S INFLUENCE

Among my most precious soul treasures, is the memory of mother's prayers by the bedside, of her affectionate touch as she tucked the bed clothes around my brother and me, and gave each a loving good night kiss. We were too young and roguish, then, fully to appreciate such devotion, but not too young to know that mother loved us.

It was this realization of mother's love, with a loyalty to the precepts of an exemplary father, which, more than once during fiery youth, turned my steps from the precipice of temptation.

If I were asked to name the world's greatest need, I should say unhesitatingly wise mothers; and the second, exemplary fathers.

If mother love were but half rightly directed, and if fatherhood were but half what it should be in example and honor, much of the sorrow and wickedness in the world would be overcome.

The home is the source of our national life. If we keep the spring pure, we shall have less difficulty in protecting the stream from pollution.

My mother! God bless you!
Your purity of soul,
Your faith, your tenderness
Your watchful care
Your supreme patience,
Your companionship and trust
Your loyalty to the Right,
Your help and inspiration to father,
Your unselfish devotion to us children—
These and every other virtue
that contributes to ideal motherhood,
I associate with you,
My Mother!

David O. McKay

Chapter 4

The First Mission

President David O. McKay was set apart as a missionary to Great Britain by President Seymour B. Young, August 1, 1897. He was then assigned to labor in Scotland. The first part of his mission was spent in Sterling, where he made many lasting friends for the Church, as well as for himself.

On June 9, 1898, he received a letter from the presidency of the British Mission about which he wrote the following in his diary: "Upon opening the letter I found it to be an appointment to the presidency of the Scottish Conference. Realizing to some extent what a responsibility this is, I seemed to be seized with a feeling of gloom and fear, lest in accepting I should prove incompetent. I walked to a secret spot in the wood, just below Wallace's monument, and there dedicated my services to the Lord and implored him for his divine assistance."

He found the Conference House in Glasgow a large, poorly furnished place. With the assistance of the elders and the sister in charge he purchased linoleum and necessary

This rare photograph shows some of the missionaries with whom David O. McKay served in Great Britain. This picture was taken while he was president of the Scottish Conference. He is seated on the front row, third from the right.

furniture to change it into liveable headquarters for the
missionaries, for their many callers, for the saints and returning European elders, all of whom sailed from Glasgow, for
the United States at that time.

During this mission Doctor James E. Talmage and Elder
George W. Palmer gave lectures on Utah with accompanying stereoptican slides in a number of cities in Scotland.
While these were not a financial success, and the elders in
the conference made up deficits, they felt that much prejudice was allayed, and many who attended became interested
investigators.

On May 29, 1899, a memorable priesthood meeting
was held in Glasgow in connection with the Scottish Conference, and it illustrates the spirit of this mission and the love
and sympathy existing among those who labored there.
President McKay records the events in his diary, excerpts
from which follow:

> A peaceful, heavenly influence pervaded the room. Some
> of the elders were so affected by it that they expressed their
> feelings in tears.
>
> Just as Brother Young sat down after giving his report,
> Elder Charles Woolfenden said, "Brethren there are angels in
> this room," and everyone present, impressed with the spirit of
> the occasion, and sensing the divine influence, could testify
> to the truth of his remarks. Elders wept for joy; sobs came
> from different parts of the room, and they were fitting, too,
> for it seemed manly to weep there.
>
> At the conclusion of the reports, all joined in a prayer of
> thanksgiving to the Lord for his blessings and manifestations.
> President James L. McMurrin then addressed the meeting and
> said, among other things, "The Lord has accepted our labors,
> and at this time we stand pure before him." He continued,
> "Yes, brethren, there are angels in this room;" and the announce-
> ment was not startling, but seemed wholly proper. Designating
> two of the brethren, he said their guardian angels were present,
> then turning to me he continued, "Let me say to you, Brother

David, Satan has desired you that he may sift you as wheat, but God is mindful of you, and if you will keep the faith, you will yet sit in the leading councils of the Church."

It was no coincidence that on July 17, 1887, when David was thirteen years old, Patriarch John Smith had also said, in his blessing, "For the eye of the Lord is upon thee—the Lord has a work for thee to do, in which thou shalt see much of the world. It shall be thy lot to sit in council with thy brethren, and preside among the people, and exhort the saints to faithfulness."

President McKay said of the meeting in Scotland, "It was a manifestation for which, as a doubting youth, I had secretly prayed most earnestly on hillside and in meadow. It was an assurance to me that sincere prayer is answered, 'sometime, somewhere.' "

On one of his regular visits to Edinborough he witnessed all the pomp and splendor accompanying the annual visit of the Prince of Wales in Scotland.

It was during this mission, also, that he visited Thurso, the birthplace of his father. Here he met people who remembered his grandfather and grandmother McKay, as well as his father, Bishop David McKay, when he did missionary work there in 1881-82.

Later he went from a conference in Liverpool to his mother's birthplace in Wales. It had been arranged that he and President McMurrin would attend the International Eisteddfodau together, but President McMurrin became ill and so David went alone to Cardiff where this annual festival of music and the arts was held. He took with him a letter of introduction from Professor Evan Stephens, director of the Salt Lake Tabernacle Choir, to Dr. Parry, the presiding officer of the festival. He was received very warmly by this great musician, who introduced the young missionary to

Dr. Edwards, assistant director, and his two daughters from Pennsylvania, as well as many other dignitaries and visitors at the festival.

After enjoying the competitive and cultural events of the festival, David went to Merthyr Tydfil where he found relatives and friends of his mother. He wrote a letter to her from the room in which she had been born.

Before he completed his missionary duties in Scotland he received a letter of appointment as a teacher in the Weber Stake Academy. He was thrilled with this opportunity to take up the career he had left to enter the mission field, and so after his missionary release in August, 1899, he went directly to Ogden to take up his new post.

In September of 1900 he was called to the Weber Stake Sunday School board, and became second assistant to Superintendent Thomas B. Evans. He was assigned the responsibility of classwork, and sensing the need for more organization, worked out a plan of graded departments with definite courses of study in each, as well as an adequately trained staff of teachers in each ward and a corresponding supervisor of each department on the stake board. These and other contributions which he made to the work of the Sunday School are detailed in Chapter 7.

Chapter 5

A Wonderful Family Life

David O. McKay and Emma Ray Riggs were married in the Salt Lake Temple on January 2, 1901. The ceremony was performed by Elder John Henry Smith. The couple had first met on the University of Utah campus, though neither had any serious thoughts of marriage at the time. However, when David returned from his mission and began teaching at the Weber Stake Academy, he learned that Ray had become a teacher at the Madison School in Ogden. Their friendship was renewed, and blossomed into a long, happy, and successful married life.

After their marriage they established their first home in Ogden, and here their seven children were born and reared as members of the Ogden Fourth Ward.

Ray was a natural homemaker—artistic, hospitable, loving, kind, and patient. David was a devoted husband and father, and their children, and all who entered their home, felt the refining influence of a united couple whose ideals conformed in every way to those taught by The Church of Jesus Christ of Latter-day Saints.

David O. McKay and Emma Ray Riggs about the time of their marriage in the Salt Lake Temple, January 2, 1901.

David and Ray reared their children in an atmosphere of love, harmony, and security, where father and mother were respected, not because they demanded their place as leaders, but because the children naturally made them their ideals and respected their judgment.

Because David and Ray lived the ideals of the Church in their home, spiritual things came naturally to their children. Typical of this is the experience of one of the sons when he was a small boy. One day he was visiting his grandfather's home, which was next door, while spring house cleaning and re-papering of the rooms were in progress. The little fellow, with his hands clasped behind his back, stood in a doorway watching the work and attracted the attention of a workman. The workman asked him, "When you are a man, would you like to be a painter and paper-hanger?" Without hesitation the child answered, "No, sir." The workman persisted, and said "Then what would you like to be?" The boy, again without hesitation, replied seriously "I should like to be a 'Twelve Apostle.'"

From the first years of his married life, David's Church duties required him to spend a considerable amount of time away from his family. Responsibilities as principal of the Weber Stake Academy, member of the Weber Stake Sunday School superintendency, and later as a general officer of the Sunday School and one of the Council of the Twelve kept him away from home a good deal of the time. During this time it was necessary for Ray to assume a large role in the home life. This she did most admirably. She could prepare and serve a delicious meal, direct the conversation at the table, and after the dining room was cleared, lead the family into the living room and entertain them by her piano artistry, or accompany them in their singing. While the family was small it seemed that every night in the McKay home was "family night." Later, when the three oldest children be-

This early, and rarely seen photograph, shows the four McKay brothers. They are, left to right, Thomas E. McKay, President David O. McKay, Morgan McKay, and Dr. William McKay.

came talented performers on violin, piano, and clarinet the home musicals continued as part of their artistic training.

While the children were young Ray did not accompany her husband in too many of his travels, saving this opportunity for later years. She remained at home, directing the education of the children, and also encouraging them in their Church activities. She always tried to be at home when the little ones returned from school, or came rushing in from the outside calling "Mother, I'm home," or "Mother, where are you?" Her assurance, "Here I am dear," was great security and protection to the growing family.

David and Ray tried to become personally acquainted with their children's teachers in public schools and in the Church. They cooperated with them in the preparation of home work and special assignments. At one time one of the boys returned from Sunday School with a firm declaration, "I am not going to that class once more because there is so much noise I can't hear what the teacher says." Ray counseled with him, and offered to go with him next Sunday to see what could be done about the matter. When she went she found conditions as he had reported them. After some private consultation with the superintendent, the inexperienced teacher was given the assistance she needed and there was no further disorder in that classroom.

On another occasion, when the boys were playing with their baseball, it inadvertently went through a basement window. As was the custom, the culprit went immediately to his father, saying, "It was an accident and I am very sorry." The wise father replied, "I am sorry, too, but just being sorry will not repair the damage."

The boy asked, "How much will a new window cost?"

"I do not know," replied his father, "but we shall have a repairman come up and he can tell us the exact amount."

A typical McKay family reunion at the "Old Home" in Huntsville. This photograph was taken in the mid-1950's.

President McKay's four sisters, in a photograph taken in 1951. They are, lower left, Jeanette M. Morrell; lower right, Elizabeth M. Hill; upper left, Mrs. Katherine Ricks; and upper right, Mrs. Ann Farr.

The child offered, "I haven't much money, but I am willing to pay what I have."

He was allowed to share in the expense, and when his mother remonstrated, "How could you take his money when he has such a small allowance?" David O. replied, "He has received a valuable lesson in the cost of keeping up a home, and now he has a monetary interest in this home which he will protect." It may have been a coincidence, but there were no more windows shattered by baseballs.

Of course there were times when differences of opinion arose, or when mischievous brothers teased sisters, or when jokes were played on unsuspecting members by older planners—all the upsetting experiences that happen in any group of lively young people. But father and mother always met these problems quietly and settled them in strict kindness.

There were no company manners in the McKay home. Father and mother were as courteous to each other and to their children when only the members of the family were present, as when the most respected guests were in the home. The same courtesy and respect for each other's rights were required of the children in their association and play together.

Besides rearing and educating their own family, the McKays invited many students to live in their home, and these they assisted in their efforts to secure an education. These young people, now with families of their own, still sing the praises of this ideal home which they were permitted to share.

There were traditions that became loving memories in the lives of all the family. Birthdays were always celebrated by special cakes and appropriate candles, and when each one reached school age, by parties in which friends participated. Summer holidays were usually spent at the Old Home in Huntsville, which was also the scene of occasional

David O. McKay and Emma Ray Riggs McKay
cutting the cake on their golden wedding
anniversary, January 2, 1951.

winter sleigh rides. There were always horses to ride on the farm, and hayrides that delighted even the smallest children.

The day before Christmas was a special occasion when the McKay children with all their cousins met at the home of an uncle and aunt to present a Christmas play, written especially for them, with a part for each child. The parents were the audience, and the party was always over in time for each family to return home before Santa's visit on Christmas Eve.

Missionary work made the first break in this ideal home life, and as each son reached maturity, he gave several years to his Church in France, Germany, England, or South America. Then followed temple marriages, until there were six new homes established on the exact pattern of the original where they had received their training.

They are still a unit, meeting with parents for birthday, anniversary, and Christmas celebrations. It would be difficult to find a more united and loving group in this world than the David O. McKay family.

Chapter 6

Weber Stake Academy

Before David O. McKay was released from his mission in Scotland, in August, 1899, he received a letter from the Board of Education of the Weber Stake Academy, offering him a position as teacher in the institution. His work commenced in September of that year, and continued until April 17, 1902, when, upon the resignation of Professor Louis F. Moench, he was appointed principal.

The school was handicapped because of the many men students who were detained on the farms in the fall, and were compelled to leave before the close of school in the spring. This meant educating the parents and students alike to the necessity of attending during the entire school year. While this meant sacrifices in some instances, the difficulties were overcome to a very great extent, and the number of graduates each year was greatly increased.

One of the first innovations made at the school was the establishment of a little paper. The staff of the paper was organized in 1903, and Principal McKay suggested that it be called *The Acorn*. The first number was published in

February, 1904, and was sent out without carrying the name of the school. When exchanges returned, addressed simply to Ogden, Utah, one of them asked, "Where does the little Acorn grow?" The first souvenir edition was dated 1905.

A lecture course was established in 1902, with the following committee in charge: Professor Wilford M. McKendrick, chairman, Dr. John G. Lind, and Jeanette McKay. The first year's program brought the best talent the state afforded. The second year Professor S. H. Clark, of the University of Chicago, supplemented the course with a series of dramatic recitals.

The Acorn of December, 1904, contained the following: "For two years past the Weber Stake Academy has offered to its students and friends, two of the finest lecture courses in the state. In fact, we have been the pioneers in presenting an outlined course of lectures from our leading home talent, and from the east."

The course for 1905, listed Professor S. H. Clark, Edmund Vance Cook, F. Hopkinson Smith, Albert Armstrong, W. J. Clarke, noted electrician of New York, and two local notables, Professor Maud May Babcock, and the Honorable Brigham H. Roberts.

In 1905, '06, and '07, the following outstanding attractions were added to the already remarkable roster of the Weber Stake Academy Lecture Course, which had now become a permanent part of the institution: Montaville Flowers, Opie Read, Sylvestor H. Long, Frederick B. Hopkins of Chicago, Jacob H. Riis, Russel H. Conwell of Temple College in Philadelphia, Whitney Brothers Quartette, Dr. Richard G. Moulton of the University of Chicago, Alton Packard, cartoonist, Van Vachton Rogers, Professor John B. De Mott, Dr. Thomas H. Green, Dr. George Riddle of Harvard University, William Jennings Bryan, and others. To accommodate the increased attendance, some of the lectures were transferred to the Orpheum Theater, where later most of them were held.

In 1903, the Domestic Arts Department was added, with Mrs. Sarah T. Evans in charge, and during the year more than fifty girls were registered in sewing and art needle work. It was not until 1906, however, that the Domestic Science Department was formally established with Eve Farr as director. Its success was assured by the large number of students who registered immediately for the classes in this practical division of vocational education.

In 1902, the school was represented by two excellent basketball teams, one of men, the other of women. The Ogden City Council granted Weber Stake Academy the use of the pavilion in Lester Park for practice, as there were no facilities for this purpose in their building. In 1903, during Field Day exercises, an interclass meet was conducted, and following this a school track team was organized. In this same year, after a successful season, the victorious basketball boys were given their W sweaters. A baseball team came into existence in 1905, and on May 20 of that year, won its game with the University of Utah.

A student body organization was perfected in 1904, and this added greatly to the group enthusiasm and support of school activities. The creation of a football team was one of the first evidences of its activity, to participate with the few teams already playing in the state. This was not a major sport, however, for some years.

In the souvenir edition of *The Acorn* for 1906, the following report was made:

> One of the most important features of the school this year, and one which has attracted a great deal of attention, is the Music Department. At the beginning of the year the choir

was organized, and has held regular weekly rehearsals. Professor Joseph Ballantyne has worked hard to bring it to a high standard, and some beautiful anthems have been rendered in daily devotional exercises.

Another feature of the school, of real importance, is the Conservatory of Music, which was established last September, with Professor Joseph Ballantyne, Professor John J. McClellen, and Professor Willard E. Wehie, as instructors. Voice culture, piano and organ, and violin, are the branches taught. It has proved to be a pronounced success, and will, no doubt, become a permanent part of the Academy. There is already a large enrollment in the Conservatory, and they have given two recitals of which we are very proud, and in which the public took a great deal of interest.

The school band has been working diligently, with Professor E. W. Nicols as Director, to maintain its excellent standard. Our orchestra is deserving of a great deal of praise. They have had regular practices all year, and the music has, at all times, been a source of great satisfaction.

One of the best and most successful musical treats we have had for a long time was the operetta, *The Witch of the Woods,* given by our students, under the direction of Mrs. Harriet Purdy Smith. The production is one requiring a great number of characters, and gives opportunity for a great variety of performance. Everything was attractive and very well worth while for the time spent in practice, and worthy of the large audience which filled the Opera House at each of the three performances. The proceeds have been given to the fund for the new building.

In 1908, the school band rendered twenty-one numbers and the orchestra eleven. The choir of eighty-five voices produced the beautiful cantata, *Father,* by William B. Bradley.

Two women's literary clubs were organized under the sponsorship of Miss Jeanette McKay, of the faculty. The HCP Club announced that its membership was open to all junior and senior girls who were willing to live up to its constitution. Men's clubs were also available to students.

A debating team brought success to the school on April 25, 1908, by defeating the Salt Lake City High School.

The school grew very rapidly, and it was not long before Principal McKay realized that the existing quarters were inadequate. When he explained to the Board of Education, and asked for additional housing facilities, they explained, "You may have a new building if you can raise the money to pay for it, but do not expect any assistance from us." Knowing that these men had mortgaged their own homes to pay for the original building, he did not blame them for taking this stand, but their decision did not alter his determination to have some more class rooms and a larger auditorium.

The problem was discussed at a special meeting of the faculty, and a plan was adopted to visit every ward in the stakes interested, besides soliciting personal assistance. In the history of education probably no faculty of comparable size ever worked more diligently or with greater determination than did David O. McKay and his teachers. The result was the erection of a $60,000.00 addition, and the board was not asked to contribute one cent. This gave the school additional class rooms, a chemical laboratory, a geological laboratory, space for a vocational training shop, and a large auditorium. This served as a community center for students and the public alike, for lectures, theatres, assemblies, and other meetings, and was still in use by Weber State College until very recently. Not one of that faculty group ever forgot the generous response of the large number of friends of the Weber Stake Academy.

While the building program was still underway, Principal McKay was called on April 8, 1906, to serve as a member of the Church's Council of Twelve. He willingly accepted the many added responsibilities as an apostle, but asked for permission to remain as principal also until the new building was completed. This was accomplished with the structure's dedication in 1908.

One distinct advantage of the new building in the Weber curriculum was the addition of a manual arts training program. The need had long been recognized, but no room had been available. Now, with the opening of a shop, and adequate new tools, instructor W. O. Ridges and some eighty students began making desks, benches, tables, and other equipment needed for classrooms. Repairs of doors, windows and other parts of the campus buildings were also possible.

When Princpal McKay left the school, the annual issue of *The Acorn* was dedicated to him, and the following are excerpts from that number.

> To him who planted our Acorn so dear,
> To him who has nurtured it gently each year,
> Discov'ring its faults with an eye but to bless,
> So ready its beauties and truths to confess.
> To him who has shared all its joys, cares, and fears,
> We dedicate now and we hallow with tears.

"Fortunate, indeed, are the students who have been registered in his classes, for when he taught religion he gave truths he believed and had proved in practice. His lessons in literature were interpreted in the light of love and charity for all mankind, and his moral teachings had behind them all the force of a perfect moral life."

During his years as principal the growth of the school was phenomenal, and with the added facilities of the new building, he left a remarkable foundation upon which to build the Weber Academy and later the Weber State College.

The resignation of Principal McKay did not terminate his service to the institution, for he was invited to become the president of the board of trustees. In this capacity he was still able to function in its development. He remained in this position until called by the Church to preside over the European Mission in 1922.

On this occasion, the *Weber Herald* of November 9, 1922, with Willard Marriott as editor, published a long article, headed, *President McKay Leaves For the European Mission,* from which the following extracts are taken:

He was connected with Weber as student, teacher, principal, and president of the board of trustees.

In the calling of Elder David O. McKay to preside over the European Mission, the Weber Academy loses the active service of the President of the board of trustees. We wish Brother McKay an earnest farewell, and wish him success in his important calling.

In doing this, however, it might be profitable for us to review some of the important incidents which connect the history of Weber with the life of David O. McKay.

Brother McKay entered Weber as a preparatory student in the Fall of 1889, the second year of the Weber Stake Academy, then occupying the Second Ward Institute. Later, Brother McKay attended the University of Utah, graduating, and took up the work of teacher. Very soon he was called on a mission to Great Britain. Here his active, energetic life asserted itself, and soon he found himself presiding over the Scottish Conference.

Upon his return home he was appointed a teacher in Weber, entering the school as head of the English department. He labored as a teacher in the school for three years, then became the principal of the institution in 1902.

The seven years during which Brother McKay was principal were years of remarkable growth for the school. Some of the buildings were entirely outgrown. Classes had to be conducted on the stairways and in the halls. Something had to be done in order to have more room. But the board remembered the hard time which it had experienced in raising the money to pay for the first building. Naturally it hesitated. It did not like to undertake a new building. In this crisis the energy and soul of Brother McKay asserted themselves. He went before the board of education with the proposition that the teachers would build an addition to the old building if they were given permission to solicit funds. Permission was granted. Brother McKay became the central figure in the campaign for money. The teachers rallied to him and assisted in the work. The money was collected. The Church assisted out of the tithing funds. Individual contributions ranging from one dollar to five thousand dollars in one case, were received. The building was built and paid for.

While this campaign was on, Brother McKay was chosen a member of the Quorum of the Twelve Apostles, but he remained as principal of Weber until after the building was completed.

Since that time Brother McKay has served the school continuously as president of the board of trustees. Although his duties as a member of the Quorum of the Twelve have taken most of his time, yet he has found ways and means to boost for Weber.

Weber is dear to the heart of Brother McKay. He loves the school, and in return is beloved by Weber and by every boy and girl who has attended the school. May God bless him as he goes from us to his new field of labor.

Chapter 7

Sunday School Activities

*T*he portion of President David O. McKay's life which he devoted to Sunday School activities is one of the most significant and interesting phases of a notable career.

He had a natural love for teaching and great ability as an organizer. Combining these with tremendous enthusiasm for the work, he was able to bring about improvements in the Sunday School programs that are still valuable today.

Like most Latter-day Saint children he was enrolled in the Sunday School at an early age, and learned to love the association and spiritual atmosphere resulting from regular attendance. His first major responsibility came on January 27, 1889 when he was called as secretary of the Huntsville Ward Sunday School. On August 20, 1893 he was sustained as a teacher in this Sunday School, and served until October 4, 1896 when he was released because of a move to Salt Lake where he was attending the University of Utah.

Following his missionary service in Scotland he was called to the Weber Stake Sunday School board in September,

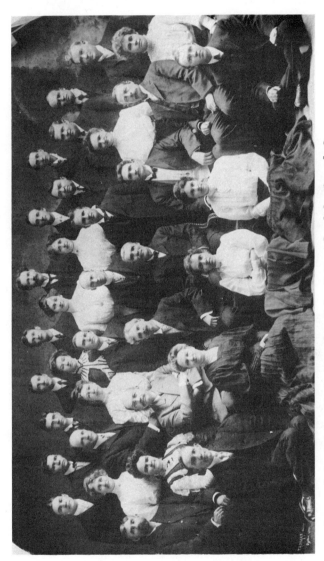

Members of the Weber Stake Sunday School Board while David O. McKay was second assistant superintendent. He is seated third from the right on the second row. Seated on President McKay's right is Superintendent Thomas B. Evans and next to him Charles J. Ross.

1899. Early in 1900 he was sustained as second assistant to Superintendent Thomas B. Evans in the stake Sunday School superintendency. It was while serving in this capacity, a position he held for six years, that his great leadership ability enabled him to make many significant contributions.

He was assigned the responsibility of Sunday School class work. Because of his educational background, and his work as a teacher at Weber Stake Academy, he sensed in the Sunday Schools a lack of proper teaching methods and little or no lesson organization. After careful, prayerful study he prepared a plan of grading students within the Sunday School, and outlined a definite course of study for each department. An adequate teaching force in each ward was specified, and corresponding supervisors for each department were included on the stake board level. He further suggested the outlining of lessons and cooperative discussion of each month's work at the stake union meeting. Thus began the real work of gospel education within the Sunday Schools.

Teachers were asked to study each lesson at home, and decide on a definite aim. They were then to arrange topics logically, suggest a timely illustration from outside the text and write a practical application of each lesson to the child's life.

There was then to be a weekly preparation meeting for all officers and teachers in each ward where every detail of the coming Sunday service would be discussed and teachers would cooperate in perfecting the lesson outline and dividing the work of the class period so that there would be no time wasted and no time for pupils to become unruly because of delays in teaching.

Then, at the monthly stake union meeting, all officers and teachers of the wards in the stake would come together, and after receiving general instructions from the stake superintendency in opening exercises, would separate for departmental work. Here, under the supervision of stake board members, the ward workers in each department would discuss problems and plans for the coming month's work. At the close of the union meeting each teacher had in his or her notebook some suggested composite outlines for the coming month's work. An example of this type of lesson outlining, taken from President McKay's notes, is as follows:

THE TEMPTATION OF CHRIST

Text: Matt. 4:1-11; Luke 4:1-13
Lesson setting: The time, place, etc.

   I. The First Temptation
      A. Physical condition after fasting
      B. Tempter seeks to have the Savior turn stones into bread.
      C. The Savior's reply

  II. The Second Temptation
      A. Tempted to cast himself from pinnacle of temple
        1. Tempter quotes scriptures
        2. The Savior's reply

 III. The Third Temptation
      A. To worship Satan
        1. Reward offered
        2. The Savior's refusal to worship or serve any but his Heavenly Father.

Suggested Aim: Resisting temptation strengthens character.
Illustrations: Stories and experiences drawn from members of the class.
Application: Suggestions from pupils as to practical application in their daily lives.

This type of Sunday School planning is taken for granted now, but in 1900 it was a major innovation. As President McKay presented it, it was first accepted by the stake board, then by the superintendencies of the wards, and most important of all, by the various teachers. Many of the teachers, even though they had served for many years, expressed their inability to outline lessons and adopt the new methods, but the great majority of them became the most ardent supporters of the plan when they saw how their lessons came alive and were so much more effective in the lives of their pupils as compared with the unorganized material of earlier years.

It was not long before each teacher felt that unless every pupil left his class with a burning desire to *do* something as a direct result of the Sunday morning lesson, he had failed in his presentation of the subject. To David O. McKay this fulfilled the admonition "Be ye doers of the word and not hearers only."

Sunday School work under the direction of Superintendent Thomas B. Evans, Charles J. Ross, and David O. McKay became a living, moving force in the lives of all who participated. Attendance, punctuality, intelligent and thorough preparation, and class cooperation became watchwords that brought the organization to heights never before realized. Many testimonies were strengthened which might never have reached maturity.

President McKay also organized and directed a parent's convention which was held in the Ogden Tabernacle, and attended by Church President Joseph F. Smith. Out of this gathering came the Parents Class, a new addition to the regular Sunday School.

With his call to serve in the Council of the Twelve came a release for President McKay from the Weber Sunday School stake board. At a testimonial given in his honor on May 16, 1906, Superintendent Evans, speaking in behalf of all the stake Sunday School workers said:

"His unusual ability and integrity in his class work have enabled all to get a clearer conception of their duty. His devotion to the Sunday School cause, his untiring zeal and purity of life and conversation have inspired all to nobler deeds and awakened in them a determination to perform their labors with an eye single to the Glory of God.

"His kindness of spirit and grace of conduct have touched the hearts and won the love of all his associates who unite in praying Heaven's greatest and choicest blessings to attend him at all times, wherever he may be."

Even after moving to Salt Lake City he returned weekly to Ogden to give an extended course of lectures to officers and teachers of the Weber Stake.

On October 6, 1906 he was called to serve as second assistant to President Joseph F. Smith in the General Sunday School superintendency. He became the first assistant in the general superintendency on April 14, 1909, and then was called to serve as the general superintendent on November 27, 1918. At that time he called his long-time friend Stephen L Richards as first assistant, along with George D. Pyper as second assistant.

Several months after the new superintendency was sustained, Elder Edward P. Kimball, writing in the *Juvenile Instructor* of February, 1919, paid the following tribute to President McKay:

> Elder David O. McKay is signally honored by his call to preside over the Sunday Schools of the Church in all the world. His appointment comes as a merited recognition for the faithfulness and zeal which he has displayed during his long association with the Sunday Schools. That confidence in his training for the great responsibility of his new calling, and in his capabilities in and fidelity to the great Sunday School cause, exhibited by his brethren in placing him at the head of this wonderful work, will find an echo in the heart of every Sunday School worker throughout the Church. His name is synonymous with the Sunday School movement, and those who are most intimately acquainted

with him know best how close to his heart are the youth of Zion, and how devoutly and indefatigably he has applied himself for their improvement and salvation. His mind is constantly busy with new problems and plans for the growth of the work. While he looks to and into the future, he is no idle dreamer; he has a wonderful capacity for making men see his vision, and then of solving the details of his plan which will make this vision a living reality. His sure and unfailing testimony of the truth of the Gospel of Jesus Christ is exemplified in his every thought, word, and deed for the young people of the Church. His kindly, gentlemanly bearing toward everyone whom he meets is proverbial; his testimony is inspiring; and his example compels admiration.

As general superintendent he began to apply throughout the Church the successful plans that had been developed in Weber Stake. Parents classes became general throughout the Church, and a progressive course of study from the kindergarten to the parents classes was instituted. The lessons were graded and the members of each department had a definite assignment to complete before being promoted to the next higher division.

Ideal class instruction which he had begun to develop in Ogden found its way into all the Sunday Schools of the Church, and there was a great general move forward in gospel instruction.

Bryant S. Hinckley, in an article published in the May, 1932 issue of *The Improvement Era,* described President McKay's work in the Sunday School as follows:

"This work appealed to the best and the finest that is in Elder McKay. He brought to it, not only an undivided heart, but the strength and devotion of all his splendid powers. He put into the organization a part of the sublime and attractive faith so manifest in his own life. Through the Sunday School he has fostered two major objectives of the Church—the development of faith and the building of character and he has left forever upon it the impress of his shining personality.

"David O. McKay has made a lasting contribution to the Sunday School cause. No history of the Church hereafter will be written that will not exalt him to a high place because of this work."

He continued as general superintendent until October 30, 1934 when he was sustained as second counselor to President Heber J. Grant in the First Presidency of the Church.

Chapter 8

World Tour

One of the most important missionary ventures of the Church began on December 2, 1920, when David O. McKay of the Council of the Twelve, and Elder Hugh J. Cannon, editor of *The Improvement Era,* were set apart by President Heber J. Grant and President Anthon H. Lund to make a tour of the missions and schools of the Church in every part of the world.

From the day of their leaving until they returned on December 24, 1921, they traveled 24,277 miles by land, and 32,819 miles by water, which is two and one half times around the earth's circumference. Among the intensely interesting experiences in every country and island visited, only a few can be mentioned here.

Christmas was spent in Japan, and after visiting the principal cities of that beautiful country, and spending a short time in Korea, the travelers entered China, with its ancient wall still standing as a bulwark, if not a protection.

Before they left Salt Lake, President Grant had instructed them, if they felt so impressed while in China, to

David O. McKay and Hugh J. Cannon in a photograph
taken during their tour of the world in 1920.

set the land apart for the preaching of the gospel. As Peking is really the heart of the country, they decided it would be an appropriate place for this sacred ceremony. On Sunday, January 9, 1921, in a small grove of cyprus trees, Elder McKay dedicated and set apart the Chinese realm for the preaching of the gospel. He wrote: "Thus was the key turned that unlocked the door for the entrance into this famine-stricken land, of the authorized servants of God to preach the Glad Tidings of Great Joy as revealed to the Prophet Joseph Smith."

Not until they returned to Tokyo on January 21, 1921, to sail for Hawaii, did they receive letters and Christmas messages from home. In Honolulu they received a royal welcome, and were shown the beauties and points of interest on all the islands of this group. Elder McKay wrote in his diary:

> I cannot describe the beauty of this tropical paradise, the trees, the gorgeous colored hedges, the profusely blooming flowers and shrubs, the sky and ocean, with bright, fantastically colored fish; all add interest to this wonderland of beauty. Later I told a reporter who came to interview us, that I had realized more than I ever thought possible, my childhood dream of fairyland.

After holding conference, attending feasts given in their honor, and blessing little children and members who were ill, it was necessary to return to the mainland to take a boat for the islands and continents of the South Seas. The Tahitian saints were visited, and several weeks were spent in New Zealand. In every town and village where meetings were held, members and non-members alike, city and government officials, joined to welcome their distinguished guests, entertained them royally, and showered them with flowers and lovely gifts. Everywhere there was beautiful music furnished by bands, choruses, and island serenaders. There were also many spiritual manifestations which strengthened the testimonies of missionaries and island people alike.

The month spent in Samoa passed all too quickly, with some of the largest conferences yet held, in preparation for which every detail had been carefully arranged. Missionary meetings were as satisfactory as the larger meetings, attended by members, investigators, and friends. When the time for farewells arrived, genuine friendships had been formed, and the parting was a sad one for the people who had never before had the privilege of meeting one of the general authorities.

At the last party there were beautiful interpretations of the island dances, in native costume, singing, and instrumental selections, and then, as they returned to the mission home, fathers and mothers brought their children to be blessed, occupying the last moments before the necessary departure. Of these last experiences Elder McKay recorded the following:

> As we came out, we found the people standing in a double column from our door out across the lawn to the street. They had prepared a farewell song for us and all began to sing. As we passed through the lines, shaking hands with them, sobs interrupted the singing. Staunch old Papo, the head of the village, sobbed like a child, and clung to us as though we were his sons. As we mounted our horses, we looked back and saw the crowd, headed by the band, coming toward us for one more parting handshake.
>
> From that spot to the dugway leading to the ocean, there was a straight, grassy roadway, lined with tall native trees and tropical vines. As we rode slowly up the gentle incline, the band leading, the people followed, as though they could not yield to parting. We had gained, perhaps, a quarter of a mile ahead of them, when I felt tempted to say, "Brother Cannon, I think we should return and leave our blessing with them here in this beautiful grove.

As we approached the sobbing crowd, I was thrilled with the picturesque setting. Hanging my folded umbrella on an overhanging limb, Kippin, our interpreter, told them why we had come back. Their sobs were louder than my voice when I commenced the prayer, but they became more subdued as I continued, and their "Amen" was distinct and impressive at the end.

An elder who remained with the crowd reported what happened after the visitors left:

The villagers watched as long as they could see their friends, then returned sadly to their homes. Kippin, the interpreter, immediately sat down and wrote the prayer as he remembered it. He and some of the others then conceived the idea of burying a copy of it on the spot where Apostle McKay had stood, and covering it with a pile of stones to mark the place. The town bell was rung, the people reassembled, and the plan was presented and approved. A copy of the prayer, together with an account of the entire proceedings, was sealed in a bottle and placed in a hole which was covered with stones, each of the heads of families throwing a handful of soil to assist in the covering. The branch on which the umbrella was hung was taken back to the village as a souvenir, and steps were taken to erect a monument at the sacred spot.

Another month was spent in visiting the missions of Australia, then on to Java, India, Egypt, and Palestine. Traveling through the Holy Land was like passing familiar towns, villages, rivers, lakes, mountains, and gardens, because of Elder McKay's long and intimate association with these places in Old Testament history, and especially because of his love of the life of Christ and his apostles.

President Grant had expressed a hope that in their travels the two could visit the Armenian Mission, which had received such harsh treatment during the great World War. On a special fast day, several thousand dollars had been contributed for the relief of these suffering people, but almost a year had passed since the brethren had left home, and they had no recent information about conditions in this part of the world. Cablegrams to the president of the European Mission and to the United States Consul at Aleppo, brought only information that J. Wilford Boothe was on his way to Aleppo. Elder McKay's diary, under date of November 2, 1921, reads:

> We have no idea where President Boothe is. We shall leave Jerusalem for Haifa, enroute to Aleppo, tomorrow morning. We have concluded to go by auto through Samaria, visiting Bible scenes. At three-thirty p. m. of the same day, we ascended the Mount of Olives, and, choosing a secluded spot, near where Jesus is supposed to have stood, we knelt in humble supplication and thanksgiving to God, asking that we might be led by inspiration on our trip to the Armenian Mission.
>
> Upon returning to the hotel, I felt strongly impressed that we should go to Haifa by train instead of by auto. When I said as much to Brother Cannon, he replied, "if you feel that way we had better take the train." Our greatest desire as we neared this mission was to meet Elder Boothe. Indeed, it seemed that our trip to Syria would be useless unless we should meet him. We were strangers. We knew no one. The branches of the Church in Syria were disorganized, and the members were scattered.
>
> During all our travels, besides giving excellent addresses at every meeting, Brother Cannon had assumed the responsibility of arranging for train and boat tickets, and hotel accommodations, and had never failed in a single instance; but shortly after leaving Jerusalem, when asked if he had the name of a hotel in Haifa, he said he had forgotten to ask about it, but would contact the Allenby Hotel runner when the train stopped at Lud.

When they changed trains at that station, and were again on their way, they both realized that they had forgotten to speak to the hotel representative.

Arriving at Haifa, Brother Cannon remained with the luggage while Brother McKay left to make inquiry regarding a suitable hotel. After some difficulty, he returned in about ten minutes reporting that there seemed to be two fairly good ones, and they would take the one whose runner appeared first. The delay caused by locating a hotel brought them to the station office door just at the same moment that another traveler reached it. He said, "Isn't this Brother McKay?" Elder McKay then records in his diary:

Astounded beyond expression to be thus addressed in so strange a town, I turned and recognized Elder Joseph Wilford Boothe, the one man above all others that we were most desirous of meeting. We had met, too, at the most opportune time and place. Having known nothing of our whereabouts, he had come from the western part of the world, hoping in his heart to meet us. We had come from the east, praying that we might meet him, and there we had met at the very time and place best suited to our convenience, and to the success of our mission to Armenia.

As we recounted to each other our experiences, we had no doubt but that our coming together was the result of divine interposition. If we had taken an auto from Jerusalem, or if we had remembered to secure the name of a hotel before we left the Allenby, or if we had thought to ask at Lud, we should not have met Elder Boothe. It is true we would have been in town that same day, but we had intended to stay at a hotel across the city from the one he decided upon, where we never should have met him, and our visit to Armenia would have failed.

After visiting missions in Italy, Switzerland, Germany, and the British Isles, they sailed for home, arriving on Christmas Eve, 1921. These two men who had been as one during this eventful year, then made a complete report to President Heber J. Grant, and received an honorable release.

On January 15, 1936, President McKay was again sent to visit the Hawaiian Mission, and since has visited nearly all the missions of the world.

Chapter 9

The European Mission

David O. McKay is one of the most effective missionaries the Church has had in this dispensation. His knowledge of the gospel, his sincerity, his courage to stand for his beliefs, his sympathetic understanding of people and their problems, his keen sense of humor, his charming personality, his exemplary life, his noble appearance, and his humility appeal alike to the great and the lowly of the earth.

When he was called by President Heber J. Grant late in 1922 to assume the presidency of the European Mission it seemed as though all the experiences of his life thus far had led up to this momentous assignment.

His early missionary experiences in Scotland, his work with young people at the Weber Stake Academy, his success in Sunday School work, and his world tour with Elder Hugh J. Cannon had all played influential roles in preparing him for this new challenge.

With his wife and five children President McKay left the Ogden railroad depot on November 8, 1922. Before sailing for Europe he wrote from the east, "Railroad officials at Chicago, Buffalo, New York, and Montreal, extended every possible courtesy, and their kind consideration contributed largely to our pleasant and comfortable journey across the continent."

After the family landed in England President McKay wrote that ". . . among the passengers aboard the S. S. Montcalm was Sir George McLaren Brown, European manager of the Canadian Pacific Railroad Company, through whose recognition and attention on the boat, our voyage across the Atlantic was made the most delightful of the many I had taken within the last two years."

The day after they landed in Liverpool President and Mrs. McKay attended their first meeting. This was one of some 525 they were to hold during the two years they spent in the mission field. They traveled in that time some 2,000 miles and visited every mission except South Africa, addressing more than 7,000 people. During their travels they also reorganized the French Mission and before leaving Europe had it flourishing with new interest aroused and new members being added.

The two outstanding accomplishments of his term as European Mission President were in overcoming the insidious attacks on the Church by British newspapers and in extending the assignment of missionary work to members of the Church as well as the full-time missionaries.

For some time prior to 1922 the newspapers of Great Britain had been publishing derogatory articles about the Church, and had refused to print refutations written by the missionaries or resident members of the Church. After studying the newspapers carefully, President McKay decided that to continue this effort would be futile, and so he embarked on a new course of action.

Without giving any information to reporters, President McKay wrote directly to the editors of the papers involved in the attacks, beginning with *John Bull,* one of the oldest and best weekly newspapers in Great Britain. His long letter appealed to English sportsmanship and love of fair play, and requested that only the truth be told about the Latter-day Saints instead of the untrue stories which had hitherto been published. To the amazement of all, the next issue of the newspaper contained a large headline which read "A DANIEL COME TO JUDGMENT," and under this caption appeared the complete text of President McKay's letter. Not another article in opposition to the Church appeared in that paper during the following two years. Similar results were achieved with the other newspapers to which President McKay wrote, and the Church enjoyed a respite from this unfair persecution.

In one town in Wales where members had been meeting in a public building the Town Council decided to prohibit any further Mormon assemblies. When informed of the matter, President McKay wrote a persuasive letter addressed directly to the Council and was effective in stopping this action against the Church. He was also effective in achieving better relations for the Church in Scotland.

The second area of significant achievement was his plan that every member of the Church should be a missionary. He traveled throughout the European mission appealing to the saints in each conference to accept the missionary work and pledge himself or herself to bring one new member into the Church each year. He suggested that the new convert might be a relative, friend, working companion, or even a casual acquaintance or a stranger. The result was a great increase in membership in the mission during 1923, exceeding that of previous years by a large margin. This same appeal for "every member a missionary" also proved successful throughout the Church after President McKay became President in 1951.

When he returned to Utah with his family in 1924 President McKay made a full report to the First Presidency, and among other things indicated the following:

> Street meetings are now held without molestation in nearly every one of the fifteen conferences, and not one interruption has occurred in a hall meeting during the last two years. Attendance at the conferences has increased from twenty to one-hundred per cent.
>
> Leading newspapers now refuse to print scandalous articles about the Mormons. The real need in Great Britain today is better meeting places. If the sum that we are now spending for rent were applied wisely in building societies, many branches might, in a few years, own their own Church buildings.

He commented favorably upon the sympathetic and able assistance given the Church by the ministers and consuls of the United States to whom it was necessary on occasion to make appeals in times of difficulty.

His report also contained a recommendation that the British Mission presidency be separated from the presidency of the European Mission. He stated that the duties and responsibilities of the British Mission were of such importance as to require the undivided and constant attention of the very ablest men in the Church.

He suggested, also, that missions be visited more frequently by members of the Council of the Twelve, adding that generally stakes were far better prepared to go without such official visits than were the missions.

Like all other returning missionaries he concluded, "This mission has been one of the most pleasant and worthwhile experiences of our lives."

Chapter 10

A White House Conference

In 1930, a White House Conference on Child Health and Protection was called by President Herbert Hoover, and, by invitation, President David O. McKay was in attendance.

The objectives, as stated by President Hoover, were "to study the present status and well-being of the children of the United States and its possessions; to report what is being done for them; to recommend what ought to be done and how to do it."

The preliminary work done in preparation for the conference was of the highest order, and required sixteen months by one hundred sixty committees, made up of the leaders in the fields of child health and welfare. The work was divided into four sections, Medical Service, Public Health Administration, Education and Training, and The Handicapped.

President Hoover, in addressing the three thousand participants of the conference, said, "Let no one believe that these are questions which should not stir a nation; that they are below the dignity of statesmen or governments. If we could have but one generation of properly born, trained, educated, and healthy children, a thousand other problems of government would vanish."

The objectives outlined by the leaders of the conference were probably the most comprehensive and ambitious ever devised for child welfare by any nation. They included spiritual and moral training, personality development, pre-natal, natal, and post-natal care; health protection in all its aspects throughout childhood; wholesome physical and men-tal training; better schools from all angles; protection from physical danger, moral hazards, and diseases; universal edu-cation along the most sensible lines for the individual prep-aration for parenthood; care of the handicapped to insure independence as far as possible; intelligent handling of the delinquent; adequate standards of living; supplementing the home in all phases of child development; and providing adequate local organizations for carrying out the welfare plans.

The program was prepared and presented by the best qualified men and women available in the nation. The work of each department was done by capable leaders, and com-prised a long-term plan of procedure destined to influence for good the entire lives of all people.

On completion of the White House Conference, state organizations were perfected for carrying out its plans. The Utah organization was effected at a meeting called by Governor George Dern, February 1, 1931, at which President McKay was appointed chairman of the state executive com-mittee. Utah was the third state in the union to perfect such an organization. It was astonishing how widely the appeal was accepted throughout the entire state. A committee for community cooperation was organized, in addition to those originally active. A partial list of those accepting responsibility follows: Boy Scouts, Girl Scouts, service clubs, social welfare leagues, Utah Federation of Labor, Utah State Kindergarten, Primary Association, Utah Manufacturer's Association, Utah Farm Bureau, Red Cross, Utah Federation of Women's Clubs, fraternal organizations, life insurance companies, transportation companies, motion picture houses, Forest Service, fish and game associations, Utah Press Association, Utah Tuberculosis Association, and Utah Education Association.

All Utah committees were filled with outstanding men and women of the state as members. The work was planned, surveys and reports made, and recommendations submitted. Local groups were organized for carrying out the work under the supervision of county committees. Reports were compiled in a single volume, which represented a mass of information never before available for study and planned activity for community benefits in the state.

With this start, it appeared that the state was on the way to great achievements in child welfare. All other states were also organized for carrying out the program. But the plans were altered when a change of administration occurred in Washington, and an entirely new plan of social activity came into being. The careful study and planning of the conference was forgotten and the organization which was set up never functioned in the manner intended. The data is still available in the combined reports, even though it was never used to any extent.

Chapter II

The Utah Centennial Celebration

In every calling or assignment which has been his, President David O. McKay has given it his best in leadership and organizational ability. His achievements have always exceeded those which he was expected to do. Such was certainly the case when he served as chairman of the Utah Centennial Celebration in 1947.

Initial steps toward a celebration commemorating the entrance of the Mormon pioneers into Salt Lake Valley on July 24, 1847, were made in the Utah State Legislature in 1938.

On April 1, 1938, members of the Twenty-Second Legislature passed Resolution No. 1, recommending the appointment of a committee ". . . to investigate the feasibility of holding a World's Fair in the State of Utah during the year 1947, and to report the findings to the Twenty-Third Legislature."

As a result of this action, Henry H. Blood, then governor of Utah, asked President McKay if he would chairman the committee for the study. Governor Blood then wrote to

seventy-five of the outstanding men in the state, asking them
to serve on the committee. His letter said in part:

> The purpose is a worthy one. The event which the centennary
> will celebrate has a tremendous significance for this state, this
> western region, and for the nation. It devolves on this state to
> assume leadership in arranging appropriate recognition of the
> anniversary. To devise an effective and practicable plan involves
> many problems. To make proper recommendations to the Legis-
> lature as to how the desirable objective may best be accomplished
> seems to call for a study by a thoroughly representative group
> of leaders from all parts of the state, and from all walks of life.
> I am therefore asking a number of persons to act on this
> committee, under the chairmanship of President David O. McKay,
> of Salt Lake City, who has consented to assume this responsi-
> bility.
> The Legislature appropriated no funds to meet the expenses
> of the committee. I feel justified to ask you to serve because
> of the great public importance of the project. I do not believe
> that the financial burden imposed on you need be very great;
> I know that the advantage to the state will be large.
> After consultation with Chairman McKay, it was decided
> he would issue a call for the first meeting. That call is enclosed.
> Sincerely yours,
> /s/ Henry H. Blood.

At the first meeting of the committee the work was
divided into nine sub-committees, and a chairman was appointed for each of these groups. An executive committee
was also formed to correlate the work of the sub-committees,
and to prepare the final report for the governor and the
legislature.

The committee's work went before the Utah Legislature
in 1939, and legislation was enacted setting up the 1947 Utah
Centennial Commission. Those appointed by Governor Blood
to the commission included President McKay, chairman; Gus
P. Backman, executive secretary; A. Hamer Reiser, corresponding secretary, and members, Samuel O. Bennion, F. P.

Champ, Delbert M. Draper, A. O. Ellett, John F. Fitzpatrick, Ward C. Holbrook, James A. Howell, Rosella F. Larkin, Donald P. Lloyd, Charles R. Mabey, Nephi L. Morris, Mary K. Mower, I. A. Smoot, and John M. Wallace.

Letters from the Commission were sent first to all civic organizations of the state asking for recommendations of scenic or historic spots where improvements or developments should be made in anticipation of the centennial observance.

With the beginning of World War II the plans for a world's fair celebration had to be abandoned, but the idea of a state-wide observance featuring the dramatic history, spiritual traditions, scenic beauties, and distinctive cultural accomplishments of the area began to take shape.

As the plans progressed, President McKay sent a letter to many leaders throughout the state, outlining the programs that were underway. From this letter it is evident that he had caught the vision of a great event which would reach into all parts of the state, and those portions of surrounding states which were settled by the Mormon pioneers.

His letter is as follows:

> Though Salt Lake City will be the hub of interest from which the centennial program of events and attractions will radiate, every beauty spot and point of absorbing interest in the state will be highlighted at some time during the centennial, and will have a share in the attraction of visitors and participants to the celebration.
>
> Already, with enthusiasm and cooperation characteristic of the people of Utah, state-wide beautification projects are being formulated. Even the most isolated communities have caught the spirit and are busy remodeling, landscaping, and planting public and private property. Much of this work has been centered around churches and other public buildings, as a result of the work of an active department of beautification set up by The Church of Jesus Christ of Latter-day Saints.
>
> Utah abounds in majestic mountain, valley, lake, and desert

scenery. Delightful recreational areas exist in abundance throughout the state. It is the purpose of the Centennial Commission to make these attractions easily, economically, and comfortably accessible to everyone by means of a system of excellent highways and comfortable lodging accommodations.

A great variety of recreational interests will be served. The already famous canyons of Cache, Weber, Salt Lake, and Utah Counties, and Zion, Bryce, Cedar Breaks, Wayne Wonderland, and in the San Juan and Uintah areas, will be enjoyed as never before. Camping, hiking, hunting, fishing, horse-back riding, will add still more to the variety offered. Swimming, golf, and other sports will be available. National athletic events and sports attractions will be sought for Utah for the Centennial year.

The brilliant and ever-changing pageantry of Utah scenery, with its flowering beauty of cloud, sunlight, and shadow, upon the wide range of form and color effects, will delight photographers and artists who find joy in capturing nature in repose or in dramatic mood.

All this Utahns plan to offer to their Centennial guests as a prelude and background for their understanding and appreciation of the inspiration which the pioneers of one hundred years ago caught from the land of beauty which was to be their home.

In this setting Utahns hope to have their Centennial re-create something of the pioneer purpose, community life and atmosphere, and by these means help their guests to recapture the spirit of the frontiers as it was expressed in the culture and life of the people of Utah in the early years after 1847.

To support this latter purpose, pioneer art, music, colonization, industry, and achievements will be appropriately featured. Museums, exhibits, pageantry, and dramatic presentations will be employed. The present facilities and resources of the state, expressive of the cultural interests of the people, such as their art centers, dramatic groups, and musical organizations, will play a major part. The organ and choir of the Salt Lake Tabernacle, and smaller but none-the-less beautiful facilities of musical groups in other towns in the state will have important places in the Centennial.

This state-wide Centennial Celebration will achieve its purpose if Utah's guests in 1947 partake of the spiritual serenity, strength of purpose, exaltation, and peace, which the pioneers experienced as they set to work to build their homes in the wilderness of natural beauty which is Utah; and if out of it their visitors can achieve the spiritual response and "peace that passeth understanding."

/s/ David O. McKay
Chairman
Utah Centennial Commission

At the general conference of the Church on April 7, 1946, President McKay delivered a major address on the plans of the Centennial Commission, outlining some of the preparations already underway for historical pageants, musical, dramatic, and educational programs, and athletic and sports events.

He said, in part:

Besides the best that home talent can produce, it is proposed to bring to the state outstanding educational and entertainment features which normally could not be presented in communities of our state—symphony orchestras, stars of stage and screen, Metropolitan Opera singers, sports events of the type our state normally could not finance. It is hoped that we might have these and other cultural entertainments that will be offered, not only in Salt Lake City, but also in other cities where large crowds can be accommodated. All towns and counties in the state are urged to unite in promoting this commemorative celebration.

Indicative of the detailed work of every division of the commission in preparation for the great celebration is this newspaper report from the *Deseret News* of November 14, 1946:

Some three hundred community planners and beautification workers are expected to attend the state-wide conference of the beautification division of the Centennial Commission, Saturday at the Newhouse Hotel.

At a general session, the five state chairmen of subcommittees, Gordon Weggeland, public relations; John D. Rice, clean-up and paint-up; A. B. Paulsen, state parks; George H. Smeath, landscaping; and Raymond J. Ashton, planning and zoning, will speak.

L. Deming Tilton, noted planning consultant of the University of California, Berkeley, will be guest speaker. Subcommittees will hold clinic sessions during the afternoon.

A general session will be held in connection with an evening banquet, at which President David O. McKay, chairman of the Centennial Commission, will preside. Carl Feiss, director of the School of Planning and Architecture, Denver University, will be principal speaker.

Each of the accredited committee members attending the session will receive a working manual containing complete and detailed outlines for their work in complete renovation, housecleaning, and beautification of the state for the centennial celebration in 1947.

When the momentous year finally came, Governor Herbert B. Maw, in an opening message to the state legislature on January 14, 1947, said in part:

> At last our Centennial year has arrived. The Centennial Commission under the chairmanship of President David O. McKay and the managership of Mr. Gus P. Backman has done a magnificent job of planning. Committees, made up of hundreds of leading citizens in every part of the state, are looking forward to events for the entire year of 1947 which will provide culture, education, inspiration, and amusement for all of us. In fact, it will prove to be one of the outstanding celebrations ever undertaken by any state—and rightly so, for it is in commemoration of one of the major events in the history of the nation.

Two days after the governor's message was delivered, the coronation of Utah's Centennial Queen, Miss Colleen Robinson of American Fork took place at the State Capitol. Forming the royal party with Miss Robinson were Mary Louise Gardner of Spanish Fork and Marie Burnett of Salt Lake City. More than 5,000 persons attended the elaborate and beautiful ceremony which was the first major event of the centennial year.

The official opening of centennial events was scheduled for May 1, and on that day a program was held honoring Utah's living pioneers. A reception was held for them at Hotel Utah, at 6:45 p.m., followed by a special meeting in the Salt Lake Tabernacle. Appropriate addresses and musical selections were presented in honor of these first citizens of the state. Each was given a pioneer certificate, indicating arrival in the valley before the coming of the railroad in 1869.

Earlier that same evening there had been a flag-raising ceremony at the State Capitol where Governor Maw and President McKay had both spoken, and then witnessed members of the U. S. Marine Corps raise a flag on historic Ensign Peak north of the Capitol where it was to remain during the entire time of the celebration. At 10 p.m., new floodlights were turned on to illuminate the Brigham Young Monument, and President McKay and Salt Lake Mayor Earl J. Glade each spoke briefly to the assembled crowd.

From this auspicious beginning there were instituted in every part of the state enthusiastic celebrations seldom equalled by the people of any community.

An inspiring pageant, *The Message of the Ages,* by Bertha A. Kleinman, opened May 5 in the Tabernacle and continued for twenty-five evening performances. It was witnessed by 125,000 people. There were six hundred in the cast, with a chorus of two hundred, elaborate costumes, (many brought from Chicago), and a plastic screen on which scenery was projected from behind the stage. This centennial production, subsidized by The Church of Jesus Christ of Latter-day Saints, was a magnificent forerunner of all that followed in quick succession.

On May 15, 16, and 17, the Centennial Commission and the University of Utah Theatre, presented Judith Evelyn in

Joan of Lorraine, by Maxwell Anderson, in Kingsbury Hall. The production was directed by C. Lowell Lees, and the cast that supported Miss Evelyn was made up of twenty local players. For the three-day run, enthusiastic audiences crowded the hall, and there were many disappointed because they could not gain admission.

On May 28, 29, 30, and 31, the Utah Centennial Commission and University Theatre, presented Orson Welles and his all-star cast in William Shakespeare's *Macbeth.* This was considered one of the rarest dramatic opportunities of Utah's theatre history. *"But Not Goodbye,"* a Broadway hit, was presented by The University Players, under the direction of Dr. Lees, as a centennial feature.

Probably the most outstanding, original, musical play ever to be produced in the west was the spectacular *Promised Valley,* given at the University of Utah Stadium, July 21, to August 9, every evening except Sundays. It was written at the request of the Centennial Commission, and sponsored by them. The book and lyrics were by Arnold Sundgaard, of New York, and the music by Crawford Gates. The dances were by Helen Tamaris and Virginia Tanner, the musical direction by Jay Blackton, and the entire production directed by Dr. Lees. *Promised Valley* was written to portray the spirit motivating the pioneer migration from Winter Quarters to Salt Lake City.

Newspapers were generous in their publicity of the production, both before the opening night and in the reviews that followed.

The Salt Lake Telegram reported on July 19, 1947:

> With more than a year of intensive preparation behind it, *Promised Valley,* centennial musical drama, was ready for its premiere Monday night in the University of Utah stadium bowl. The play which will cost approximately $150,000, will hold

performances every evening except Sunday until August 9. In addition to the initial cost, improvements have been made in the form of a $20,000 transportable stage, a $10,000 sound system and a $12,000 lighting system. Another $10,000 has been donated to the University of Utah stadium for improvement of seating facilities and general construction. The new improvements and changes will remain in the stadium after the show closes.

Stars Alfred Drake, Jet McDonald, Barton Mennan, and Nellie Fisher, have been working eight hours a day on rehearsal since their arrival in June. Helen Tamaris, noted choreographer, selected twenty candidates from the Salt Lake City applicants to fill ballet roles in January. Returning from London in June, she added ten more artists.

The total cast of the production will number 225, including orchestra, choruses, ballet, and leading players, and the show will be one of the largest outdoor attractions of its kind ever to be exhibited.

Following the opening night performance, the *Deseret News* said in a review, July 22:

> *Promised Valley* is almost unbelievable. Not even the richest phrases of a Hollywood press agent could do justice to the great centennial production that opened before an audience of more than five thousand last night. You can go to the show expecting to see a spectacular Broadway musical, and actually see one.

During the eighteen-night run, highest praise was given by critics and audiences alike, and the memory of a thrilling, artistic, historical, musical drama will live always in the minds of the thousands who were fortunate to witness it.

The Salt Lake Tabernacle Choir gave brilliant performances of *The Creation*, *The Restoration*, and *Elijah* during the celebration, and the Utah Symphony Orchestra gave special concerts in cities and counties throughout the state. A light operetta, *Blossom Time*, was presented in roadshow performances all over the state.

On June 2 the Centennial Exposition at the state fairgrounds was opened formally for a sixteen-week exhibition. Queen Colleen Robinson snipped a green satin ribbon across the south gate, and Governor Maw escorted her and her attendants to a nearby stage where the festivities began. The governor and President McKay both congratulated the fairgrounds committee for their work in preparing the grounds for the opening-day crowd of more than 7,000. President McKay noted the addition of cement walks, new landscaping, and many general improvements.

Twenty-four of Utah's twenty-nine counties prepared exhibits which were housed in a newly remodeled Industrial Building at the fairgrounds. Displays were also sent from Colorado, Wyoming, Idaho, Nevada, San Francisco, and Los Angeles.

An editorial in the *Salt Lake Telegram* of June 3, 1947 indicated some of the work done at the fairgrounds:

> A gigantic facelifting job has been done at the fairgrounds to make it into a worthy center of Utah's Centennial Celebration. All drives and walks have been paved. Low cement brick walls have been built to enclose patios where there are comfortable seats for exposition visitors. The grounds are all landscaped, with lawn, shrubs, and flowers. All the buildings have been painted, and there has been much interior remodeling and redecorating. This was a permanent contribution by the Centennial Commission. While the midway attractions, Holiday on Ice, light opera performances, Walter Follies, rodeo, auto races, etc., will be of interest, the major emphasis is still the presentation of one hundred years of Utah progress.
>
> The Centennial Exposition is a big project. It is not by any means just another state fair. It will continue to run until September 20, sixteen weeks of interesting exhibitions, entertainment, contests, stock shows, art exhibits, music auditions, floral displays and many other attractions.

The million-dollar show, One Hundred Years of American Painting, opened at the fairgrounds June 30, and continued through July 29. Its gorgeous paintings received a warm welcome by Utahns. Students in schools throughout the state received special invitations to enjoy the rare pieces of art included in the exhibit.

Throughout the state, in every county and in most cities and towns, individual celebrations were held, and whenever possible, President McKay made it a point to be on hand for these.

One of the most colorful spectacles on the centennial sports program was held at Pine View Lake in Ogden Canyon, on July 4, and 5. It was directed by the Ogden Pine View Yacht Club. Fifteen thousand visitors viewed the races during the two-day celebration.

The historical pageant, *A Link in a Mighty Empire,* written and produced by Mr. and Mrs. M. W. Smith, and presented at the Sevier County Fair Grounds, at Richfield, Utah, was sponsored by that county's centennial committee.

July 15 to 19, marked the date of the Black Hawk encampment at Heber, Wasatch County, which was witnessed by thousands of visitors.

Santaquin's contribution was *The Centennial Town Frolic,* a two-day celebration under the direction of Mrs. R. J. Peterson, centennial chairman. A four-day celebration was held in Wayne County, *The Rainbow Land.* One of the many features was a pageant depicting the Wayne County pioneers.

Pleasant Grove, Utah County, adapted the annual Strawberry Festival to the centennial celebration.

Ogden's *Loyalty Fete,* with eleven thousand students marching in parade, was given in honor of approximately fifty Weber County pioneers, who, with President McKay, witnessed the spectacle from a grandstand erected for their convenience.

Smithfield's annual *Health Day,* was also adapted to the centennial theme, with President McKay as the principal speaker.

Hyrum, Cache County, dated its celebration for July 19 to 24. Beaver County's was on July 22. Spanish Fork's rodeo was also on July 22.

Saga of Sanpete, historical outdoor pageant, presented August 29 and 30 at the Sanpete County Fair Grounds, was dedicated to the Mormon pioneers.

Davis County Days included a unique parade shown in every major center in the county. The Salt Lake County Fair, at Murray, with a parade of centennial events, commenced August 25. Summit County held its celebration at Coalville August 28, 29, and 30, and Duchesne County at Roosevelt, on August 30.

Over the Labor Day holiday, vacationers had a choice of three celebrations, Bountiful's *Cantaloupe Day,* American Fork's *Steel Day,* and Payson's *Golden Onion Day,* the latter being extended to a five-day event for the centennial year. Brigham City's annual *Peach Day* started September 4. The Grand County Fair was scheduled in Moab for September 11 to 13. Iron County's celebration was held at Parowan September 15 to 19. In the south-western part of the state, the *Deseret Rodeo,* with honest-to-goodness cowboys, was held September 22 and 23. Richfield sponsored the *Southern Utah Junior Livestock Show* on September 3, 4, and 5.

These are but a few of the outstanding events sponsored locally and illustrating the extent to which the centennial celebration reached the remotest corners of the state, uniting as one the descendants of the pioneers who bequeathed a noble heritage to the sons and daughters of this vast western area.

The most important week of the centennial was that of July 24. On Sunday, July 20, President McKay delivered an address, *Faith Triumphant*, over the Columbia Broadcasting System's *Church of the Air* program, in which he paid tribute to the Mormon pioneers. Many congratulatory letters poured into his office from near-by and distant parts of the country following the address.

Tuesday, July 22, marked the date of arrival of the Sons of Utah Pioneers' Trek, from Nauvoo, Illinois, to Salt Lake City. Re-enacting drama of a century ago, 148 Sons of Utah Pioneers Centennial Trekkers followed the trail of their forefathers across more than half a continent. Along the 1,400 mile trail, spectators lined the streets of every town to watch the novel covered-wagon-topped and oxen-drawn cars —an excellent replica of the original wagon train of 1847. Elder Spencer W. Kimball, of the Council of the Twelve, who accompanied the caravan all the way, said: "Citizens all along the trail, from Nauvoo to Salt Lake City, will have a higher regard for Utah and her people as a result of this trip."

President McKay met the company at Fort Bridger, Wyoming, and addressed them at their last encampment. President George Albert Smith and Governor Maw, met the caravan at Henefer, and led them into the city, where an appropriate welcome was given them.

Members of the Sons of the Utah Pioneers taking part in this unique contribution to the centennial celebration, made the trip at their own expense.

On July 24, at 9:30 a.m., the great *This is the Place Monument* was dedicated. The monument was commenced under the direction of President Heber J. Grant, the Monument Commission carrying on and completing their great task under the leadership of President George Albert Smith, who presided at the dedicatory exercises. President McKay addressed the fifty thousand people in attendance at the ceremony.

At 12:15 p.m., a formal luncheon honoring the Utah pioneers was served at the Hotel Utah, ushering in the use of the Centennial Stamp. Joseph J. Lawler, the Third Assistant Postmaster General, and R. E. Fellers, Stamp Superintendent of the United States Post Office Department, from Washington, D. C., were present for this occasion. Mr. Lawler lauded the hardy Mormon pioneers who elected to settle in the new-found freedom of the far west. He said that in selecting a design for the new Utah stamp, the Post Office had endeavored to bring a motif symbolic of that memorable and historic scene of the first wagon train arriving on this spot, July 24, 1847.

President McKay pointed out that the Centennial Stamp had done much to publicize Utah, and commended the Post Office officials for issuing a most appropriate commemorative stamp. Already half a million stamp collectors had requested stamps. Three million stamps were issued to Utah for the Centennial, and 125 million stamps had been printed. This was one of the largest and most popular issues the Post Office Department had witnessed.

At 4 p.m. that day the Immigrant Pioneer Plaque in the State Capitol was unveiled. A message of congratulation was received from President Harry S Truman, and he was sent a special centennial medal, which he acknowledged with appreciation.

On July 23, at 8:30 a.m., the long anticipated parade swept magnificently through down town Salt Lake before a thrilled crowd of two hundred thousand people.

Heralded by a flight of army pursuit planes, the giant street pageant swung into its march and for two hours kept a firm grip on the crowd which lined the sixteen blocks of march. More than seventy colorful floats, supported by more than twenty bands and some four thousand marching Boy Scouts, made it the longest parade in the city's century-long history.

Brigadier General J. Wallace West, state adjutant and marshall of the day, led the parade, followed by the color guard and the United States Marine Band from San Diego, California. They were followed by official cars carrying Governor and Mrs. Maw, the First Presidency of The Church of Jesus Christ of Latter-day Saints, Mayors Lowell Horton, of Nauvoo, Illinois, and Earl J. Glade, of Salt Lake City, and The Centennial Commission. Then came the Boy Scouts, interspersed with Utah high school bands. The first division of floats drew expressions of appreciation from the massed onlookers.

Fourteen horsewomen in colorful Spanish costumes, followed by the Pasadena City College Tournament of Roses Band, brightened the marching column. Twenty nations of the world were represented by some of Utah's loveliest girls, dressed in elaborate national costumes, each carrying the nation's flag.

Centennial queen, Colleen Robinson, dressed in her coronation robes, and seated on her sego lily throne, with her two attendants, brought murmurs of approval. Then followed floats depicting every phase of Utah's one hundred years of history, interspersed by colorful bands.

The parade was repeated on July 24, at 6 p.m. The *Salt Lake Telegram* on July 25, said: "It was indeed a great parade—one that not only outranked anything hitherto presented in this state, but one which also ranks well with any parade ever presented in the West."

A *Deseret News* editorial, September 8, 1947, said:

"Although the Centennial year still has a part of its course to run, it has become plain to us here in Utah, and to many people the world over, that no people has ever had before the kind and caliber of celebration that has graced our efforts here in these mountain valleys.

"To President David O. McKay and the Centennial Commission, to Governor Herbert B. Maw, to Gus Backman, and to a host of others too numerous to mention, the people of Utah owe a vote of deep appreciation for the planning and management of the thousands of special Centennial events. The good that has come to Utah and the West as a result of their planning and leadership is difficult to estimate."

"No state has ever received greater publicity through an undertaking," says a Salt Lake Chamber of Commerce announcement, "than has the State of Utah through its Centennial."

Nearly every major magazine in the country has told the story of our history and achievements. Newspapers everywhere have done likewise. Hours of radio network time have been devoted to Brigham Young and his followers, and to the things being done here today to memorialize their achievements.

Utah has gained much from her centennial. Our greatest rewards, however, will come through the years as we practice what has passed before our eyes this year in one grand panorama.

The *Salt Lake Tribune* of July 30, 1947, carried the following: "Rodney C. Richardson, Coordinator of California centennial affairs, came to Salt Lake City to study Utah's Centennial, which, he said, was conceded to have 'the best planning in the nation. Lack of commercialism is one of the outstanding features of the Utah Centennial. It has been a true historical celebration.' "

Mr. Richardson expressed great appreciation for the way Centennial officials have worked with cities and counties to extend the celebration to all corners of the state. He said that an astonishing job had been done in getting organizations to work together.

Many other states wrote for plans and other literature of the celebration.

When all reports were in, the results showed many permanent improvements left in different parts of the state, besides the ones already noted. Instead of a deficit, as is often the case, at the close of the celebration, the Centennial Commission returned to the state the half million dollars appropriated by the Legislature as a revolving fund. This was a procedure entirely unique in the annals of finance.

Saturday evening, September 20, the Exposition gates were closed, after a summer-long tribute to the pioneers, emphasizing the theme of the Centennial—"One hundred years of Empire building." On October 15, the entire program ended.

During all these months of strenuous work, President McKay had kept up his Church duties and responsibilities, making a double load for him to carry. He did it in his usual cheerful and efficient manner, making a success of both.

In the *Salt Lake Tribune* of Sunday, September 21, 1947, there was a report of a letter in which President McKay praised sincerely the men and women whose indefatigable labors contributed so much to the success of the Centennial. He wrote: "Perhaps never before in the history of our state have so many people willingly, energetically, and ably, united to accomplish a single purpose. Thank you one and all for your loyalty to a great cause. Your masterful efforts in planning and in execution have been a worthy tribute to the pioneers, and have brought credit and honor to Utah and her surrounding commonwealths."

Then, commencing with the governor and legislature, he mentioned all committees and individuals, county committees and Church committees who worked so valiantly for the success of the great celebration. No one was omitted from this letter of generous and sincere appreciation.

That President McKay's efforts in heading the planning and administration of the details of the celebration were appreciated, is evident from the many tributes received. A few of these are quoted:

"Dear President McKay:

I spent an hour last Saturday in reading the General Report of the 1947 Utah Centennial Commission. The work of the Commission was ideally well-done, artistically and financially. The good results will be felt for years to come.

This is just a word of congratulation to a man, yourself, who has done more for the public welfare, within and without the Church, than any person should be called upon to do. May life in health and strength long wait upon you.

Cordially your friend and brother,

John A. Widtsoe."

"Dear President:

This is to acknowledge with sincere thanks your wonderful letter of December 13. I can only say in reply that the privilege of having served under your direction for the last two and a half years, provided the greatest happiness I have ever experienced in my business life. I only hope that at sometime in the very immediate future, I shall have the privilege of again serving under your direction.

The success of the Centennial was possible only through your great leadership, and the unselfish work done by all of the members of the Centennial Commission. It has been a real joy to me to have been associated with these fine people who served so efficiently with you.

Sincerely Yours,

Gus P. Backman."

Salt Lake City, Utah, Nov. 3, 1949.

David O. McKay, Chairman,
Utah Centennial Commission,
Salt Lake City, Utah.

Dear President McKay:

It was indeed with mixed feelings that I received your letter of Oct. 25, as the last official communication of the Utah Centennial Commission. It is with keen regret that I note the passage into history of the Centennial Commission; and yet, at the same time, I have a feeling of real pride in having been permitted to take part in the great work of the Commission.

No state has yet presented a finer or more artistic Centennial Celebration Program, and no state can even approach the financial handling of this great program. The physical improvements made throughout the state, the spiritual awakening, the community pride, to say nothing of the tremendous national publicity gained for the state and its people, can be marked up as a credit to the Centennial that will live and enrich the state and its people for many years to come.

The greatest personal satisfaction to me, however, was the knowledge of working with you, and under your inspirational leadership. To you must go the individual credit for the brilliant success of this grand undertaking.

Personally, I know some of the heartaches, disappointments, and obstructions, that you encountered, but never once did you falter or give up that radiant hope and enthusiasm which you imparted to every individual connected with the project. It was a fine job, and I am proud and happy indeed, to have been connected with it. I salute you as a great leader, and would be willing, and feel honored, to be chosen to follow you in any undertaking.

With all good wishes to you, and with my warm personal regard, I am,

Yours Very Sincerely,

J. F. Fitzpatrick.

At a meeting of the Centennial Commission held January 2, 1948, a scroll expressing appreciation of President McKay's outstanding leadership as Chairman of the Centennial Commission, together with a gold fountain pen, were presented by their representative, Judge James A. Howell, who stated:

> Apart from the consciousness of a task well done, your reward, Sir, for this outstanding service you have thus rendered, will be the practically universal satisfaction that the celebration you have led is as worthy of the pioneers whom it honored, as it could be. However, the committee felt that you should have some memento that you can always keep as a commemorative of the fine association which has been established between the members and you as we have worked together throughout the years of this common cause.
>
> This scroll symbolizes the sentiments I have endeavored to express and which is signed by members of the commission, and also this gold pen, which typifies in the purity of the metal, the purity of the affection which is ours for you. The inscription on the scroll reads: "In appreciation of David O. McKay, from co-workers on the Utah Centennial Commission. To know you is a joy, to work with you is a privilege, and to be guided by you is an inspiration. There is no finer man."

In President McKay's response he said:

> It has been truly said that there is no thought which cannot be expressed, but that there are feelings too deep for expression. I know this is true. This is one of those moments in my life in which I sense the inadequacy of words to express the feelings of my heart.
>
> The tribute you have given me comes wholly unexpected and uninvited, and I say that sincerely. Every word of commendation in your beautiful, impressive presentation, I should like to apply to each member of this Board. All you have said to me, I want to say to you, because you are the men and women who have made this Centennial Celebration successful, and have carried out the high ideals to which Judge Howell has referred.
>
> Nine years have passed since Governor Blood and the State Legislature appointed this Centennial Commission, and assigned to me the task of chairmanship. At that time, I knew some of

you intimately; others of you I had not met, and I knew you only by reputation. I knew little about your ability, and nothing about your innermost feelings and thoughts; but I want to tell you that tonight I can say with all my soul, I love you, and I esteem as one of the greatest experiences of my life the opportunity I have had to associate with you on this Centennial Commission.

I believe we can truly say that no celebration of events in the history of Utah has been supported more unitedly by the people of the state than has our Centennial Celebration. The counties have united; the people have reflected unity.

Letters of congratulation came to President McKay from every member of the Commission, from mission presidents, from chambers of commerce, from governors of states, from organizations, local and national, from the Utah State Legislature, and from hundreds of citizens.

Chapter 12

A Solemn Assembly

The year 1951 was momentous in the life of David O. McKay.

As plans were being completed for the April Conference of the Church that year, President George Albert Smith's health weakened, and his doctors advised that he rest in bed. Then his condition took a turn for the worse, and death came at 7:27 p.m. on Wednesday, April 4, his 81st birthday anniversary.

President Smith's counselors, President J. Reuben Clark, Jr., and President McKay, carried on with the sessions of the general conference, while plans were made for President Smith's funeral services on Saturday, April 7.

Following the impressive funeral service and the regular Sunday sessions of the conference, a Solemn Assembly was held on Monday, April 9 at 10 a.m. in the Salt Lake Tabernacle for the sustaining of a new Quorum of the First Presidency of The Church of Jesus Christ of Latter-day Saints.

The arrangements for the Solemn Assembly were the same as those that had been held since John Taylor was

The First Presidency of The Church of Jesus Christ of Latter-day Saints as sustained in the solemn assembly of April 9, 1951. From left to right, President Stephen L Richards, first counselor; President David O. McKay; President J. Reuben Clark, Jr., second counselor.

sustained as President of the Church in 1889. The entire lower floor of the Tabernacle was reserved for bearers of the priesthood, and they were seated in quorums. They voted in their respective groups.

Before the names were presented, the vast audience was reminded that, as individuals, they were free to express themselves for or against any one named for the offices to be filled. A sincere spirit of love pervaded the assembly, and a unanimous vote was offered in sustaining David Oman McKay as Prophet, Seer, and Revelator, and the ninth President of The Church of Jesus Christ of Latter-day Saints. Sustained as counselors in the First Presidency were President Stephen L Richards and President J. Reuben Clark, Jr.

After this unanimous vote of confidence, President McKay told the members of the Church assembled in the Tabernacle:

My beloved brethren and sisters, fellow workers:

I wish it were within my power of expression to let you know what my true feelings are on this momentous occasion. I would wish that you might look into my heart and see there for yourselves just what these feelings are.

It is just one week ago today that the realization came to me that this responsibility of leadership would probably fall upon my shoulders. I received word that President George Albert Smith had taken a turn for the worse, and that the doctors felt that the end was not far off. I hastened to his bedside, and with his weeping daughters, son, and other kinfolk, I entered his sick room. For the first time he failed to recognize me.

Then I had to accept the realization that the Lord had chosen not to answer our pleadings as we would have had them answered, and that he was going to take him home to himself. Thankfully, he rallied again later in the day. Several days preceding that visit, as President Clark and I were discussing problems of import pertaining to the Church, he, ever solicitous of the welfare of the Church, and of my feelings, would say,

"The responsibility will be yours to make this decision," but each time I would refuse to face what, to him, seemed a reality.

When that reality came, as I tell you, I was deeply moved. And I am today, and pray that I may, even though inadequately, be able to tell you how weighty this responsibility seems.

The Lord has said that the three presiding high priests, chosen by the body, appointed and ordained to this office of presidency, are to be "upheld by the confidence, faith, and prayers of the Church." No one can preside over this Church without first being in tune with the head of the Church, our Lord and Savior Jesus Christ. He is our head. This is his Church. Without his divine guidance and constant inspiration, we cannot succeed. With his guidance, with his inspiration, we cannot fail.

Next to that as a sustaining potent power, comes the confidence, faith, prayers, and united support of the Church.

I pledge to you that I shall do my best to live to merit the companionship of the Holy Spirit, and pray here in your presence that my counselors and I "may indeed be partakers of the divine spirit."

Next to that we plead with you for a continuation of the love and confidence as you have expressed it today. From you members of the Twelve we ask for that love and sympathy expressed in our sacred Council. For the Assistants to the Twelve, the Patriarch, the First Council of the Seventy, the Presiding Bishopric, we ask that the spirit of unity expressed by our Lord and Savior when he was saying goodby to the Twelve, may be manifest by us all.

You remember he said as he left them:

"And now I am no more of the world, but these are in the world, and I come to thee. Holy Father, keep through thine own name those whom thou hast given me, that they may be one as we are.

"Neither do I pray for these alone, but for them also who shall believe on me through their word:

"That they all may be one, as thou, Father, art in me and I in thee, that they also may be one in us, that the world may believe that thou hast sent me." (John 17:11, 20-21.)

Brethren and sisters, brethren of the general authorities,

God keep us as one, overlooking weaknesses we see, keeping an eye single to the glory of God and the advancement of his work.

And now to the members of the Church. We all need your help, your faith and prayers, not your adverse criticism, but your help. You can do that in prayer if you cannot reach us in person. The potency of these prayers throughout the Church came to me yesterday when I received a letter from a neighbor in my old home town. He was milking his cows when the word came over the radio which he had in his barn, that President Smith had passed. He sensed what that would mean to his former fellow-townsman, and he left his barn and went to the house and told his wife. Immediately they called their little children, and there in that humble home, suspending their activities, they knelt down as a family and offered prayer. The significance of that prayer I leave for you to understand. Multiply that by a hundred thousand, two hundred thousand, half a million homes, and see the power in the unity and prayers, and the sustaining influence in the body of the Church.

Today you have by your vote placed upon us the greatest responsibility, as well as the greatest honor that lies within your power to bestow as members of The Church of Jesus Christ of Latter-day Saints. Your doing so increases the duty of the First Presidency to render service to the people.

God bless you brethren and sisters. May the spirit of this session remain in your hearts. May it be felt throughout the uttermost parts of the earth, wherever there is a branch in all the world, that that spirit might be a unifying power in increasing the testimony of the divinity of this work, that it may grow in its influence for good in the establishment of peace throughout the world.

I bear you my testimony that the head of this Church is the Lord and Savior Jesus Christ. I know the reality of his existence, of his willingness to guide and direct all who serve him. I know he rendered, with his Father, to the Prophet Joseph Smith, the gospel of the Lord Jesus Christ in its fulness. I know that these brethren whom you have sustained today are men of God. I love them. Don't you think anything else. God's will has been done.

May we have increased power to be true to the responsibilities that the Lord has placed upon us, and I pray this in the name of Jesus Christ, Amen.

Thus, with a great spirit of humility and placing his trust in God from whom he knew would come the needed strength, President McKay assumed the greatest honor and responsibility that could come to him in the Church.

This new responsibility came forty-five years after that April in 1906 when he was called as an Apostle—forty-five years of devoted service and unexcelled leadership in the Restored Church of Jesus Christ. Of those years, nearly seventeen were as second counselor in the First Presidency, first to President Heber J. Grant from 1934 to 1945 and then to President Smith since 1945.

Now the mantle of presidency had fallen on his shoulders. He was the rightful successor to the Prophet Joseph Smith. As prophet, seer, and revelator since 1951, President McKay has truly brought inspired direction to the Church, and has won the trust, love, and respect of a vast Church membership.

Chapter 13

A Visit to Europe

On Wednesday, May 28, 1952, the announcement was made through the press that the members of the Church residing in the British Isles and on the European continent were to have the rare privilege of a visit from the President of The Church of Jesus Christ of Latter-day Saints. It was also stated that he was to fly from New York on June 1, and arrive in Scotland on June 2. The special purpose of the trip was not to be announced until after his arrival in Europe.

Accompanying President McKay on this trip were Mrs. McKay and their son and daughter-in-law, David Lawrence and Mildred C. McKay, the former an assistant general superintendent of the Deseret Sunday School Union, and the latter a member of the Primary Association general board.

Before leaving home President McKay was advised by his physician that it was imperative that he have time to rest each day; otherwise the trip as outlined would prove too strenuous for him. Instead of taking time out for relaxation, however, the itinerary was enlarged to include additional cities and many more meetings than were included in the original plan.

President Stayner Richards, Assistant to the Council of the Twelve, and president of the British Mission, had arranged the tour, and he and Mrs. Richards met the President and his party when they landed at the airport in Glasgow, Scotland, on Monday, June 2, at 3:30 p.m. At 7:30, they arrived for the dedicatory exercises of the new Glasgow chapel, and were greeted by more than 300 people.

A group of Primary boys presented President McKay with a gold McKay crest fastened to a McKay tartan, and a book of scenes of Scotland. The president was deeply touched by this presentation, and by the hearty welcome given him by the audience. He spoke of his previous visits to Europe, first as a missionary to Scotland in 1897, then on his world tour with Elder Hugh J. Cannon in 1921, and as President of the European Mission in 1922-24.

The Glasgow press heralded the dedication of the first chapel of the Church in Scotland. One newspaper, commenting on President McKay's visit, said, "It will probably surprise most people to learn that Mormon missionaries from America have been working in Scotland for more than one hundred years."

All the papers made much of the fact that President McKay, world leader of the Mormons, made the trip to Scotland from America in order to dedicate the Glasgow chapel. Some recounted the history of the Church in Scotland, and others gave fair treatment of some of the doctrines of the Church.

On Wednesday President McKay addressed the members of the Edinburgh Branch and dedicated their chapel. As an introduction to his address he said:

108

Before I tell you how grateful I am for the hearty welcome extended to Sister McKay, our son and daughter, and me, in Glasgow and Edinburgh, let me just briefly state that it has been more than one hundred years since my grandfather, William McKay, and grandmother, Ellen Oman McKay, left Thurso, Scotland, having become converts to The Church of Jesus Christ of Latter-day Saints.

They settled in Ogden, Utah, and so, in the same year, did the Evans family from, Wales. And William McKay's second son, David McKay, met a little girl nine years of age, Jennette Evans, who nine years later became his wife.

About 1877, William McKay, my grandfather, returned to his native land as a missionary, and went up to Wick, Thurso, and Aberdeen, bearing witness that the gospel had been restored, and that he knew it to be true.

About 1881, his son David, my father, came over here as a missionary. He, too, labored in Glasgow, Dundee, Aberdeen, and in Thurso, and he appointed president of the Glasgow Conference.

And so as I look back in reminiscent mood upon those events, and many others that have crowded my mind, there is gratitude in my heart that a humble elder, a hundred years ago, knocked on a door in Thurso, and testified that the Gospel of Jesus Christ had been restored. I am thankful that my grandfather and grandmother believed that, because that was the beginning of the events that have happened in the century leading to this moment.

After a powerful sermon on the subject, "Happiness, the Aim of the Gospel of Jesus Christ," the President dedicated the chapel in the beautiful city of Edinburgh.

On Thursday morning he and his party arrived in London. Here he spent several busy days attending to special business matters, meeting with missionaries and members of the Church. On Sunday, conference sessions were held, attended by approximately one thousand members of the British Mission.

Through a slight change in his previously planned itinerary, President McKay was in Basel, Switzerland, on

Tuesday, June 10, where he attended to special business pertaining to the purpose of his European trip.

From Berne, President McKay and his party arrived at the Schiphol Airport, in Holland, on Wednesday. They were met by President and Mrs. Donovan H. Van Dam, who traveled with them to Scheveningen, to their suite in the Palace Hotel.

On Thursday morning, the President and his party were taken to Soestdyk, where Queen Juliana entertained President and Mrs. McKay at her palace. During the visit President McKay gave her greetings from the thousands of Dutch saints in America, and explained the missionary system of the Church. He told his royal hostess, the Queen, he would like to present her with a Book of Mormon, which she said she would be very happy to accept.

The visit, which lasted for more than half an hour, was arranged by the Dutch Consul General in San Francisco, through the cooperation of the Vice-Consul, Bas Van Dongen, in Salt Lake City.

After this visit, President McKay had several interviews with news correspondents from Holland's leading papers, and also from the United Press and Associated Press.

On Friday, June 13, there was a mission-wide conference of missionaries and members in Rotterdam, attended by 1,024, which represented one third of the membership of the mission. At this meeting there was a presentation of a Delft Blue China plate to President and Mrs. McKay, and one also to Elder and Mrs. David Lawrence McKay.

During his remarks, the President said:

> Today, Sister McKay and I stood on the ruins of the place where thirty years ago a very remarkable experience occurred to me. I was speaking to an audience here in Rotterdam, and President Zappey was interpreting, when it happened that the gift of interpreting tongues was given to me. There may be some

here today who were present at that time. President Zappey was making a statement following my remarks, and even though I could not understand the language, I knew that he had given the wrong interpretation, and I told him so, and corrected him. He turned to me and said that I really had no need for an interpreter, since I understood the language so well. This is an illustration of the spirit directing the minds of each.

Now that building is gone—destroyed by the power of man. May the Lord hasten the day when there shall be no more war. Nobody is helped by it. The victors are losers and the innocent suffer.

As I stood on that barren spot, I felt moved to offer a prayer to the Lord to hasten the day when peace may once more come to the world.

That evening President and Mrs. McKay were guests of honor at a banquet of all missionaries in Holland, held in the Palace Hotel in Scheveningen. He addressed the gathering following the dinner program.

The President's arrival in Copenhagen, Denmark, on June 14, was a thrilling experience for hundreds of Latter-day Saints, many of whom awaited his arrival at the Copenhagen airport. As the plane arrived from Amsterdam, his tear-blurred vision beheld a large Danish flag, and at its side, the Stars and Stripes floating proudly in his honor. Reaching his ears were the lovely strains of the famed Mormon hymn, "Come, Come, Ye Saints."

As the last notes of the hymn faded, the President, visibly moved by this greeting, waved to the group and went with his party into the Customs office. While they were going through the customs, the large crowd assembled in the waiting-room of the administration building and sang, "Now Let Us Rejoice . . . ," then as the President came through the door-way, all joined in singing, "We Thank Thee, O God, for a Prophet." This was not just a song. It was a sincere expression of appreciation and gratitude that the Prophet of the Lord had set foot on Danish soil. One of the newspaper reporters present, later wrote, "The President of the Mormon Church, David O. McKay, received an exceptional welcome at the airport as several Danish Mormons sang welcome songs and completely drowned out the loud speaker's announcing the arrival and departure of planes."

President McKay took time, before leaving the airport, to greet personally and shake hands with everyone who came to welcome him. Then he and his party were taken to the mission home to be the guests of President and Mrs. Edward H. Sorensen.

Then began a busy week-end. A concert was presented in the evening. An hour before the concert began, the hall was filled and many were standing. President Ejnar Nielsen of the Danish Mission Presidency presiding, reminded the audience that it was just one hundred years to the day, June 14, 1852, that the first Apostle, Erastus Snow, came to Denmark, to bring the gospel to the Danish people.

Sunday, June 15, was a spiritual feast for the hundreds who packed the Copenhagen chapel, and listened to words of inspiration from President McKay. Four outstanding meetings were held—priesthood meeting at 8:30 a.m., Sunday School at 10. Bouquets of roses were presented to Sister Emma Ray McKay and Mildred C. McKay. At the conclusion of the Sunday School session, President Sorensen, in behalf of the missionaries and members, presented to President and Sister McKay a sterling silver salt and pepper set and a figurine, "The Harvest Girl," of world-famous Copenhagen porcelain. A beautiful sterling silver berry spoon was given to Brother and Sister David L. McKay.

A special missionary meeting was held in the afternoon, and the evening service climaxed an outstanding day, typical of the busy days the President was spending in each of the European missions visited during the tour. As he closed his address, he said: "Goodbye my friends, we must leave in the morning to visit the Saints in other missions. Let me assure you that as we take the plane, and leave this lovely land of Denmark, we shall carry with us the love and fond memories of one of the choicest people in all the world. God bless you."

After the closing prayer, while the President and his party were still seated, the congregation arose and sang, "God Be With You Till We Meet Again."

After each of the meetings, opportunity was given members and friends to shake hands and receive greetings and blessings from President McKay.

On Thursday, June 19, in the late afternoon, a large group of members and missionaries assembled at the Stockholm airport to greet the Presidential party. Press and newsreel representatives joined the welcoming crowd as President and Mrs. Clarence F. Johnson welcomed the President to the land of the midnight sun, and presented the traditional floral bouquet—a token of welcome.

On arrival at the Hotel Malmen, President McKay, in spite of a tiring journey, just completed, met the news representatives for nearly an hour at an official conference.

The Swedish Mission Mutual Improvement Association Conference scheduled to meet July 10 to 14 was changed to June 20 to 25 to coincide with this visit. There was also a conference of Swedish missionaries, followed by an evening's entertainment presented by various Mutuals of the mission, which received the warm congratulations of the President.

At the Sunday morning session the message was a beautiful admonition to the Saints to remain true to their covenants with their Heavenly Father; that with all their power they live in accordance with those principles of righteousness on which a true Latter-day Saint's life is based and dependent.

At the Sunday evening meeting, held in one of the largest auditoriums in Stockholm, and at which members of the Swedish Church, representatives of the national press, and non-members from every walk of Swedish life were present, President McKay delivered a powerful and highly impressive address in the packed hall. His theme was the burning need in the world for a return to a belief in the existence and power of our Heavenly Father. He said, "The most ominous threat to the peace and happiness of mankind is not the probable misuse of the atomic bomb, but the dwindling in men's hearts of faith in God." With a brilliant insight into the true situation of the world today, he portrayed a picture so true to life, that no one present was left in doubt as to the veracity of his message. On this pertinent and inspiring note ended probably the most significant public meeting held so far in the Swedish Mission.

Next morning farewells were said to the Swedish saints and missionaries to the strains of "God Be With You Till We Meet Again," when the party continued on to Helsinki where the Finnish members were awaiting their arrival.

For the first time in history, a president of The Church of Jesus Christ of Latter-day Saints visited Finland. What a royal welcome the more than 350 members of the Church in that comparatively young mission gave to President and Mrs. McKay and his party at the Malmi Airport, Helsinki!

June 23 was a special day for Mrs. McKay as she was celebrating her 75th birthday, and as the party left the airport in Stockholm about 300 people waved goodbye and sang "Happy Birthday." President Henry Matis of the Finnish Mission escorted the party to the mission home where an American dinner was served, complete with birthday cake and candles, and the missionaries and members of the Relief Society sang "Happy Birthday" in Finnish, and then all repeated it in English.

After the dinner, the party drove about ten miles to Vihtijarvi, a lake, on the edge of which the Latter-day Saint youth of the mission were gathered for the first Scout encampment in Finland. The camp was sponsored by the Mutual Improvement Associations and ably directed by Mr. and Mrs. Martti Hartiala, who were formerly active in scout work for the state. They were assisted by Elder Don Brown, a missionary from Salt Lake City.

As President McKay approached the camp, one of the girl scouts stepped forward, very formally and in good English, welcomed the President and his party to Finland and to the scout camp. Then, successively, different girl scouts each brought a rose to Sister McKay, wishing her a happy birthday. Other girls pinned corsages of wild lilies of the valley on each of the party. Twenty-five missionaries then presented Sister McKay with birthday roses. The group then sang some Finnish songs, and "We Thank Thee, O God, for a Prophet," and "Come, Come, Ye Saints" in the Finnish language.

By this time all were in tears—they were tears of gratitude, for they realized that they were singing to a true prophet of God.

The following day was mid-summer "John's Day"—a holiday—and the streets of Helsinki were deserted. President McKay and his party were staying at the new Vaakuna Hotel, and all restaurants were closed during the day, so the Utahn's were guests of President and Mrs. Matis. Members of the Church from outlying districts were coming in all day to Helsinki for the general meeting which was to be held in the evening, and all brought their own food.

That evening a public meeting was held at which 450 members of the Church and their friends were inspired by the wisdom and counsel from the lips of their beloved and revered prophet.

On Wednesday, June 25, President McKay and President Matis flew to Turku, where they were escorted to the summer estate of Finland's President, T. H. Paasikivi, who welcomed them cordially, and visited with them for some time. On their return to Helsinki in the late afternoon, they met with Minister John Cabot at the United States Embassy for a pleasant visit.

The following day, as President McKay and his party were at the airport to take a plane for Germany, many members of the Church and their friends were there to say goodbye, and as the plane left Finnish soil, the strains of "God Be With You 'Till We Meet Again" floated with them into the air.

From Helsinki President McKay went to Hamburg, Germany, where he was met on June 26, by President and Mrs. Edwin Q. Cannon of the West German Mission, missionaries of the Hamburg area, as well as representatives of the press.

That evening he addressed a capacity crowd of 900 members and friends in Hamburg's Gewerbehaus, appealing especially to the young people of the group. He said, "Let us make our ideals in life the Kingdom of God." He also stated that next to life itself, man's free agency is the greatest gift from God, and after free agency is the sense of mastery over the evil of the world—abstinence from intoxicating liquors and other poisonous substances, and keeping one's self pure from sexual indulgence. These will determine if a man will be master of himself or be subject to his passions.

"Young men and women, yes, old men and women also, who resist temptation, grow in strength of character, and place themselves in a position to respond to the influence of the Holy Spirit. Strength of character and service to mankind are attributes of nobility we can take back to God," he said.

After this brief visit to Hamburg, the Presidential party left for Berlin where they spent the week-end.

In reporting this visit, the secretary of the East German Mission wrote: "A fitting climax to one of the greatest weeks of activity in the history of the East German Mission was the long-awaited visit here of President David O. McKay. He came in time to complete a combined missionary and mission conference which had extended from Tuesday, June 24, through Sunday, June 29.

"Many factors combined to make this conference an unusual one. About 1,500 members of the Church, and German missionaries, came from beyond the Iron Curtain, from the Russian Zone of East Germany, at great personal sacrifice. Their unusual comment was, 'Although we don't have sufficient to live on here, we will see our president and prophet at any price.' "

Another factor making the conference a success was the technical delays in putting through a government order preventing the East Germans from crossing their border into the Berlin sector.

Incidental to the signing of the German peace treaty, Communist dictators had sealed the borders so that nobody could cross into West Germany from the Soviet Zone. They tried to carry out a similar order to stop the flow to Berlin from East Germany, but on technical grounds were unable to stop trains coming into the city. At least they were not able to do so until Tuesday, July 1, the very day members of the Church were safely returned to their homes.

If these measures had been successful three days earlier, most of the 1,500 from the Soviet Zone would not have been able to come to the conference.

Climaxing this missionary conference was the testimony meeting held with President McKay on Friday, June 27.

Without resting or even going to his hotel room from the Berlin Templehof Airport, where he had arrived from Hamburg, President McKay was driven directly to the missionary meeting. For most of them it was the first opportunity they had ever had to meet a President of the Church, and all were overjoyed at the experience. As these missionaries were singing "We Thank Thee, O God, for a Prophet," tears were streaming down many cheeks.

President McKay expressed astonishment at the presence of so many missionaries from the East Zone. He spoke to them on the subject of authority and restoration of the gospel, and the obligations of a missionary.

On the next day, Saturday, June 28, he dedicated one of the small chapels located in Charlottenburg, in Northwest Berlin. More than 600 crowded into the two small assembly rooms, and on the surrounding grounds where an elaborate public address system had been installed by Radio Station RIAS.

The highlight of the entire conference was the session for all the members of the West German Mission, which was held on Sunday morning in the Mercedes Palast, the largest hall in North Berlin. Although the capacity of the hall was about 1,850, a total of 2,600 persons crowded into the building, filling the stage, aisles, and every available space. The Berlin police permitted members to stand in the aisles, although it was contrary to the city ordinances. The President expressed appreciation for this special privilege, and for other courtesies extended by the officers.

Another chapel was dedicated on Sunday morning in Dahlem, South West Berlin, where another overflow crowd gathered to hear the President. The same public address system carried his message to the entire audience.

The subject of the address was, "The Immortality of the Soul," and he called on the nations of the earth for obedience to the Gospel of Jesus Christ. Everyone present had an opportunity to shake hands with President McKay.

The party left Monday morning for Hanover where a third chapel was dedicated. They were accompanied by President and Mrs. Glaus of the German Mission.

From Hanover the President went to Frankfurt, and then to Switzerland, Paris, and thence to England and Scotland.

Wednesday evening in Frankfurt President McKay bade a formal farewell to West Germany's ten thousand members of the Church, in an address before more than one thousand, including eighty missionaries and about three hundred servicemen and their wives. He said in part, "I have been greatly impressed with Germany. When I came here twenty-nine years ago I had a great respect for the German people, but now I have even a greater regard for them."

The party flew from Frankfurt to Zurich, Switzerland, where they were met by President and Mrs. Samuel E. Bringhurst. They were driven by car to Berne where they remained until Friday. They then proceeded to Basel, the place of the conference on Saturday and Sunday.

At the Sunday morning session, all members of the President's party spoke, representing the Sunday Schools, the Primary, and the mothers of the Church. During the President's address he said:

> Membership in The Church of Jesus Christ of Latter-day Saints and obedience to the restored gospel, will make a man nobler, will make him a better husband, will make his wife a better and truer wife, will contribute to happier homes, will help discouraged people to rise above discouragement, will prove by actual experience that religion, rightly lived, as preached and expounded by the Church, is at once the most delightful and most useful experience in the world.

Now, there are many people right here in Basel who do not believe that. But whether they believe it or disbelieve it, what I have said is an actual fact, and I have experienced it in all parts of the world.

It has been my privilege to travel a good deal in the world, and to meet members of the Church in the islands of the sea and on every continent and in every place. We found that those who lived up to the teachings of the Gospel are happy, cheerful, and useful.

In another talk he said in part:

"May the Stars and Stripes of the United States and the White Cross of Switzerland, with its red background, ever wave together in defense of individual liberty, and in opposition to dictatorship and tyranny in any form."

At the Sunday evening session, President and Mrs. Bringhurst and the missionaries presented President and Mrs. McKay with a beautiful oil painting of one of Switzerland's most famous peaks, the Matterhorn. Before leaving Switzerland, the party, accompanied by President Bringhurst, visited Interlaken, Zurich, Luzerne, Wengen Scheidegg, Lausanne, and Geneva.

President McKay left by plane for Paris on Thursday, July 10, where he remained for four days. Among other duties, he inspected the new mission home, and held conferences with missionaries, members, and their friends. He addressed a meeting held in the Pleyal Concert Hall on Sunday afternoon where over fifty percent of the membership of the entire mission was in attendance, some coming from as far distant as Nice, Lille, Liege and Brussels in Belgium and Geneva in Switzerland. The meeting was also open to the general public.

While in Paris the President visited the United States Ambassador to France, the Honorable James Dunn, who received him and his party most graciously.

President McKay told an inquiring audience that the main purpose of his trip was to investigate the possibility of setting up chapels throughout Europe—to encourage Church members to remain at home and not to emigrate to America.

President McKay and party left Paris Tuesday morning, July 15, and arrived in London on the last stage of a six weeks' visiting tour of the missions of the Church in Europe. After a hurried trip to Wales, where he visited his mother's birthplace, and addressed a large assembly at Cardiff, he returned to London to be in attendance at a party at Buckingham Palace, given by Queen Elizabeth II.

While in London, President McKay explained the Church's genealogical project being carried out in Europe. He said hundreds of thousands of dollars are being spent to enable nearly fifty full-time researchers to microfilm every scrap of information dating back for centuries in Great Britain and on the Continent. He explained that the project is rooted in the Church's belief that one's ancestors can be "baptized for by proxy," even though they died long ago. Salvation, thereby, is not denied to ancestors who had no opportunity to receive divine revelation.

He pointed out that the Mormons' great gathering together of data on millions of Europe's inhabitants down through the centuries will prove of priceless value in cases where war and other disasters destroy the original records.

From London the President's party returned to Scotland, and on July 22, in Glasgow he made the announcement that he had obtained a site in Berne, Switzerland, for the first European temple of the Church.

During the fifty days in Europe, President McKay visited ten missions, nine countries, addressed forty-five meetings, dedicated five chapels, selected a temple site in Berne, Switzerland, and held numerous conferences with mission presidents and with the press. He visited the president of Finland, Queen Juliana of The Netherlands, several American ambassadors, and attended a Royal Garden Party given by Queen Elizabeth II of Great Britain.

Only the European members of the Church can realize fully the extent of the comfort, guidance, and inspiration which President McKay's visit brought to the Saints in a troubled world.

The President and his party left Glasgow's Prestwich Airport at 1:00 a.m. on Wednesday, July 23, on their return home. They arrived in Salt Lake City on July 26, receiving a royal welcome from the nearly two thousand relatives, friends, and associates gathered at the Union station to greet them. President McKay said in appreciation of this sincere demonstration of affection, "Our trip everywhere has been glorious, but it is wonderful to be home with you all again."

Chapter 14

The Mormon Pioneer Memorial Bridge

In response to an invitation from the North Omaha Bridge Commission, President David O. McKay traveled to Nebraska in June, 1953, to dedicate a bridge across the Missouri River at the site where thousands of Mormon pioneers had crossed the river to begin the journey west.

Accompanying President McKay on a special train from Salt Lake to Omaha were President J. Reuben Clark, Jr., of the First Presidency, President Joseph Fielding Smith of the Council of the Twelve, Elder Eldred G. Smith, patriarch to the Church, and fifteen other of the general authorities, as well as more than a thousand members of the Church. Many of the members traveled to Omaha in chartered buses.

The $3,500,000 steel bridge which President McKay was to dedicate, connected Florence, Nebraska, the site of the pioneer encampment known as Winter Quarters, and Council Bluffs, Iowa.

It was in February, 1846, that the Latter-day Saints, driven from their homes in beautiful Nauvoo, Illinois, had commenced their journey westward under the leadership of Brigham Young. It was late in September when they reached the banks of the Missouri River, near Council Bluffs, and were advised to camp there until spring before beginning the long and hazardous journey to the Rocky Mountains.

A temporary camp was established near Council Bluffs, but the group decided to seek higher ground for a more permanent location. A ferry boat was constructed, and President Young and others crossed the river and located the site they called Winter Quarters. In addition to serving as a winter encampment site, Winter Quarters also became the major outfitting point for the thousands who followed the pioneer trail to Utah in the next two decades before completion of the railroad.

The new community was laid out with streets at right angles, and crude log cabins were built. The camp was divided into wards, each having a bishop to preside over its affairs and the worship services. While those in the first company used it only as a winter resting place, the surrounding land was put under cultivation so that those who would follow could harvest crops to sustain their travels. This policy was continued as long as the pioneer companies used the site.

Since this was the first white settlement in Nebraska, the Indians of surrounding areas began to make trouble. The established policy of Brigham Young, however, was to make friends with their new neighbors, and trouble was kept at a minimum.

Because the homes were hastily constructed and the conditions quite primitive, many illnesses and deaths occurred during the long winter months. Food was also scarce. More than six hundred pioneers were buried at the Mormon Cemetery in Florence.

President McKay and his party arrived at Union Station

in Omaha on Sunday morning, June 5, 1953. They were greeted by members of the Bridge Commission, Union Pacific officials, and many civic leaders. Signs of welcome were in evidence everywhere, and the facilities of the city were placed at their disposal.

Sunday's events were climaxed by a public meeting and pageant at Omaha's huge Ak-Sar-Ban Coliseum. More than 7,000 were in attendance to hear a narration of the history of the pioneers who began the journey westward from this point. Events connected with the settlement of Winter Quarters and Council Bluffs in 1846 were depicted, and the place of the pioneers in blazing the way for other western migration was emphasized.

Music for the meeting was furnished by one hundred singers from Brigham Young University. Stirring tributes were paid to the pioneers by President Clark, Elder Matthew Cowley of the Council of the Twelve, and Marvin G. Schmid, general chairman of the Bridge dedicatory services and a prominent Omaha attorney.

A special meeting was also held at the Mormon Cemetery near Florence, and tributes were paid to the memory of those who died during this trying period. President McKay and President Clark participated in the services, along with Elder Spencer W. Kimball of the Council of the Twelve, Omaha Mayor Glen Cunningham, missionaries from the Northern States Mission, and some 2,000 spectators.

The Monday activities began with a one-hundred car motorcade across the bridge to Council Bluffs, Iowa, then back to Omaha and to Winter Quarters. As the motorcade neared the starting point it became the first section of a colorful parade through the streets of Florence to the bridge entrance. Included in the parade were members of the Sons of the Utah Pioneers, dressed as soldiers of the Mormon Battalion. Their wives were dressed in appropriate pioneer costumes. Also participating were members of the Weber County Sheriff's Posse, with the men and horses having made the trip to Omaha in a special train.

The bridge dedicatory services were directed by Mr. Schmid as master of ceremonies. Tributes to the Mormon pioneers were given by Governor Robert B. Crosby of Nebraska and Governor William S. Beardsley of Iowa.

A tribute to Brigham Young was given by a grandson, Gordon C. Young. There was a bronze plaque unveiling at the bridge entrance by Kate B. Carter, president of the Daughters of the Utah Pioneers, and Richard A. Lambert, president of the Sons of the Utah Pioneers. The plaque was officially accepted by W. F. Schollman, past chairman of the Bridge Commission. A companion plaque on the Iowa approach to the bridge had been previously unveiled by Elder George Q. Morris of the Council of the Twelve when the motorcade made a brief stop there for that purpose.

President Joseph Fielding Smith gave an historical sketch of the Latter-day Saints from Nauvoo to Winter Quarters, narrating some of the tragedy of the flight from their enemies in the winter and spring of 1846.

In his remarks President McKay congratulated the North Omaha Bridge Commission members, Governors Crosby and Beardsley, the mayor and city council of Omaha, and all associated with the project for their suggestion that the bridge be made a memorial to the Mormon pioneers.

He termed the bridge another memorial to the faith and undaunted heroism of the Utah pioneers. He said, in part:

> Their undying fortitude and heroism have been, and will continue to be a guiding light to all who read their simple but incomparable story. It was their faith in God who could guide them as a loving Father, through inspiration and revelation, if they sought him in sincerity, which supported them in this trying time.

It was a sublime confidence in inspired leadership that caused 15,000 Mormons to seek refuge on the plains between Nauvoo and Winter Quarters in 1846—men and women who offered their lives in maintenance of a great cause, just as truly as former-day Christians faced death in the Roman arena.

The trek of the Mormons from Nauvoo to Winter Quarters, and thence onward to Salt Lake City, is one of the most outstanding feats in all history of colonization. Bancroft, the historian, avers that "There is no parallel in the world's history to the migration from Nauvoo."

To these intrepid, faith-inspired lovers of liberty and freedom to worship God as conscience dictates, we shall formally and reverently dedicate the Mormon Pioneer Memorial Bridge.

The dedicatory prayer offered by President McKay follows:

With gratitude and praise, we come to thee, O God, the Eternal Father, in prayer on this auspicious occasion. Nearly a century ago, men of vision dreamed of the possibility of what tens of thousands witness today as a reality. We are grateful for these forward-looking men. They are the leaders of empires, contributors to the world's progress.

We are grateful for the government of the United States that fosters individual initiative, and thereby makes such achievements possible. We are grateful for the architect and the engineers, members of commissions, for the workmen, skilled and unskilled, who, day after day, month following month, have, through intelligence and industry, made this bridge a reality.

We are grateful for the spirit of true brotherhood manifested by the members of the North Omaha Bridge Commission that designated this great steel structure 'The Mormon Pioneer Memorial Bridge,' thereby commemorating the faith, dauntless courage, and unflinching heroism, of these pioneers who early founded settlements in this area and ferried across the Missouri River in a matchless trek westward. May that spirit of brotherhood become more potent in human hearts, until all will worship thee as Father, and recognize every man as brother.

In its designation as the Mormon Pioneer Memorial Bridge, this mighty steel structure becomes an unbreakable link uniting the past generation with the present, and the hope that the faith, industry, and undying fortitude of the pioneers will continue to be a guiding and encouraging light to all who read their simple but incomparable story.

From the ferry to this strongest bridge across the Missouri River, there has passed a century of progress. We pray, O Lord, that thou wilt inspire men to desire to make equal advancement in preserving and making applicable to society the principles of individual liberty and freedom of worship brought by the pioneers and vouchsafed by the Constitution of the United States.

May these ideals ever be connoted with this inspirational occasion, as we invoke thy protecting care upon this Memorial Bridge, and dedicate it for the convenience and use of millions whose progress and pleasure will be enhanced thereby.

For this realization of a dream come true, we praise thy holy name, and pray for desires and strength to emulate the faith and high ideals of the pioneers to whose memories we now dedicate it as a fitting memorial.

This we do reverently in the name of our Savior, Jesus Christ, Amen.

The climax of the visit to Omaha was a special Chamber of Commerce luncheon at which President McKay and President Clark were invited to speak. They extended the appreciation of the entire Church for the greeting, reception, and hospitality extended to the party by the officials and people of Omaha. There were expressions of brotherhood and friendship which will never be forgotten by the Church.

Chapter 15

Visits to South Africa and South America

The Church Section of the *Deseret
News* of December 26, 1953, contained the significant announcement that for the first time in Church history a
president of the Church would visit missions in South Africa
and South and Central America.

The announcement stated that President and Sister
McKay would leave Salt Lake City on January 2, 1954, their
fifty-third wedding anniversary, and would travel first to
London and then on to South Africa and from there to South
and Central America.

The entire trip was to be by air except for the train ride
from Salt Lake City to New York City. When completed
it would mark completion of an official visit by President
McKay to every existing mission of the Church.

President and Sister McKay reached London on schedule
where they were met by President A. Hamer Reiser of the
British Mission. Meetings were held there with officials
of the British and Swiss Missions concerning the forthcom-

ing construction of temples in England and also Berne, Switzerland.

With business completed in London, President McKay, his wife, and President Reiser left the London airport on January 7, 1954 headed for South Africa by way of Madrid, Lisbon, and Dakar on the West African coast. They spent the night at Lisbon, and left the following morning for Africa. Along the African coast they rode in sunshine, the first they had seen since landing in London. Fog and overcast skies had covered all of England and the continent for several weeks. Because of some rough air conditions along the coast the pilot had to detour over the Atlantic Ocean, and this caused a one-hour delay in their arrival at Dakar.

Dakar, located in Senegal, French West Africa, is the most westerly point of the African continent, and the departure point for trans-Atlantic flights to the eastern coast of South America. As President McKay and his party arrived there and reviewed their itinerary, President McKay noted that he had to return to Dakar after his trip through Africa and spend a two-day layover there before leaving for South America. Anxious to make every minute of the trip as worthwhile as possible, he was pondering what could be done about the delay when an official of Pan American Airlines approached him, introduced himself, and asked the President if it would be permissible to shorten the layover at Dakar from two days to four hours. This, of course, met with instant approval.

From Dakar the group traveled to Johannesburg, an arduous trip of some twenty-four hours, with three stops enroute. The trip was through many rough storms, and was a trying one for President McKay. President Reiser, who described the trip for the press, said there were many thrilling experiences, the clouds and lightning being almost beyond description.

The plane landed at Johannesburg at 7:30 p.m., and was greeted by a huge crowd of saints and friends who had never before seen one of the general authorities, and were beside themselves with joy. They sang, "We Thank Thee, O God, for a Prophet," and "Come, Come, ye Saints," and they really meant every word of it. A touching greeting was given the party, flowers presented, and the visitors were then taken to their hotel.

The following day two sessions of the general conference of the Transvaal District were held in Duncan Hall, with about 450 people in attendance. The meetings were described by President Reiser as wonderful, but the greatest thrills came after the meetings, when everyone who desired had the privilege of greeting President and Mrs. McKay, and shaking their hands. These experiences were especially touching and would remain as treasured memories for a lifetime. The effects of the day's contacts could never be over-estimated in the lives of men, women, and children, who had hungered so long for such an experience. Now it had come with even greater pleasure than they had ever anticipated.

The entire experience was so touching and heart-warming that President Reiser said the language he was capable of using was inadequate to describe it. Presents were given, and appreciation expressed for the visit and the messages spoken by President McKay.

A side trip was made to Pretoria, only a short distance from Johannesburg, where government officials were visited, as well as the United States Ambassador to the Union of South Africa, Mr. W. J. Gallman. Visits were made to places of interest and they then returned to Johannesburg.

Capetown, at the very tip of the continent, and nine hundred miles south of Johannesburg, was the next place visited, and here a three-day conference was held. The missionaries from all the surrounding territory, some hundreds of miles distant, attended. The meetings with the missionaries and the local saints were inspirational, as were all the other meetings arranged for the President. Every word spoken was heard in deepest silence, and with the greatest interest and reverence. It is difficult to get a full appreciation of the meaning of this visit of the Prophet of the Lord to these remote places. The people had longed for such a contact for so many years, but had felt little hope that it would ever materialize.

President McKay had had a longing while in South Africa to see something of the wild life so attractive to all Americans. There was no time, however, to make any extended trip. From Johannesburg the journey to the famed Krueger National Park required three days. It was impossible to make this trip because of the meetings already planned. From Capetown, however, a short ride was arranged into the country where some thrills were experienced in seeing some zebras and a few families of baboons. The latter were encountered after all hope of seeing them had been lost. They had looked for them in vain, when, on returning toward Capetown they spotted a male baboon sitting atop the bonnet (hood) of an automobile, with others, adults and children romping about. The call to duty, however, precluded any extensive sight-seeing, here as elsewhere.

The intensity of the devotion to the spiritual program of the visit is apparent from the fact that the concluding day of the conference at Capetown was devoted to a testimony meeting. This meeting lasted ten hours, with a short recess for lunch, and two ten minute intermissions at mid-morning and mid-afternoon. Fifty-three elders spoke feelingly of their work, in such manner as is never apparent in any other gatherings of the saints. Youths, mature men, and some aged, all evidenced the wonderful influence of the contact with President McKay.

Personal contact was made, so far as was humanly possible, with every member of the Church, by President and Sister McKay on this South African visit. The difficulties and dangers of the trip were forgotten in witnessing the gratitude of the saints who had experienced the joys of the visit. It is typical of all the visits made to all the other isolated missions of the Church, where devotion and sacrifices of many years were rewarded by the intimate contacts with the President and his wife. In Capetown a visit was made to a woman member of the Church who was hospitalized, which made contact with the saints of that area almost one hundred percent.

The return trip to Dakar was made without inconvenience except for one violent storm which tossed the plane about as it flew over the equator. President McKay was thrown from his seat, but not injured.

The arrangements at Dakar, made at the previous visit, were followed, and there was only a four-hour delay instead of the two days. This gave President and Mrs. McKay an extra two days to spend in Rio de Janeiro, which they appreciated. The Pan-American manager, Joseph Makowski, who had arranged this convenience for them, also introduced them to The United States Consul-General, Charles Ferguson Jr., who informed them that arrangements had been made for their comfort at Dakar's best hotel, and for interesting entertainment while they were waiting the departure of their plane.

President Reiser bade them goodbye at Dakar, to return to London. He wrote enthusiastically of the trip to South Africa as a never-to-be-forgotten experience, with incomparable companions, on a significant and prodigious mission.

President and Mrs. McKay then made the trip by plane from Dakar to Rio, reaching their destination on Friday, January 22, at 1 a.m. The change in schedule had been made known by cable to the president of the Brazilian Mission, but was not transmitted to their son, Robert R. McKay, who was to meet them at Rio and serve as guide, interpreter, and secretary, for the South American part of the journey. Robert was at a hotel only a block away from his parents before he learned of their arrival. He then found them in excellent health and spirits.

The two extra days in Rio gave President and Sister McKay an opportunity to see some of the beauties of this famed city. This included the immense statue of Christ at Corcovado. To get close to the monument, it was necessary to climb eighteen flights of steps, a total of 220 steps. This they did without hesitation, in spite of their age and warnings they had received from relatives at home before leaving.

The Brazilian Mission headquarters are at Sao Paulo, a beautiful city about 75 miles south of Rio. Through a misunderstanding, plane reservations had been cancelled to that city, and a later plane was engaged for the President to make this trip for scheduled meetings. This gave him an extra evening in Rio which he might have used to rest, but instead he insisted on making a trip to a meeting with a few members of the Church at Tijuca.

Sunday morning they left Rio at 5:30 a.m. without breakfast, and with no prospect of dinner until after an afternoon meeting. Robert described the trip as one in which the steward told them in poor English that this would be the last trip the plane would make. The startled passengers asked what he meant, and were relieved when they learned that the plane was to be converted to a cargo ship. They had already viewed the plane with some apprehension, and were all relieved when they landed safely at Sao Paulo.

A touching greeting was given them at the airport, where the assembled saints sang the usual "We Thank Thee, O God, for a Prophet," and a little girl, with a beautiful bouquet for Sister McKay, planted a kiss on her cheek. This was typical of the receptions arranged everywhere.

It was a full day of meetings, with only a forty minute intermission for hand-shaking, until after 3 p.m. During the recess, the people were most expressive in their greetings. Robert described it thus: "A hand-shake and a clap on the back with the other hand, is the usual greeting between friends, but today the whole act of affection was shown, which included hugs and kisses on both cheeks. Mother was so busy being kissed, that she didn't notice all the girls and women adoring her husband."

The meetings went on into the night, and at midnight the town was at the height of a celebration of its fourth centennial, and the confusion and noise promised to go on uninterruptedly through the night.

The meetings during the day included one for a group of German-speaking saints. Another group had come from an outlying district, expecting to meet the plane from Rio. Due to the schedule change, with the plane not arriving until the following morning, the group asked permission to roll up in their blankets on the floor of the meeting house. Such was the devotion and interest of these people.

The following day was taken up with meetings and hearing reports of the missionaries. The work was found to be growing favorably and all were encouraged with the progress being made. A reporter for the United Press was given an hour and a half of the President's time, with President McKay explaining the work of the Church in Brazil. It seemed incredible to the reporter that the missionaries as well as the saints in Brazil did not drink coffee, this being the coffee-growing capital of the world.

135

Montevideo, Uruguay, was the next scheduled stop, and here again President McKay was met at the airport by the strains of a most beautiful chorus singing "We Thank Thee, O God, for A Prophet." An orchid was pinned on Sister McKay.

An appointment had been made for the afternoon with the President of Uruguay, but because of illness he could not keep the appointment. Instead, he sent his secretary, a person of great influence in the nation. With him were two sub-secretaries and an army official. The meeting was most cordial, and President McKay was told that Church missionaries were welcome in Uruguay, and would be given full religious freedom. He was also told that church and state were entirely separate in Uruguay, differing in this respect from nearby Argentina. It was agreed by all that this was very beneficial to Uruguay.

When President McKay's plane had arrived in Uruguay it was met by a member of the American Embassy who arranged a meeting for President McKay with the ambassador. A delegation from the embassy later came and escorted him to the appointment. Here he was most cordially received by Ambassador McIntosh. The ambassador had shown every possible courtesy and consideration to the missionaries in Uruguay, for which President McKay expressed appreciation.

One of the highlights of the trip in Uruguay was President McKay's visit to a new chapel under construction in Montevideo. Since this was the first new chapel of the Church in South America, President McKay was vitally concerned with its progress. He emphasized the great asset it would be to the work of the mission, particularly in attracting young people to the programs of recreation and culture which could be carried out in the new facilities.

On January 30, 1954, President McKay officiated at the laying of the cornerstone on the new chapel, and offered a special prayer on this occasion for the growth of the work in this part of the world.

That evening, President McKay met with the members of the priesthood in Montevideo, about one hundred in number, and told them of the authority of the Church and of their responsibilities in the priesthood. Most of those present had been bearers of the priesthood only a year or two, and President McKay's words were a great help to them in learning their duties.

The following day a conference was held in the nearly completed chapel, but it was not adequate to accommodate all who desired to attend. President McKay spoke fervently on the Ten Commandments, and asked some newer members of the Church to participate with him in a discussion. Reporters from the Uruguayan press were present for the meeting also.

While in Montevideo, President McKay was the guest for a ten minute interview on Radio Expectador. He commented on the wonderful climate of the country, its great resources, the charm and graciousness of its people, and the fair attitude of the government in granting freedom of worship, one of the greatest boons to humanity. The interview was a fitting climax to President McKay's successful visit in the country.

Leaving Montevideo by plane, the party flew across the LaPlata River, and in fifty minutes landed at Buenos Aires, Argentina, listening again to the welcoming strains of "We Thank Thee, O God, for a Prophet," sung by the saints who had gathered at the airport.

The day following his arrival in Buenos Aires, President McKay addressed a group of 200 businessmen and their wives in the American Church. He was introduced by Dr. William B. Giles, who was familiar with the life and activities of President McKay, and gave a thorough and accurate description of him and of the Church. He passed through the congregation three envelopes with cancelled stamps from the Utah centennial celebration. He spoke of the great success achieved by the Centennial Commission under President McKay's chairmanship.

Since the Group represented many Christian faiths, President McKay spoke on American Christian ideals, and the responsibilities of Americans to the rest of the world in achieving a stronger brotherhood. He quoted from the *Book of Mormon* that ". . . this is a land choice above all other lands." In a question-answer period he explained many points about the Church, especially in regard to recreational and welfare programs. One questioner, with an evident Scottish brogue, asked, "And how many members of your Church would you have in Scotland?" From this question President McKay was able to relate some of his own experiences in Scotland, as well as the progress of the Church there.

Many of the women in attendance were members of the Mother's Club, a group associated with the English school in Buenos Aires, which had just elected the wife of the Argentine Mission president, Sister Valentine, as its president. She was the only Latter-day Saint among the more than 300 members of the group.

On the day following this meeting Mr. Gilbert Chase of the United States Embassy called to say that President Juan D. Peron would grant President McKay an interview at 9:55 that morning, and that one other person could be present. Through circumstances too complicated to narrate, four persons, President McKay, President Valentine, Robert R. McKay, and Mr. Chase, all were received by President Peron. He was most gracious to them, and exhibited a considerable knowledge of the Church and its activities. He knew its history and said he had respect for a people who had to work and fight for what they had. He said he would like to offer them refreshments, but knew they neither drank nor smoked, so his hands were tied. President McKay replied that he had already given much in his gracious reception. He then said he was happy to have our people in his country.

President Peron knew that a conference was to be held in Buenos Aires on the following Sunday, and said the building in which it was planned to hold the meeting was not suitable. He then offered the Cervantes Theatre, the second in rating in Buenos Aires. The offer was gratefully accepted, but when the building was inspected, it was discovered that repairs were being made, and all the seats had been removed. This was not known by President Peron. It was then decided to return to the original plan, but those in charge of the remodeling, after a meeting, said they would have the theatre ready for the conference. A group of sixty men was put to work and the building was ready as promised.

President McKay and his associates were delighted with their reception by President Peron, and the visit received wide publicity over the air and through the press. The benefit to the work of the mission could readily be appreciated. On concluding the visit President McKay presented President Peron with beautifully bound copies of the *Book of Mormon, Doctrine and Covenants,* and the *Pearl of Great Price,* in Spanish. These he gratefully accepted and promised he would read.

It was the general feeling among the Americans that President McKay rendered a splendid diplomatic service for the United States, one which would have a wholesome effect in improving relations between the two countries.

Following this interview, there was another with the United States Ambassador to the Argentine, Mr. Alfred F. Nufer. Mrs. McKay and Mrs. Valentine were included in this fifteen minute interview. They were impressed by a picture of Temple Square in Salt Lake City which hung on a wall of the embassy.

A seven hour automobile trip was made to hold a conference at Rosario, 250 miles distant from Buenos Aires. This was a fatiguing journey but was much appreciated by the 250 people who could attend. On returning to Buenos Aires, a Time-Life reporter, Mr. R. A. McCoy, was awaiting an interview. He became so interested in the discussion of the missionary system, and the Church in general, that the interview was extended to two hours. This ordeal, at the end of a trying day, left President McKay extremely fatigued.

The conference was held as scheduled in the Cervantes Theatre, with eight hundred members and investigators in attendance. This was 250 more than could have been crowded into the original chapel. No charge was made for the use of the theatre, an offer to compensate them for the special services being likewise rejected. This was a radical change from anything previously known in the Argentine.

The conference was a great success, and the audiences were thrilled with what they had heard. Afterward, the Radio Excelsior gave a ten minute tribute to President McKay, and played two of Crawford Gates' arrangements as sung by the Tabernacle Choir.

The President and his party left Argentina on February 8, and made the flight over the Andes to Chile. They were met at the airport in Santiago by the only Church member in that nation. The Church then maintained no mission in Chile, and the stay there was only brief. They next visited Peru, where much of the history of the Nephites transpired. There were only a few North American Church members living there at the time. These families were congregated in Sunday School at Lima, where a meeting was held and a pleasant visit enjoyed. There was hope expressed that a mission could soon be opened in Peru.

The homeward journey was begun on February 10, with stops planned for Panama, Guatamala, and Mexico. Three days were spent in Panama City, where meetings were held, and one day in Guatamala City. Here plane trouble developed, the regular flight to Mexico City was cancelled. As it was impossible to reach there in time for the scheduled meetings, it was decided to fly direct to Los Angeles, and visit Mexico City at a later time.

Thus ended the epoch-making visit to the two Southern continents with such far-reaching possibilities. The extension of the missionary programs into other countries of the Southern Hemisphere now seemed nearer. The party returned home safely, with President McKay beginning at once the busy administrative duties always awaiting him.

The visit to the Mexican Mission was made during the week of March 20-28, by plane from Los Angeles. The saints of that country had been keenly disappointed because of the postponement of the conference. President McKay was determined to complete the tour of the missions as originally planned, and so scheduled this special visit to Mexico City. Sister McKay, and their son Robert accompanied the President, and an inspirational conference was conducted.

Chapter 16

David O. McKay Day in Ogden

The Biblical statement that ". . . a prophet hath no honour in his own country," was effectively refuted by the citizens of Ogden in a community-wide tribute paid to President David O. McKay on July 16, 1954.

The celebration, designated as "David O. McKay Day" was a heartfelt display of the love and esteem held for President McKay by those in his native Weber County.

The event was planned by a citizen's committee headed by Arthur V. Woolley, Ogden attorney. Included on the committee were representatives of city and county offices, ministers from every denomination in the area, presidents of men's and women's civic and service clubs, educational administrators, and life-long friends of President McKay.

It was as if the community had but one heart beat that day—and that was one of appreciation for the outstanding accomplishments of a native son, David O. McKay.

The event began as a committee of civic and church officials met President McKay on his arrival in Ogden. They escorted him to the Hotel Ben Lomond where more than five hundred had gathered for a luncheon in the hotel ballroom. Master of ceremonies for the luncheon was The Reverend A. Cadman Garretson of Ogden's First Presbyterian Church. In this capacity he expressed the love and admiration for all of the people of Ogden and Weber County for President McKay. The invocation at the luncheon was offered by Catholic Monsignor Patrick F. Kennedy, who also paid a tribute of friendship to President McKay.

Following the luncheon, the program consisted of tributes to the various phases of President McKay's life. He was extolled as "The Farmer," by Chairman Woolley; "An Educator," by Dr. Henry Aldous Dixon, president of Utah State Agricultural College, Logan, and former president of Weber College; "Churchman," by A. Walter Stevenson, Ogden businessman and assistant general superintendent of the Young Men's Mutual Improvement Association; and "World Citizen," by The Reverend Henry C. Beatty, pastor of the First Methodist Church in Ogden.

Typical of the tributes paid to President McKay are the following.

Mr. Woolley said in part:

> The tributes and hosannas to him, our most distinguished and revered citizen, are innumerable and have sprung from the hearts of people from all over the world.
>
> We of this community, his home-town folks, have not been unmindful of his great distinction. We cannot hope adequately to express the warmth of our esteem and our pride in his greatness, which reflects upon us, his neighbors.
>
> He grew tall and straight as a pine tree grows, the light of joy upon his face, that joy that comes from good deeds done. It is this kind of man that the Lord God made in his own image, to have dominion over sea and land. . . .
>
> To his kind is given the blessing to multiply, and the command to replenish the earth and subdue it . . . to have dominion over every living thing that moveth upon the earth.

In the rough work of subduing the new land, he was a good hand. He ploughed fields. He sowed seeds. He harvested the crops. He was a logger and brought timber from the canyons to build houses, barns, and fences. He was a horse man, and played the games strenuous men play. That life did not produce "the man with the hoe" but it produced the man who does not forget the hoe.

As an educator, Dr. Dixon said:

President McKay has always had the power and the eagerness to give something extra, something higher in his teaching. . . . He has shown leadership in education. He was president of his class when he was graduated from the University of Utah in 1897. He became principal of the Huntsville School. After his mission to Great Britain he began teaching in the Weber Stake Academy, and three years later became principal of that institution. Although he was a young man, he was a strong spiritual force in the community as well as in the Academy. Suffice it to say that four institutions of higher learning have recognized his high merits by granting him honorary degrees.

No one in the west has helped more to keep schools better aware of their true aims than has President McKay. No one has come out as courageously in favor of education in Utah during the darkest hours than he, and no one is as devoutly beloved and revered in the educational profession.

As a churchman, Mr. Stevenson said:

This man we are honoring today established his true greatness as a churchman. . . . Throughout his life, President David O. McKay has been a living example of keeping the commandments. His rich life is filled with service to God and to his fellowmen. Behold, truly, here is a man in whom there is no guile.

President McKay, I salute you! You are a Christian gentleman. Your soul-piercing eyes can melt the hardest heart. Your smile gives encouragement to the most dejected. I admire your fearless courage in standing for the right, your sense of humor, your devout love for your fellowman. Many to whom you have given comfort and inspiration will ever call you blessed. You are a great churchman. More than that, I can say in all sincerity, that surely there has never been a greater prophet in Israel.

Reverend Beatty paid an eloquent tribute to President McKay as "World Citizen:"

With a dedicated sense of vision, David O. McKay has endeavored, with unique success, to build everywhere a community of good will, sympathetic tolerance, and creative humanitarianism. Actually this virile pioneer became a world figure back in 1920-21, when he, in response to the needs of his Church, made an around-the-world tour of its missionary undertakings into which he injected inspiration, direction, and purpose, through his profound personal conviction that the Kingdom of Heaven must be promoted and projected into the hinterlands of this planet. During these days, the pulse of the world started pounding within his sensitive ears.

Like the Prophet of ancient Galilee, whose life our honored guest magnetically emulates, he had come to feel so keenly the agony and aspirations of men that his life became, to the discerning mind, an enactment of dedication.

With calmness rooted in mature faith, a forcefulness animated with vision, and a firmness fortified with an appreciation of the principles of righteousness, President McKay has traveled through the world as an exponent of a spiritual heritage which alone possesses the historic positiveness, social drive, and spiritual grip sufficient to curtail and crush the atheistic forces of materialism, and the dangerous distortions of communism.

In President McKay's dedicated concern to the promotion of a righteous world community, there is a blending of three elements, namely, the latitude of his vision of human need, as a steward of opportunity; and the magnitude of his compassion as a disciple of the creative Carpenter of Nazareth who insisted, 'If I be lifted up, I will draw all men Unto me.'

Five times during the last thirty-four years, our esteemed citizen, who, once upon a time, bridled his horse to the hitching posts at Weber Academy, in his quest for culture, has ridden the sea and the sky lanes to remote places to exemplify, through his attitude, and action, the force of his teachings on Christian culture.

In brief, President McKay has discovered the heart-beat of the world and has come to stimulate it by the courageous commitment of his life to a mission which, apparently, continues moment after moment, to stretch his imagination. . . . Qualities so richly incarnate in President McKay clearly made him a world citizen extraordinary.

"The Woman at his Side" was the subject of a tribute paid to Sister McKay by Mrs. Francis L. Lund. She said:

> I wish it were in my power to express the love and admiration we feel for this great man and his partner. Two great women, inspired the life of our beloved friend, President David O. McKay, the wife by his side, and his mother.
>
> The spirit of love and harmony have ever been present in the family home at Huntsville. On holidays, as a magnet, it draws the families even unto the second and third generations, from far and wide, to rejoice and celebrate together. We can appreciate what family solidarity means.
>
> No less can be said for the home in Salt Lake City, where all the family gather at every opportunity. There Mama Ray reigns. She presides graciously when the president entertains notable guests, or she sweetly and kindly ministers to the needs of her family, or those needing understanding, seeking her advice or just a shoulder to weep on. Our congratulations to a wonderful couple whose lives together have been idyllic.

Igor Gorin, of New York City, sang "Prayer for a Safe Journey," from "All Faces West," by Roland and Helen Parry.

Sister McKay responded to the tribute given her, and told of President McKay's tenderness toward Ogden and her people: "His grandparents were among the early settlers of this community; and we spent the first twenty-five years of our married life here. All of our seven children were born here. It was here also that he started his intensive religious work. Only he and I know how hard he worked at it."

In his response, President McKay told of his courtship with Emma Ray Riggs as she taught in the Madison School, near Weber Academy where he taught. He told of his worry over the anticipation of this hour because "I was coming into the hearts of old friends and cherished, whom I love as I love my own." He declared he was deeply touched by the things said which came from the heart, although he did not merit the praise. With marked emotion the President said:

> I am trembling because of appreciation.
> This day is one of those rare occasions which are delightful to experience and to be treasured sacredly in memory forever. It is one of those experiences which awaken the heart to a realization of two great attributes of the soul—the first, appreciation, the other a sense of responsibility.
> I thank you with all my heart. No person can associate with the nobility of souls in their homes or anywhere, without a greater sense of responsibility than ever before.

He paid a glowing tribute to the spirit of brotherhood and love present on this occasion. "I could but hope that a little of this spirit manifest here today, could enter into our international relationships."

President and Mrs. McKay were presented with a beautiful painting of the La Platta Valley in the mountains beyond Huntsville. It was done by Farrell E. Collett, chairman of the art department of Weber College. Its presentation touched President McKay, because here was the scene of his labor of earlier years. When La Platta was a boom mining town of some 3,500 miners and their familes, he carried mail to them on horseback.

An expression of appreciation also marked President McKay's remarks at the laying of the corner stone of the Ogden Tabernacle which followed the luncheon. His message on this occasion stressed the full value of the great contributions of those who have preceded us, and hoped that those who come after will have an equally strong foundation on which to build.

Services at the tabernacle were under the direction of the stake presidents of the area, with President William J. Critchlow Jr., of the South Ogden Stake officiating.

Following an informal reception held in the open court of the building, President and Mrs. McKay retired with members of their family for a buffet supper at the "Old Home" in Huntsville.

A climax to the day was their keen enjoyment of the performance of "All Faces West," Ogden's Pioneer Day festival program, with Igor Gorin depicting the character of Brigham Young.

Chapter 17

Dedication of the Swiss Temple

In his two visits to Europe, described in Chapters 13 and 15, President David O. McKay had arranged for the construction of a temple near Berne, Switzerland and had carefully followed its progress.

For many years members of the Church had been looking forward to the time when a temple would be built on the European continent. The announcement to build the first temple in Europe at Berne had been made by President McKay in July, 1952, at the completion of his first tour of the European missions. President McKay officiated at the ground breaking services in August, 1953, and actual construction work on the building began in October of that year from plans drawn by Elder Edward O. Anderson, temple architect. The cornerstone was laid on November 13, 1954 by President Stephen L Richards of the First Presidency.

By mid-1955 the work had progressed sufficiently that the *Deseret News* carried an announcement in its editions of May 21, 1955, that dedicatory services were planned for

September 11, 1955, and that President McKay would officiate.

The newspaper article indicated that Elder Anderson, the architect, had just returned from a month's visit at Berne, and had reported that, while it would require heroic effort on the part of the builders, the structure would be completed by September. Also scheduled to be completed were a chapel for the Berne Branch, and a home for the temple president. President McKay would also dedicate these buildings.

The Swiss Temple was the first in a series of edifices begun under the direction of President McKay. Others either were contemplated or were under construction near London, England, in New Zealand, and at Los Angeles, California. It was expected that while he was in England on this trip President McKay would break ground for the temple near London.

It had long been planned that the Salt Lake Tabernacle Choir would participate in the dedicatory services of the Swiss Temple. This would be the crowning event of a tour and a series of concerts which would take the choir to Scotland, England, Wales, Holland, Denmark, Germany, and France. The choir would be accompanied by many relatives and friends of the members, and by Elder Richard L. Evans of the Council of the Twelve, announcer for the Tabernacle Choir broadcasts over the Columbia Broadcasting System.

It was arranged that the choir would make the trip by boat from Montreal, Canada, ahead of President McKay. He would fly, arriving in Scotland before them, and would meet them when they arrived at Greenock, Scotland, the port near Glasgow, where their first concert would be given. The tour was arranged by W. J. (Jack) Thomas, the tour manager of the choir.

Arrangements for a trip of this magnitude were difficult to complete, and at times when it seemed almost a hopeless project President McKay would lend his encouragement and the spark necessary to go on, for he clearly saw the results that would be obtained from such an undertaking.

As it was finally arranged, the choir, along with many of the traveling party, were permitted by the Soviet government to go behind the Iron Curtain and give concerts in Berlin. This was an unprecedented event in the cold-war relations between the Soviet Union and the United States.

President McKay indicated to the choir that he would travel with them on a large part of their tour, and emphasized to the members their responsibilities in representing not only the Church but also the United States.

Press response to the announced choir tour was overwhelming, and the newspapers, as well as radio, television, national magazines, and many national leaders hailed the event as a major effort in diplomatic relations and world affairs, apart from its cultural and entertainment value. It was noted that no other American group of comparable size had ever undertaken a similar tour through the countries of Europe, and certainly not at such a critical time in cold-war relations. But the Church leaders and members of the choir felt they were equal to this responsibility, and were determined to be ambassadors of good will wherever they traveled.

The financing of the tour itself was a tremendous undertaking. *The Salt Lake Tribune* of August 10, 1955, listed some of the sources from which this support was obtained. Salt Lake City business men had raised approximately $30,000. The Mutual Improvement Association's dance festival brought $15,000. A Lowell Thomas concert realized $9,000. Many concerts and other benefits were given, private contributions made, too numerous to mention, and many groups and organizations raised funds in various ways. The Church contributed unknown amounts to complete the necessary budget. *The Tribune* estimated the amount to exceed $100,000. Many felt that it perhaps would reach much more, possibly double that amount.

The choir left Salt Lake City by Union Pacific train on August 10, accompanied by about two hundred relatives and friends. Ted Cannon, columnist of the *Deseret News*, went along to provide day to day comments for the readers. They reached Montreal without incident, and sailed on the S.S. Seconia on Saturday, August 13, for Scotland. The sailing from Montreal was preceded by the singing of *God Save the Queen*, from the decks of the Seconia.

President and Sister McKay, with their son and daughter-in-law, Dr. and Mrs. Edward R. McKay, and his secretary, Miss Clare Middlemiss, left the Salt Lake City airport for New York City, on Tuesday, August 16, at 9 a.m., and were scheduled to leave New York City's International Airport August 17, at 4 p.m., arriving at Prestwick Airport, Glasgow, the following day at 9 a.m. This gave the President one day to meet the choir, which arrived at Greenock, Scotland, on Friday, August 19.

President McKay's itinerary called for several appearances with the choir, particularly at Glasgow and Edinburgh, in Scotland; Cardiff, Wales; and at the groundbreaking ceremonies for the London Temple. From there President McKay planned to go to Berne to prepare for the dedicatory services on September 11. The choir, in the meantime, planned concerts at Amsterdam and The Hague in Holland; Copenhagen, Denmark; Berlin, Frankfurt, and Wiesbaden, Germany. After these appearances the Choir would participate in the dedicatory services at Berne, and then conclude their trip with concerts at Zurich, Switzerland, and Paris, France.

This schedule was carried out with notable success, by both the choir and President McKay. Crossings of the Atlantic were made without incident. The President met the choir when the Seconia steamed up the Clyde to dock at Greenock. From that time it was a busy period for both parties to meet the schedule planned, and to save a little time for sight-seeing by the choir members, most of whom were visiting Europe for the first time. For President McKay the trip was no novelty, and he could direct the plans with the confidence of long experience. The thrill of having the great choir participate at so many places was a new one, and there was some apprehension as to how their concerts would be received.

The choir trip had been well publicized by the American and European press, and the national magazines of both continents. There had been radio and television broadcasts from the Tabernacle, and through *Voice of America,* and other channels. The choir was also widely known from the publicity given by Lowell Thomas and "Cinerama." All the favorable impressions gained must now be justified by personal appearances before critical audiences, and austere professional critics. The choir would be judged in comparison with the great professional musical organizations of the world, and they were yet to demonstrate their ability to meet the test.

The degree of favor extended to the choir by the audiences and the press would determine the probable extent of its missionary influence. That the impressions made would be favorable few Latter-day Saints doubted. Probably none was prepared, however, for the extravagant praise heaped upon the entire organization from the beginning to the end of the trip. The good it did, not only for the Church it represented, but also for the entire nation, cannot be overestimated. It was widely hailed as an ambassador of peace and good will, and by some as the greatest gesture for good relations sent by America to Europe in a trying period.

The concerts were presented to capacity audiences in the great music halls of Britain and the continent. The first, at Glasgow's Kelvin Hall, was watched with unusual interest. The critics were extravagant in praise of the renditions, and doubt of the success of the tour was dispelled. Equal praise was given to the rendition of the religious numbers by the great composers, patriotic songs, and the beautiful old Mormon hymns. The reception by the audience of all numbers was tremendous, with numerous encores demanded.

The success of the initial concert was duplicated throughout the entire tour. There were variations in the comments made at the different concerts, but the general reaction was always the same, a wonderful and gracious organization, well-trained and capably conducted, and a credit both to the Church and to the nation it represented. Speeches of welcome and approval were given at receptions arranged at various places, and additional praise given to the choir and officials accompanying the singers.

The Church members, in the various countries visited, experienced new thrills in the singing of the choir, and in contacts with President McKay and the general authorities who were also seen and heard. Elder Richard L. Evans of the Council of the Twelve was with the choir at all concerts and served as contact man and commentator in his usual, impressive manner. Elder Ezra Taft Benson, also a member of the Council of the Twelve, and Secretary of Agriculture in President Eisenhower's cabinet, joined the party at Copenhagen, and also attended the dedication exercises at Berne.

The relatives and friends of Church members who had migrated to Utah came to the concerts and meetings, and many remained to seek information regarding friends and loved ones, or to learn of the Church and its teachings. All seemed to be stimulated by the favorable receptions and the press comments, and wished to add their personal approval of what they had seen and heard.

This was a new experience for the Church leaders and the missionaries present, who remembered the difficulties of past years in getting hearings for their Gospel messages. People never before contacted now seemed anxious to hear, and to extend praise and favors. The favorable impression created will remain and become more apparent with the years, in the easier approach for the elders in the mission fields. The singing of the choir will be an opening wedge for conversations, which will, in turn, offer opportunities for teaching the Gospel.

The official receptions were especially heart-warming to the Church leaders who were invited to attend. Each city seemed to be anxious to out-do the others in its welcome. The Lord Mayor of Cardiff called the group "brothers and sisters," and various presents were given to individuals. President McKay noted that in Glasgow, where, as a missionary fifty-seven years before, he had been barred from the marble halls of St. George Square, they now were received and extended honors by the Lord Provost. In London the County Council entertained President McKay and other members of the party at an official function, where they also were interviewed by the press. Similar favorable welcome was also extended to them in all cities of the continent where they visited.

In Amsterdam, the concert was dedicated to Queen Juliana and her mother, the former Queen Wilhelmina. A tribute was paid by Elder Evans to the Netherlands for its great contributions to America, in the outstanding leaders developed from its emigrants. Holland had also served the Church nobly in the quality of its people who had accepted the gospel and migrated to Utah.

The soloists with the choir, Miss Ewan Harbrecht, with

her superb singing, and Alexander Schreiner and Frank W. Asper, organists, came in for constant praise. The capable directing of the choir by its leaders, J. Spencer Cornwall and Richard P. Condie, was noted by the writers in every city visited. That no great body of singers had ever shown more capable training was the universal comment.

The concert given at Copenhagen received the same enthusiastic reception extended to the choir in Great Britain and at Amsterdam. The trip by train from Holland, which began at 4 a.m., was especially trying, but the singers reacted with the same enthusiasm as always. The concert was attended by the American Ambassador, Robert Coe, and by Elder Benson. Because the scheduled concert was completely sold out long in advance, and many had been unable to hear the choir, a special concert had been arranged at Copenhagen's famed Tivoli Park for the men's chorus, where thousands were able to hear and applaud, who otherwise would have been denied the pleasure they had looked forward to for so long. They said that the most enthusiastic reception given to the choir, thus far, was that given them at Copenhagen.

The visit of the choir to Berlin was a notable one in many ways. The difficulties encountered in getting permission from the Russian government to pass through the Soviet zone to Berlin, were finally overcome, and the first body of American civilians granted that privilege, passed by train into Berlin, escorted by a party of United States' State Department officials. They were met at the station in Berlin by the Singing Mothers of the Berlin Branch, with the chorus, "For the Strength of the Hills." A tour of the war-damaged, formerly beautiful capital of Germany, caused many heartaches for the choir members.

The concert in Schoenberg Sport's Palace was sold out, and many were turned away. Hymns and numbers were sung from German composers, including Bach, Beethoven, and Handel, which pleased the audience greatly. A splendid feature of the visit to Berlin was the presence at a rehearsal, of especially invited guests, refugees from East Germany who were unable to attend the regularly scheduled concert. This, like the extra concert given in Copenhagen, brought unstinted praise. The German critics were generous in their praise of the choir, a source of satisfaction from this center of music for generations. Officials of Berlin extended a welcome to the delegation of choir members. The Berlin concert was broadcast over the Radio Free Europe network to unseen millions behind the Iron Curtain. East Germany, and all the satellite countries heard the special message of greeting and hope, and prayers for the people from the lips of Elder Evans.

From Berlin the choir went by special train for concerts at Frankfurt and Wiesbaden. On arrival at Frankfurt they were given a reception by Obergeburgmeister Waldo Kolb, at the City Hall. They enjoyed a day of rest and sightseeing in Frankfurt, before their concert the following day in nearby Wiesbaden.

There is much of interest in the neighborhood of Frankfurt, and the time was spent visiting Heidelberg, Baden-Baden, and other places with interesting histories. The concert at Wiesbaden was described by Ted Cannon as "another climax in a never-ending series of climaxes." There were hundreds of servicemen from the surrounding areas who were in attendance under the supervision of General William Turner, the Commanding General of USGFE; Oscar C. Holder, Consul General; and Wiesbaden's Ober ger Hoister, Dr. Eric Mix. The General was so impressed that he said that if he had had any idea of the scope and magnitude of the performance he would have arranged for an outside setting where ten thousand servicemen could have attended.

As it was, many servicemen from home were contacted, and the wonderful effect of the concert was apparent to all.

The trip from Frankfurt to Berne was made in twenty busses, and it was a trying ordeal. One writer described the more than five hundred people as being "groggy" when they reached Berne. They were greeted enthusiastically by President McKay who had been in Berne for several days, making final arrangements for the most important work of the tour, dedication of the first temple to be built by the Church in Europe.

President McKay had left the choir in London, and had gone to Berne by way of Paris, to direct the final work of preparation for the dedication of the temple. There was so much still to be done in the final days that it seemed to be a hopeless task to have it ready at the time specified for the dedicatory services. President McKay, however, was the inspiration, as always, in the face of obstacles, and assured them that it could and would be ready, and on time. By working around the clock for the last few days, everything was in order. This was the crowning event of this epoch-making tour, and all were prepared to make it the impressive feature its importance demanded.

This event was to climax the tour of President McKay and the choir. The services were conducted on Sunday, September 11, as planned. Members of the Church from all the countries of Europe were in attendance, as well as the large group from America accompanying the choir, their relatives and friends. There were also four members of the Council of the Twelve, Richard L. Evans, who had been continuously with the choir, and Spencer W. Kimball, Ezra Taft Benson, and Henry D. Moyle, who were already in Europe on other assignments, and were now participating in the dedicatory exercises.

Two sessions were held on Sunday, September 11, one

at 10 a.m. and the other at 2 p.m. Two sessions were held each day thereafter through Thursday, September 15. At each session all available space was occupied, the six hundred permanent seats being supplemented by nine hundred folding chairs. The choir participated at all sessions, and talks were given by President McKay, the members of the Council of the Twelve who were present, and others, including President William F. Perschon, of the Swiss-Austrian Mission, and Samuel E. Bringhurst, president of the temple. A number of addresses were delivered in German by former missionaries of the German speaking countries. President McKay spoke at all the sessions and gave the dedicatory prayer. In addition to English, services were also conducted in German, French, Dutch, Swedish, and Finnish languages.

The President expressed his personal gratitude, and that of the entire Church, to all who had worked so valiantly from the time of the selection of the site for the temple, the acquiring of the property, the struggles of the building, and the completion of the structure and final arrangements for the dedication. It was a valiant service.

The choir was most impressive, the singing of the solo by Ewan Harbrecht, "Bless This House," the inspirational talks, and the dedicatory prayer, all impressing the President to note that there was a great unseen audience from the spirit world participating in the solemn exercises. He felt that the veil between earth and heaven was very thin at the time.

The prayer expressed gratitude for many blessings enjoyed by the Latter-day Saints, for the restoration of the Gospel in its fullness, with its priesthood authority, the freedom-loving governments of the United States and Switzerland, where man's free agency and his rights to worship were all respected, for the great leaders who had guided the Church in this dispensation, and for the cooperation of the

Church members in making possible the building of the temple. An appeal was made for the hastening of the day when peace would come to the world. That the temple would serve all good purposes, and eventually the immortality and eternal life of man, were the hopes anticipated, and the temple was dedicated to the Lord to these ends. The plea was made that the temple would be regarded by all who enter as sacred, and respected as the House of the Lord.

Ordinances were begun on the day following the dedication, with three sessions. President and Mrs. McKay and some of the choir members participated in the first session which was conducted in German. The second was also in German and the third in French.

Following the dedicatory exercises the choir left Berne for Zurich, for another concert. President McKay was present at this concert, and, as with all the others, the choir sang to a full house. Liberal praise was given by all the critics.

The final concert of the tour was given to an audience of three thousand in Paris. Here, too, the reception was most cordial and the praise liberal for the quality of the singing. One Paris newspaper summed up the reaction to the recital thus: "With the Parisians, the Mormons will have left the memory of a marvelous vocal ensemble of incomparable quality."

President McKay went from Paris to London, and left by plane for New York after what he described as "one of the most inspiring weeks of my life." Of the choir he said, "nothing we have ever done—nothing that I know of, equals the choir trip for encouraging good will." He described the entire trip as "a highly successful European visit."

Chapter 18

Dedication of the Los Angeles Temple

A prophecy by President Brigham Young in August, 1847, that "In the process of time the shores of the Pacific may yet be overlooked from the temple of the Lord," was fulfilled in part at least by President David O. McKay when he dedicated the Los Angeles Temple on Sunday, March 11, 1956.

Land for the temple site had been purchased as early as 1937 while President Heber J. Grant was President of the Church. But it was not until January, 1949, that any plans were begun by the Church architect.

Ground-breaking ceremonies for the temple were conducted by President McKay on September 22, 1951, and he also presided at the laying of the cornerstone on December 11, 1953, with some 10,000 persons present at the exercises.

It was an important milestone when the temple was ready for dedication in 1956, for the Los Angeles Temple was the largest to be built by the Church in this dispensation.

The building is beautifully situated on a hill in Westwood village, towering 257 feet, with the spire rising 30 feet from the center, topped by a statue of the Angel Moroni ascending another 15 feet. It is visible to ships twenty-five miles out at sea, and is an addition to the Los Angeles sky line that awakens pride in every Southern California Saint.

The building has a structural steel framework, and is fire proof and earthquake resistant. The sparkling white exterior, made of crushed Utah and Nevada quartz and cement, is self-cleaning. Grills covering the long vertical windows, provide maximum light, while cutting down the direct rays of the sun. The head of the architecture department of the University of Southern California, when asked to describe the type architecture of the building, used only one word, "everlasting."

An almost unbelievable result in landscaping was accomplished during the weeks of completing the building, by transplanting twelve species of full-grown trees, shrubs, gorgeous lawns, and flower gardens. Palms, which had taken many years to grow, were transplanted to the grounds as rapidly as the planting area could be made ready. Twenty specimens of olive trees line the main walk, and there is also a beautiful rose garden. It all seemed a miracle to the thousands visiting the great temple, knowing how recently the building had been completed.

The temple contains ninety rooms, furnished in excellent taste, including a chapel which will seat 380 persons, and an assembly room on the third floor which will accommodate 2,600.

In many of these rooms there are beautiful murals depicting scriptural scenes, harmonizing with the rich furnishings, making the interior as attractive and impressive as the first glimpse of the noble building itself. The modern baptismal font, patterned after the one in Solomon's Temple, is made of stainless steel, and rests upon the shoulders of twelve bronze oxen. The mural depicting Christ's baptism by immersion, in the River Jordan by John the Baptist, adds much to the impressiveness of this room.

Prior to the dedication, the building was opened to the public, and from December 1955, through February 18, 1956 some 682,361 persons walked through the magnificent structure. The old and the young, people from all walks of life, government leaders from this and many other countries, visitors from near and far, some in wheel chairs, came to view the new addition to the Los Angeles sky line. During the week-end following the "open house," a crew of workers swarmed over the six-million-dollar edifice, cleaning the rich carpets and the rooms generally, in preparation for the dedication which began on Sunday, March 11.

The dedication rites were held in the Assembly Room, using closed circuit television for members assembled in other rooms, with a total attendance of 6,700. In the days following, with two assemblies each day, more than 50,000 members were privileged to participate in these sacred ceremonies.

There was absolute silence in the building until the sweet strains of the choir rose in a sacred hymn, "The Morning Breaks—The Shadows Flee." The hymn was followed by the opening prayer, given by Elder Eldred G. Smith, Patriarch to the Church. The second song by the choir was "Joseph Smith's First Prayer."

President McKay, in his introductory remarks said: "This is one of the most memorable dedicatory services, if not, in many respects, the most memorable temple dedicatory service ever held in the Church. All the general authorities are present, or will be, in one or more of these sessions. Only one is absent this morning, because of the illness of his wife. This is probably the largest congregation ever assembled at a dedicatory service. Every one of the fifty thousand persons in attendance at this and succeeding sessions, will have increased responsibility as never before, in the words of an ancient prophet, 'to do justly, and to love mercy, and to walk humbly with thy God.'" (Micah 6:8)

President McKay then read, or referred to several telegrams and resolutions: From the Honorable Norris Poulson, Mayor of Los Angeles:

> Congratulations upon the selection of Los Angeles as the site of your magnificent Mormon Temple, and allowing the citizens an opportunity to view the building before the dedication. Both Mrs. Poulson and I will be ever grateful that we were among your guests. The stately building, rising as it does majestically into the sky, has already enhanced the city as a tourist attraction; thousands more visitors will daily tour the premises, but more important still are the spiritual values and the great labor of love that will proceed from the sacred edifice. Best wishes to you and the Latter-day Saints of the area on this magnificent and important period.

The Honorable J. Goodwin Knight, Governor of California, sent the following wire:

> I am glad to join in extending greetings upon the occasion of the dedication of the new Latter-day Saint Temple in Los Angeles. It was a privilege for Mrs. Knight and me to have the opportunity to inspect the magnificent edifice a short time ago. This temple truly reflects the profound devotion and dynamic force of your faith on the side of justice, morality, and human dignity. The entire aspect is indeed one of grace, solidarity, harmony and serenity. Our visit was one of the most impressive and inspiring experiences we have ever enjoyed.

Congratulatory resolutions were unanimously passed by the Los Angeles City Council, and also by the Board of Supervisors of the County of Los Angeles, and sent to the temple exercises at this time.

President McKay referred to three men who were instrumental in securing the land upon which the temple stands:

President Heber J. Grant, Preston D. Richards, former counselor in the Los Angeles Stake presidency, and Bishop David S. Howells. He said:

> These names will ever be associated with the early history of this temple, and their hearts are full of rejoicing at these messages and for this eventful hour of dedication. One of the most appreciative feelings I shall ever associate with this temple is the faith, loyalty, and devotion of the people of this Los Angeles district in their voluntary contribution of one million six hundred thousand dollars in addition to their participation in building chapels during this same period.
>
> To all assembled I extend a hearty welcome, and with all my soul I pray God to bless us this day with a rich outpouring of His Spirit, and with a realization that He is near us, as He was to the Prophet Joseph when He answered that boy's prayer.

President Noble Waite, of the South Los Angeles Stake, representing the members of the Los Angeles area, said: "This morning our dream has come true. We have waited for this moment for four years." He thanked the general authorities for building a temple in Southern California, and for their patience, kindness, and encouragement. He continued: "Of course we had our moments of discouragement, and when these seemed darkest we would wire or call President McKay, who would immediately respond and meet with us to discuss our problems. Always after such a meeting the clouds would lift and everything would proceed smoothly again. For the most part, however, it has been no sacrifice for our people, but rather a glorious opportunity with many resultant blessings."

He praised the local temple committee, Presidents John M. Russon, Hugh C. Smith, and Howard W. Hunter, with all the other stake presidents and their counselors, and all who had assisted in any way. "We can never give enough to have the Lord in debt to us." He said he had been instructed by the people of Southern California to promise that they would do everything possible to make the temple fulfil the purpose for which it was built.

After remarks by President Stephen L Richards and President J. Reuben Clark Jr., Ewan Harbrecht, standing in the pulpit, sang, "Bless This House." Then came the inspiring dedicatory prayer by President McKay.

There were few dry eyes in that vast congregation of more than six thousand as the services were concluded by the choir singing "Hosanna," followed by the congregation singing "The Spirit of God Like a Fire is Burning." The closing prayer was offered by President Russon of the Los Angeles Stake.

There were many prayers of gratitude both during and following the session for the privilege of participating in such a sacred service. Those present felt it a great spiritual experience, and one that carried them as near to heaven as is possible while still on the earth.

The other seven sessions of the dedication resembled the first, with members of the general authorities as speakers, and with music furnished by various choirs. President McKay gave an address before repeating the dedicatory prayer at each of the sessions.

Following is the impressive dedicatory prayer which he offered:

O God, Our Eternal Father, Creator of the Earth and of the teeming manifestations of Life thereon, we, Thy children, assembled in dedicatory services in this House built to Thy most Holy Name, plead that we may be accepted by Thee.

May we feel Thy presence and the presence of Thy Beloved Son Jesus Christ, by whom all things were made and only through whom will the consummation of Thy Divine purposes pertaining to the inhabitants of this earth be wrought. That we may thus sense Thy Presence, and have assurance that our prayers are heard by Thee, may every heart in this Edifice this day be clean and pure before Thee, and every mind be willing to do Thy will, and to work for the accomplishment of Thy purposes.

When our first parents chose to take upon themselves mortality, they knew that they would be driven from Thy divine Presence, and that their only hope of ever regaining it would be dependent upon Thy revealing Thyself to them through Thy Beloved Son, who would give to them the Plan of Salvation. Today, we express heartfelt gratitude to Thee for having given in the Beginning the Gospel plan, the power of God unto salvation, and with it man's Free Agency, a part of Thy divinity wherein man may choose the Right and merit salvation, or choose the wrong and merit condemnation.

Down through the ages men have been free to accept or to reject Thy Righteous Plan. Thou knowest, and history records, how many in wickedness yield to the enticements of the flesh, and how few, comparatively, follow the path of Light and Truth that leads to happiness and eternal life.

But, Thy mercy, Thy love, Thy wisdom are infinite! And in dispensations past Thou hast pleaded, as Thou dost now plead, through chosen servants for Thy erring children to repent and come unto Thee.

We thank Thee that Thou, O Great Eloheim, and Jehovah, Thy beloved Son, didst appear to the Prophet Joseph Smith, and through the subsequent administrations of angels didst enable him to organize the Church of Jesus Christ in its completeness with Apostles, Prophets, Pastors, Teachers, Evangelists, etc. as it was established in the days of the Savior and His apostles in the Meridian of Time.

In keeping with the unwavering truth that Thy Church must be established by divine authority, Thou didst send Heavenly Messengers to bestow upon the Prophet Joseph Smith and others the Aaronic and Melchizedek Priesthood, and subsequently all the Keys of the Priesthood ever held by Thy Prophets from Adam through Abraham and Moses, to Malachi, who testifies of the authority of Elijah to "turn the heart of the fathers to the children, and the heart of the children to their fathers," down to the latest generation. For this completeness and consistency of restoration of authority, we express gratitude today, and praise Thy Holy Name.

We are grateful for this land of America, "choice above all

other lands." The freedom vouchsafed by the Constitution of the United States, which guarantees to every man the right to worship Thee in accordance with the dictates of his own conscience, made possible the establishment of the Church of Jesus Christ of Latter-day Saints. Oh, may the American people not forget Thee, Our Father! Help us to see the greatness of this country, and to mini-mize its weaknesses. We express gratitude for the right of the people to resort to the ballot, and for freedom to meet in legisla-tive halls to settle problems and disputes without fear or coercion of dictators, secret police, or slave camps. Help people everywhere to sense more clearly that government exists for the protection of the individual—not the individual for the government.

Bless, we beseech Thee, the President of the United States, his Cabinet, the Houses of Congress, and the Judiciary. Give the President health and wisdom needful for the world leadership now placed upon him.

We express gratitude to Thee for the men whom Thou hast chosen to lead the Church from the Prophet Joseph Smith, his brother Hyrum, and other associates, their successors through the years down to the present General Authorities—The First Presi-dency, the Council of the Twelve, the Assistants to the Twelve, the Patriarch to the Church, the First Council of the Seventy, the Presiding Bishopric.

Continue to reveal to the President and his counsellors, The First Presidency, Thy mind and will concerning the growth and advancement of Thy work among the children of men.

We have felt Thy presence, and in time of doubt and per-plexity have hearkened to Thy voice. Here in Thy Holy House, in humility and deep gratitude we acknowledge Thy divine guid-ance, Thy protection and inspiration. This is truly Thy Work. Help us to be able representatives, faithful and true!

Bless the Presidencies of Stakes, the High Councils, the Presi-dencies of Missions, the Bishoprics of Wards, Presidencies of Branches, Presidencies of Quorums—Melchizedek and Aaronic; Presidencies and Superintendencies of Auxiliary Associations throughout the world—make them keenly conscious of the fact that they are trusted leaders, and that they are to keep that trust as sacredly as they guard their lives.

This edifice, as eleven other Temples dedicated to Thy Holy Name, is a magnificent monument testifying to the faith and loyalty of the members of Thy Church in the payment of their tithes and offerings. Not only the building of Temples is thus made possible in different parts of the world, but the proclaiming of the Restored Gospel, and the carrying out of Thy purposes by the building of Chapels, Tabernacles, Recreation Halls wherever needed by churches organized in many lands and climes.

In this respect, we invoke Thy blessing particularly upon Thy people and their friends in this Temple District who have so willingly and generously contributed their means, time, and effort to the completion of this imposing, impressive House of the Lord. May each contributor be comforted in spirit, and prospered a hundred fold! May all be assured that they have the gratitude of thousands perhaps millions on the Other Side for whom the prison doors may now be opened, and deliverance proclaimed to those who will accept the Truth and be set free.

For this purpose Thou has revealed that the Gospel is to be preached to those who have passed beyond the Veil, as well as to the millions now living whose faith in Thee and in Thy Gospel is faltering and unstable, who are now being influenced by false ideologies, which are disturbing the peace of mind and distorting the thinking of honest men and women. May the Temples, Tabernacles, Churches, wherever a Branch or Ward of the Church is organized, declare even in silence that Jesus Christ is the Way, the Truth, and the Light, and that "there is none other name under heaven given among men, whereby we must be saved."

Guide us, O Lord, in our efforts to hasten the day when men will renounce contention and strife, when "nation shall not lift up sword against nation, neither shall they learn war any more." To this end, we beseech Thee to influence the leaders of nations that their minds may be averse to war, their hearts cleansed from prejudices, suspicion and avarice, and filled with a desire for peace and righteousness.

Temples are built to Thy Holy Name as a means of uniting Thy people in bonds of faith, of peace, and of love.

Today, therefore, we come before Thee with joy and thanksgiving, with spirits jubilant and hearts filled with praise that we are permitted to participate in the dedicatory service of this, the twelfth Temple to be dedicated to Thee since the organization of Thy Church. Millions have had their attention drawn to it—many through curiosity, some because of its beauty in structure, others because of its lofty purpose. Help all, O Father, to realize more keenly and sincerely than ever before that only by obedience to eternal principles and ordinances of the Gospel of Jesus Christ may Loved Ones who died without baptism be permitted the glorious privilege of entrance into the Kingdom of God. Increase our desire, therefore, to put forth even greater effort towards the consummation of Thy purpose to bring to pass the immortality and eternal life of all Thy children.

To this end, by authority of the Holy Priesthood, we dedicate this, the Los Angeles Temple of The Church of Jesus Christ of Latter-day Saints and consecrate it for the sacred purposes for which it has been erected. We ask Thee to accept this edifice and to guard it from foundation to statue. Protect it from earthquakes, hurricanes, tempestuous storms or other devastating holocausts. We dedicate the ground on which it stands and by which it is surrounded. May the Baptismal Font, the Ordinance Rooms, and especially the Sealing Rooms be kept holy that Thy spirit may be ever present to comfort and to inspire. Protect all mechanical parts pertaining to lighting, heating, ventilating system, elevators, etc. Bless the persons who are charged to look after all such installations and fixtures that they may do so faithfully, skillfully, and reverently.

Bless the President of the Temple and his wife as Matron. Let humility temper their feelings; wisdom, and kind consideration guide their actions. May they, and others, who will be appointed as assistants and custodians, maintain an atmosphere of cleanliness and holiness in every room. Let no unclean person or thing ever enter herein, for "my spirit," saith the Lord, "will not dwell in unclean tabernacles"; neither will it remain in a house where selfish, arrogant or unwholesome thoughts abide. Therefore, may all who seek this Holy Temple come with clean hands and pure hearts that Thy Holy Spirit may ever be present to comfort, to inspire, and to bless. If any with gloomy forebodings or heavy hearts enter, may they depart with their burdens lightened and their faith increased, if any have envy or bitterness in their hearts, may such feelings be replaced by self-searching and forgiveness. May all who come within these sacred walls feel a peaceful, hallowed influence. Cause, O Lord, that even people who pass the grounds, or view the Temple from afar, may lift their eyes from the groveling things of sordid life and look up to Thee and Thy Providence.

Now, dear Lord, our Eternal Father, through love for Thee and their fellow men, faithful members of Thy Church, and others who believe in Thee, by tithes and other generous contributions, have made possible the erection and completion of this Thy Holy House, in which will be performed ordinances and ceremonies essential to the happiness, salvation, and exaltation of Thy children living in mortality and in the spirit world. Accept of our offering, hallow it by Thy Presence, protect it by Thy Power. With this prayer, we dedicate our lives to the establishment of the Kingdom of God on earth for the peace of the world and to Thy Glory forever, in the name of Thy Beloved Son, Jesus Christ, Amen.

Chapter 19

A Tabernacle in Ogden

Just prior to the dedicatory services of the Los Angeles Temple, President David O. McKay officiated at the dedication of the new Ogden Tabernacle, an occasion for him which was filled with much personal satisfaction and reminiscence.

As a young man, and later as an educator and leader in the area, President McKay had participated in many meetings in the old tabernacle. The structure, dedicated on October 10, 1859, had served for many years as the center for stake conferences and special meetings in the area. There was much respect and reverence for the historic structure, but it had become inadequate to accommodate the conference audiences of the eleven stakes now using it.

Though the need for a new tabernacle was long recognized, it was 1953 before financing and other details could be arranged and approval obtained from the First Presidency of the Church to proceed with plans.

At a meeting early in 1953 the eleven stake presidents

utilizing the old building met to begin planning for the new tabernacle. A special committee was appointed to supervise the building, with President Scott B. Price of East Ogden Stake selected as chairman. Chosen to assist him were Albert L. Bott, president of the Mount Ogden Stake, and Laurence S. Burton, president of the Ogden Stake.

Planning proceeded rapidly with cooperation from all concerned, and the ground-breaking services were set for July 24, 1953. Elder Harold B. Lee of the Council of the Twelve represented the general authorities, and participated in the services with many local Church and civic leaders.

The site selected for the new building was in the north half of the old tabernacle square, and was a beautiful spot adjoining the business section of the city.

Work began at once, and in a year the building had progressed to the point that the cornerstone could be laid. As indicated in Chapter 16, this event was planned to coincide with "David O. McKay Day" in Ogden, July 16, 1954, so that President McKay could officiate. At the services he placed a sealed box filled with memorabilia in the cornerstone and placed the stone bearing the date of the occasion over the opening. In his remarks the President noted that ". . . this stone is laid for the erection of a tabernacle where the priesthood can meet, and for stake conferences and other appropriate purposes."

Completion of the building, with its many details, continued through 1955, and it was then ready for dedication on February 12, 1956.

The tabernacle, a beautiful structure of white cast stone, faces the Wasatch Mountain range, only a few miles to the east. At the east end of the building is a majestic spire extending some two hundred feet into the sky. The furnishings of the building include 2,000 opera-style seats to facilitate the comfort of those attending meetings. Cost of the building, when completed, was approximately $725,000.00.

The dedicatory services were very impressive. Obviously all those from the eleven stakes desiring to attend could not be accommodated in the building, but as many as possible filled the beautiful auditorium. A choir of 145 voices was chosen from the eleven stakes, and included many of the members of the old Ogden Tabernacle Choir, a group which had given many years of musical service to the area. Choir director was Lester H. Hinchcliff, with Wayne N. Devereaux at the organ. The music for the service was particularly impressive and thrilling to the large audience.

The new pipe organ in the building, heard for the first time by the public at the dedication, gave promise of much beautiful music to be heard in the ensuing years. The organ included 2,280 pipes, housed in special chambers behind a grill designed as an appropriate background for the choir.

President McKay delivered the principal address and offered the dedicatory prayer. Present with him from the general authorities were President Stephen L Richards of the First Presidency, Elders Henry D. Moyle and Richard L. Evans of the Council of the Twelve, Thomas E. McKay, Assistant to the Council of the Twelve, and the Presiding Bishopric of the Church, Joseph L. Wirthlin, Thorpe B. Isaacson, and Carl W. Buehner. Many civic leaders were also present, including Ogden Mayor Raymond S. Wright, and E. J. Allison, city manager.

President McKay's address was most stirring. He spoke of the tabernacle as an important building, having a particular radiation. He told of other great buildings throughout the world, each with a special purpose. This tabernacle, he said, "is a house which stands for a message which 2,700 other chapels throughout the Church give to the world—the message of Peter, 'There is none other name under heaven given among men, whereby we must be saved.' "

He spoke of United States Ambassador to the United Nations, Henry Cabot Lodge, attempting through a letter to the various delegations, to have the existence of God as a Divine Being recognized officially by the United Nations. He spoke of the day as a memorable one in the history of the United Nations. The desire to have the Lord's support in the affairs of this body, almost was a re-enactment of a scene in the Constitutional Convention, when Benjamin Franklin made a similar plea to the delegates to invoke the blessings of God upon the efforts of that body to frame a constitution.

President McKay spoke of Lincoln's reliance upon Deity for wisdom in guiding the affairs of the nation during the Civil War, and the security he felt in the knowledge that his prayers were heard. He then cited the rejection by Russia of Mr. Lodge's suggestion as "unnecessary."

This fact in recent history, President McKay felt, was an adequate reason why we should want this tabernacle to stand as a testimony to the divine mission of the Savior, and his sacrifice for us. He lauded the united action of eleven stakes, where only one functioned originally, in declaring the message, "There is no other name under heaven given among men, whereby we must be saved. We must have faith in him as a divine Being, as our Lord and Savior. Such faith enabled the doubting Thomas to say, 'My Lord and my God,' and which also brought a glorious vision to Joseph Smith, enabling him to declare beyond question that God lives. The same faith prompted Peter to say, 'Thou art the Christ, the Son of the Living God.' It also sustained Paul when he stood before King Agrippa.

"The restored Gospel of Jesus Christ proclaims that he

lives, that he is the Son of God, our brother and Savior, the Everlasting Father, the Prince of Peace."

In the dedicatory prayer, President McKay expressed gratitude for the testimony of Joseph Smith's mission, for the true plan of salvation, for the organization of the Church, offering opportunity for so many to serve and to assume responsibility, and for America, with its inspired constitution. He made a plea for the preservation of the government, that freedom should still be guaranteed through the constitution.

He dedicated the tabernacle to the Lord, with all its physical properties, to be regarded with reverence by all who entered. He prayed for blessings upon all services therein, that faith would be established, and good accomplished by what was done.

A spirit of unity was invoked for all who served here. "Keep them one, as thou, Father, and thy Son are one," he prayed.

President McKay spent more than an hour greeting all who came to the stand, shaking their hands, and giving each a word of encouragement. He saw and greeted many old friends from his years of residence in Ogden and Weber County.

Chapter 20

The New Zealand Temple

A significant step forward in the Church's program of temple building was taken in 1958 when, in that one year, two new temples in opposite parts of the world were completed and dedicated by President David O. McKay.

The New Zealand Temple, at Hamilton, was dedicated by President McKay on April 20, 1958. Dedication of the London Temple in Great Britain came on September 7, 1958. Both were constructed under the careful direction of President McKay.

The general authorities had felt for some time that a temple should be constructed in the South Pacific. Missionary work among the Polynesian people had met with continuing success since it first began in 1851. Thousands had accepted the gospel during the ensuing years, and proved to be loyal and faithful members of the Church. However, lack of contact with a temple was a serious deterrent to the growth of these individuals. Some had been able to reach the temple in Hawaii, but this involved considerable expense and much loss of time for a people who generally were of meager circumstances.

Discussion of a temple in the South Pacific was underway even at the time President McKay and Elder Hugh J. Cannon made their world tour in 1921. The Hawaiian Temple had been completed and dedicated in 1919, and it was hoped that this would help somewhat among the members in the islands of the South Pacific. However, it became apparent as the work continued to grow that a temple would have to be built nearer these faithful saints.

In 1954 the general authorities approved the building of a temple at once somewhere in the South Pacific. The location could not be determined so easily, since there were many Church members in all of the islands, as well as on the continent of Australia. All must be given consideration, but since only one temple could be built it would have to be located where it could serve the most people to the best advantage.

Accordingly, it was decided by the general authorities that President McKay should visit all the missions involved, and make a careful survey of conditions and needs and then determine the location of the new temple.

Such a trip was planned, and on January 1, 1955, President and Sister McKay left Salt Lake City by plane, accompanied by President Franklin J. Murdock of the Highland Stake who was to serve as secretary of the tour. Plans called for them to visit all of the missions of the Pacific Islands and make the trip a missionary tour as well as a fact-finding trip. Some of the islands had been visited by previous presidents of the Church, and President McKay had visited all of them in 1921. This visit, however, would be the first to all of the missions by the President of the Church.

First stop was San Francisco, where the party remained until January 4, 1955, then leaving by plane for Honolulu, Hawaii. As they left the airport they were informed that a hurricane warning was posted for the mid-Pacific area, and undoubtedly would alter their plans. Some concern was expressed about continuing the flight, but President McKay expressed no worry at all and insisted that they continue. He recounted his travels over almost all of the globe without any serious trouble, and said he felt secure while on this important mission.

The flight to the Hawaiian Islands was made without any difficulty. Only a few hours were spent in Hawaii since they planned to tour these islands on their return trip. They left Honolulu in the evening, with President and Mrs. Wendell B. Mendenhall of the San Joaquin Stake joining their party there.

During the night a stop was made at Canton Island, a small spot in the Pacific, where they were warned of the dangers of hurricane weather. Their next scheduled stop was at Nandi, in the Fiji Islands, and the plane's route was directly in the path of the storm. The pilot was apprehensive about continuing, but while they were waiting, an unexplainable thing occurred. Reports were received that the storm had suddenly changed its course, almost reversing itself, and they could proceed to Fiji with no concern.

This peculiar action of the hurricane caused a good deal of comment at Nandi and Suva, on the Fiji Islands. Weather officials explained in detail the abrupt change of the storm's path, but could offer no explanation for it, and called the typhoon "The Screwball." This was not the only instance of favorable changes in the weather during the trip. President Murdock, in his narration of the trip, referred often to sudden changes, cessation of violent storms at the last minute, and other happenings which enabled parts of the trip to continue or open air meetings to be held as planned. He reported that President McKay always anticipated good weather, and occasionally referred to some lack of faith on the part of those who worried. President Murdock said that such changes

179

came with so much regularity that as far as he was concerned they were not accidental.

On Fiji an automobile trip of 135 miles was made from Nandi to Suva, where they would embark for the Tongan Islands. At Suva they were still talking about the typhoon and its unexplainable action. President McKay and the entire party felt that there was a protecting influence in this, as well as in so many other things on the trip, that made for security in the face of great danger.

One of the prime purposes of the detailed inspection of the island missions was expressed by President McKay at Suva. When asked specifically by a reporter, he answered that it was to be able to better the educational facilities of the natives. Agricultural and mechanical training would be stressed, "for here we realize that their destiny lies." He said further, "We come to give, not to take away."

Here on this Fiji Island the President remained quietly over Sunday; that is, it was so intended. But the few saints and missionaries had planned some interesting activity, and the results were typical of the personal interest President McKay has always shown in those he meets. There is no place so isolated, nor group so small, but that he shows the same interest that he would give to the largest congregation in the most beautiful chapel in the Church. And how he is loved and admired because of that tender feeling for everyone!

Here, near Suva, lived a brother, C. G. Smith, who had been on the island for many years, and had kept a little group of twenty-eight members together, with frequent meetings at his home. He had planned a meeting for 10 o'clock, at which all members, and the two missionaries on the island, would be present to meet the visitors, and welcome them to Suva. All were present when the President and his party arrived, and they were greeted wth the usual, "We Thank Thee,

O God, For a Prophet," with feeling sufficient to bring tears to many eyes. A man and woman were present who, as youngsters, had seen President McKay on his first visit to the island in 1921, and who had witnessed the calming effect of a prayer he uttered during a storm at sea, when the boat was threatened with destruction.

President McKay explained that conditions on the Fiji Islands were such at the first visit, 34 years ago, that the mission could not be opened. He was not aware that active work was yet going on there. Now to find a few faithful members, and the work under way, was truly a pleasure. He was happy that circumstances had brought them together.

The intimate, spiritual session, at which many expressed themselves, brought them very close together, and when the "good-byes" were said, another sacred memory was left to be cherished until the next visit.

Before sailing for Tonga, the few Saints came aboard ship for a final visit of two hours with President and Mrs. McKay. It was an intimate and loving farewell from a small, isolated group, alone in the midst of the great Pacific Ocean, trying to maintain their faith under trying conditions.

The next step of the tour was made by boat to the Tongan Islands, and the landing was made at Nukulofoa. Each island visited brought back memorable hours spent by President McKay and his companion, Elder Cannon, on that first visit. Well-remembered faces still greeted them at almost every stop, and the wonderful experiences were re-lived again and again. Everywhere the stimulating evidences of the gospel appeal were apparent. Schools had been built, and new ones were ready for dedication. Appreciation was constantly being shown for what had been done, not alone by Church members, but also by non-members and by government officials.

The landing was made at Nukulofa at 5:30 in the morning. The party was greeted by President and Mrs. M. V. Coombs, and by four Tongan members who had come 140 miles by open sailboat to meet them. After breakfast they were taken to the newly completed Liahona College. Here more than a thousand people greeted them, seated in a bowery in a beautiful coconut grove. Songs were sung, native rites and ceremonies conducted, and costumed dances given by the members. Following this a religious meeting was held, with the usual fine feeling, and the long hand-shaking period always given for an hour or more after such assemblages.

As the party left Nukulofa, two thousand or more friends were on hand, including the British Consul, and all joined in singing, "God Be With You Till We Meet Again." A stop was made at Vavau, and another at the Tongan Islands, where they were greeted with songs by almost fifty members. A meeting was held in a branch chapel, built in 1912. A greeting was given by a member of parliament, who was not a Church member. President McKay gave them a wonderful message, with the usual responses of appreciation.

The Samoan Islands were next visited, and the first stop was made at Paga Paga. Here they were met by the Governor and the Crown Prince. The prince had been very friendly to the Church leaders, and offered the President a private car for his use at Paga Paga. He said he would soon make a trip to Europe, and hoped to see President McKay in Salt Lake City on his return trip through the United States.

One of the outward expressions of the love of these people for President McKay, was the erection of a monument at Suniatu, Samoa, to commemorate a touching incident of his first visit. The white shaft stands in a beautiful spot amidst trees of various kinds, at the place where the people had their last glimpse of him on that memorable first visit, and where he had given them a blessing. This is a shrine to which they have come again and again to live over the loving memories of those wonderful days. Another school was also dedicated before they left Suniatu, to be added to the many already in operation on these islands.

There were three Church schools on the Island of Upola, with new schools constantly being opened on the islands of the Pacific. A beautiful new school site was dedicated at Maupasago by the President. It was a 360-acre tract of choice land. The Pesaga school at Apia, is another fine example of Church schools, with good buildings and class rooms, and is called the "Garden Spot of Apia." A banquet was tendered the party here, arranged by the members, and attended by government, Church, and civic officials, and given in the recreation hall of the school. A new school at Suniatu was also dedicated by President McKay.

The schools dedicated or visited by President McKay were typical of Church efforts to better the education of those in the islands. Good teachers were provided in addition to the missionaries who spent quite a bit of their time teaching in the schools. The results of their efforts were seen in the building of strong Church members who were educated, capable men and women. President McKay expressed the thought that here was truly where the pure in heart dwelt.

The boats were now replaced by planes for the visits to the Tahitian Islands. These were usually short trips, with many stops in these island groups. Meetings were held early and late, with saints and missionaries, according to the time of arrival or leaving. Early or late, the President was always given enthusiastic welcomes, with songs, flowers, and leis. It was an opportunity of a lifetime to be able to see the President under any conditions, and to be permitted even a few moments to show their devotion. The weather was often hot and humid, but all possible time was given to these visits, which held such meaning for the people.

The return plane flight included short stops at the Cook, Samoan, and Fiji Islands, with brief visits at each stop. There was time to work in Sunday afternoon meetings at Suva and Nandi. Nandi was the last stop before leaving for the final leg of the journey to New Zealand.

The Auckland airport was twenty miles from the town, but a large crowd was there and ready with a greeting. The change in temperature was refreshing, for here it was early autumn, and already light wraps were needed. An enthusiastic welcome was given them here. They then motored to Auckland, and after only a short stay for an inspection of the new Auckland chapel, they were on their way for a seventy-mile ride to Hamilton, where the Church had a three-million-dollar college under construction. This impressive project promised to become a real landmark in the progress of the Church, as well as for the people of New Zealand.

The college campus is part of a beautiful 215-acre tract, with a rock quarry about seven miles distant. There was great building activity going on, utilizing mostly Maoris, who were using all kinds of American machines. Most of them had learned the intricacies of the various jobs from capable supervisors, and had become skilled workers. They were mostly serving two year work missions, and were apparently happy with what they were doing.

The Church has a large farm of 729 acres, near to the college campus. Here they raise cattle, horses, and sheep, as well as all the products useful in their economy. The rolling hills and wooded areas made an impressive landscape for the travelers.

The workers on the college buildings had their families with them, living in individual cottages, and having small tracts of ground for growing vegetables. They were interested, even fascinated, with the work they were doing, and were looking happily to the time when their children would be attending the college. They began the day with prayer, and were cheerful and happy with their work.

The party visited the city of Tauanga, only a short distance away, which was the center of activities of Elder Matthew Cowley, who spent so much time in this land, and who was regarded with such intense devotion. His wonderful influence seemed everywhere apparent.

A tour of the adjoining country was made with stops at various places where meetings had been scheduled. Local and government officials were usually present, and the greetings spontaneous and impressive. There was always the feeling that the nation was happy with what the Church was doing for the people of New Zealand, and they expressed their gratitude in many ways.

The Church officials and their wives had arranged all the details of the tour of New Zealand, with the greatest care. This had also been the case in all of the Pacific Islands, and as a result the programs everywhere were carried out smoothly and impressively.

At the schools and colleges under construction, the efficiency of the contractors and workers was everywhere evident. The long experience of the Church in its work in the missions all over the world, has resulted in economical construction and management. The loyalty of all was evident, with their attitude based on the conviction that all is planned by a divine source, and is being directed by inspired prophets of God. It would not be possible to carry on this massive program of spiritual and secular education otherwise. There is nothing comparable to it in the world. Here in the Pacific, alone, many observers have stated frankly that the Mormon

Church is doing more for the spiritual, moral, and economic development of the people, than all other churches combined.

The President and his party left Auckland for Sydney, Australia, on January 31, just one month after leaving home. It had been an eventful trip, so far, probably one of the most productive ever made to these missions. The great continent of Australia would be the last to be visited, except for short stops on the homeward journey.

The plane ride to Sydney was made without incident. A large body of Church members and representatives of the Australian government greeted them at the airport. Only a short stop was made at Sydney at this time, as they would return at a later time for a longer visit. They left for Brisbane, and enroute encountered a violent storm. The pilot expressed concern because of the violence that appeared certain to be faced. The lights of the plane switched off and as suddenly returned. The storm melted almost miraculously, and the plane flew into the Brisbane airport in calm weather at 10 p.m.

A chapel was dedicated at Ipswitch, near Brisbane, at which the President spoke to a large congregation. He advised the people not to incur too great expense in order to go to the temples at Hawaii or on the continent, because it was very likely that a temple would be built nearer to them. This was the only public reference to the probability of another temple being built in the Pacific area, but it was generally understood that such a temple was in contemplation by the general authorities.

The President's party then returned to Sydney, but emplaned at once for a long trip to Adelaide. The route followed the coast-line generally, which is the productive area of Australia; the interior being largely desert. The passenger list on the plane included a group of young athletes who were to participate in a track and field meet at Adelaide. They were interested in the attitude of the Church toward athletics, as they were aware of the record of the Church missionary basketball team having won the Australian championship. They also commended the Church's attitude toward the use of tobacco and alcoholic beverages. Many of them did not indulge, and felt that they were benefitted as a result.

On reaching Adelaide, the athletes became excited when they discovered a large crowd at the airport. They naturally assumed that a great reception awaited them, and rushed off the plane. They were chagrined when they learned that the people were awaiting the arrival of President McKay, and greeted him with "We Thank Thee, O God, For a Prophet." They took it all good naturedly, however.

In the greetings in Australia, reference was made to the Tabernacle Choir's broadcasts. These had been used for more than twenty years over the entire system of stations in Australia, and were much appreciated. The vastness of this country can be appreciated when it is known that many saints had driven eighteen hundred miles, from Perth, on the west coast of Australia in order to see and hear the President. The nature of the country is also appreciated from the fact that one railroad leading to Adelaide had a stretch of track of four hundred miles without a curve or a hill.

Immigration is encouraged to Australia by the making of government loans to desirable European families who are unable to finance their passage. If they remain for two years, the loans become a gift. If they return sooner, they must repay the loan. Good citizens are thus acquired.

On leaving Adelaide the usual large crowd assembled at the airport. Many were in tears. One reporter asked the meaning of so much emotion. It was explained that the affection for their President was genuine and universal. This was their first experience of meeting their great leader, and it would be the last for most of them, in all probability. This last glimpse, a loving goodbye, and his blessing that would be the last event of the visit, would be cherished by them as long as memory lasted. The parting was always sad, but an experience of only a day, or even a few hours with him, would be a highlight in the lives of all of them.

President William Edward Waters explained further, that he had never met President McKay before, but he had been praying for his protection and success as his leader for many years, just as all these people had. The experience of seeing and hearing him now was wonderful beyond expression.

On the trip to Melbourne from Adelaide, the plane flew over vast areas of sand—sand and nothing else. President Murdock, in his fine narration, lapsed into a reverie of the things that impressed him most. The vastness of the Australian country stood out as he flew over this desert. He thought also of the waste, as he saw it everywhere, especially in the expenditures of twenty-one percent of the income of the people for tobacco and liquor.

At every airport on this trip, President McKay's party was greeted and assisted by government officials in every possible way. Many courtesies were extended, with solicitations for their comfort and convenience. Interviews by the press were the rule, and fellow travelers often were amazed, and asked many questions as to why so much attention was given by so many.

Missionary meetings were held at all places where elders were stationed, and these usually lasted for hours. Many young elders had never met President McKay personally, and these intimate meetings were appreciated beyond expression. The President's counsel in these conferences was always so helpful and inspiring that they were invaluable in the experience of the missionaries.

Visits were made at many places to the Governors or the offices of local officials. Many courtesies were extended at these visits, which would react in many ways for the good of the missionary work. Always the objective of the President was the creating of greater interest and respect for the Church and its representatives. The many similar foreign tours of President McKay have had that effect in great measure, and he has been in every respect the great missionary of the Church.

The greatness of the New Zealand and Australian countries was impressed upon the President more strongly than he had ever experienced it before. The change in sentiment in Australia was often commented upon. The gospel was introduced into Australia in 1851, by John Murdock and Charles Mandell. With world sentiment almost universally hostile at that time, one can easily appreciate the obstacles they faced, in order to find the few for whom the message would have appeal. It required courage and determination to carry the gospel message at that time, but the work was done, and without it, President McKay's tours of the world would have been of no avail.

The trip by plane from Melbourne to Sydney was the last leg of this epoch-making tour of these great countries. Sydney is a city of three million people, and is probably the greatest seaport, in some respects, of any in the world. It has 230 miles of shoreline, and handles easily all the greatest ocean liners.

The stay in Sydney concluded with a visit to the Zoological Gardens, one of the finest in the world. Australia is noted for its many strange animals, found nowhere else. The zoo was under the direction of Sir Edward Hallestrom, who was also its builder. He accompanied the party, explaining the various kinds of animals, with something of their habits and history. It was a revealing and most worthwhile visit.

During this tour President McKay had spoken twenty-two times, including responses to welcoming addresses, farewell speeches, and sermons. The largest audience was more than two thousand, in Samoa. There were twenty-six press conferences. The President talked intimately with officials of all ranks, explaining the ideals and objectives of the Church, and was received courteously and warmly everywhere. The one pleasing thing so often referred to was the great work that the Mormon Church has done for the welfare and advancement of the Polynesian people.

The effect of Mrs. McKay's presence on this tour, was noted especially by President Murdock. Her appeal to the people generally, was always apparent and her visits with missionaries brought a feeling of the presence of their own mothers. Her talks always carried a message of practical value.

The party left Sydney on February 8, 1955, reaching Honolulu on the following day. The plane flew low over the island of Molakai, where a view was had of the leper colony, and where twenty-four Church members were patients. They were anticipating an air visit from the President, and the group waved a greeting to the plane, which made a second circuit of the colony, and the passengers waved in return. Several stops were made at the different islands, where crowds always greeted the travelers. At one point, arrangements had been made for a broadcast by the President to all the Hawaiian groups of islands. The President, accordingly, gave a greeting and told of his impressions of what he had seen and heard thus far. He was given a huge, highly polished, key to the City of Maui in token of his visit. Various entertainments were provided at Maui, and a meeting held with eighteen missionaries.

Similar greetings were given by large crowds on the Island of Hilo, with sumptuous entertainment. Here the beautiful flowers intrigued him, gorgeous beyond description because of the wonderful climate, and the two hundred inches of rainfall each year. Seven hundred persons attended a meeting to listen to President and Mrs. McKay.

On the Island of Maui, President McKay and a number of others visited the little village of Puleli, where there is a monument commemorating the first baptisms in the Hawaiian Mission, and the first branch of the Church, organized in 1851. President McKay had some interesting narrations to tell of his historic visit to the same spot, with Elder Cannon in 1921.

The Island of Hawaii, which the group also visited, is known as the orchid island, with beautiful orchid gardens in every direction.

The last island visited was Oahu, on which Honolulu is located. The distance was one hundred miles to Honolulu, and it was made by plane in just thirty-two minutes. The President arrived just in time for a scheduled meeting, a habit he has had all his life. He never has a minute to spare, but he always arrives.

This special meeting was called to discuss plans for a Church college at Laie, forty miles from Honolulu. Laie had long been a Latter-day Saint community, and was the locale of the Hawaiian Temple. It is a beautiful spot in the great Pacific, all buildings clean and white, in a gorgeous setting of flowers. A feast of wonderful food was served amid striking native costumes and sweet Hawaiian music. A pageant followed, with an evening of varied entertainment.

The population here is a mixture of many nations and races, the Hawaiians, Caucasians, Chinese, and Japanese predominating. They get along well together, and, as Church members, support each other valiantly, to build up the work on these islands. This night they were at their best, to show their President what they were capable of doing.

Laie was to be the seat of the new college, and ground

was broken by President McKay. The exercises were witnessed by a large crowd, including the mission and local officials, with the local members and some visitors from Utah.

A meeting with the missionaries was held at Honolulu, and this, as in all other places, proved to be the inspirational part of the visit. These meetings were always of three to six hours duration, and no time was wasted.

The tour of the Pacific Missions ended officially with this meeting. The departure from Honolulu was delayed three hours, however, because of some minor engine trouble experienced by the plane at Guam. Even though the leaving was at a late hour, a large crowd of officials and Church members was at the airport to see them off. This, President McKay said, was the climax to a continuous series of demonstrations of affection since they had left for the orient. It was necessary to spend a night in San Francisco, making their arrival back in Salt Lake City about twelve hours behind schedule.

After reviewing his tour with the Council of the Twelve, President McKay recommended that the temple in the South Pacific area be constructed at Hamilton, New Zealand. Here, it seemed, everything was ideal. The setting in the immediate vicinity of the Church college seemed perfect for a spiritual and educational center.

There was no need now for delay, and plans for the building matured rapidly under the direction of the Church architect, who had designed so many other wonderful structures for the Church.

It was not difficult to transfer the building activities from the college to the temple. There were now competent foremen, supervisors, and workers available, skilled and equipped with the necessary machinery to make good progress. "Work missions" would supply most of the labor on the temple, and the workers were eager to begin. There would be various ceremonies, and official inspections, in the course of building the temple, which, it was estimated would require about three years time. The material used would be the same as that used for the college structures, and it was certain that a beautiful and harmonious center would ultimately emerge. It would compare favorably, perhaps even surpass, many of the attractive centers built by the Church throughout the world, which had created so much comment and had done so much to change world sentiment for the better.

The work of building progressed favorably and without interruption. When the construction had advanced sufficiently to estimate the time for its probable completion, the date for the dedication was set for April 20 to 23, 1958. It is always necessary to set such dates as far in advance of completion as possible, so that all interested persons could plan ahead for their attendance. Here there would be many who would travel thousands of miles, and for all it would mean planned adjustments in order to meet the expense.

When the date was set for completion, all plans were directed toward that end. Like all other similar projects, however, unlooked-for difficulties arose, and there was fear that completion would be delayed. As the date for the dedication grew nearer, it seemed impossible that the structure would be ready. Postponement, however, was unthinkable to all concerned, as so many had made arrangements for the trip. The only thing was to speed up the work, and it seemed that already the pace was about as great as human effort could make it.

Just how serious this effort was to the workers is shown by one incident. The many Maori workers, who were on work missions, felt that the great responsibility for completion was theirs. One of the supervisors came unexpectedly upon a group, who, before beginning work for the day, were engaged in fervent prayer for help. They were appealing to the Lord that they might be given extra strength, that they might be able to go on continuously, without rest, or even food, if necessary, in order to complete the work. All said they had been blessed, so far, and that they were better off than when they began the work.

The temple was ready when the day set for dedication arrived.

President McKay again led the party from Salt Lake City for the temple dedication. He was accompanied by Mrs. McKay, and also by Elders Delbert L. Stapley and Marion G. Romney of the Council of the Twelve, Gordon B. Hinckley, Assistant to the Twelve, Rulon S. Tingey, secretary for the President, and Theodore L. (Ted) Cannon, who would write up many of the events of the trip. The wives of all these men accompanied them.

The party left Salt Lake City by plane on April 14, 1958. There were short stops at San Francisco and Honolulu before the longer ride over the vast Pacific. Short stops were made at Canton Island, and at Nandi in the Fijis. Arrival at Auckland brought the same enthusiastic reception accorded the President at airports all over the world. Crowds of Church members were on hand, as well as officials of Church and government. Songs were sung and welcoming addresses given. President McKay made a brief response, and then the party was on its way by auto to the home of the mission president, Ariel S. Ballif, twenty miles away.

There were other officials present including Wendell B. Mendenhall, chairman of the Church Building Committee, Edward L. Clissold, president of the Oahu Stake, George R. Biesinger, project supervisor, and E. Albert Rosenvall, president of the temple. All of the officers present went into conference with the President, to discuss the details of the many events impending.

On April 18, all made the eighty mile trip by automobile to Hamilton, to witness a program arranged by the Church members. They arrived just in time to witness a terrifying mystical performance by costumed natives, in a huge, natural amphitheatre, between the temple and the college. It was estimated that about eight thousand people witnessed this spectacle, lounging on the surrounding hillsides. The object was to determine whether there would be peace or war. In the ceremonial portrayal, a fierce-looking individual, with beaded skirt and head ornament, struck a defiant attitude before the President, and threw a long, carved staff on the ground, an emblem of authority. If the President picked it up, there would be peace. When the President complied, in the interest of peace, the defiant one picked up a carved hatchet and placed it on the ground before Mrs. McKay, which she recovered. This brought smiles to the fierce-looking face, but outlandish yells from an old woman who ran up and down before the assembly.

This was followed by an elaborate program put on by the Maoris, Samoans, and Tongans, in great numbers. There were songs, dances, and ceremonials, given partly in the native languages, and partly in English. At the conclusion, President McKay expressed his gratitude for the welcoming and interesting demonstration.

In the evening, a pleasing meeting was held in the two large connecting halls of the chapel. Singing Mothers were in one, and a mixed choir in the other. There were about five hundred singers in all. Short talks were given by the general authorities who were present, and those who had been in charge of the activities at the temple site. All the talks indicated the intensity of the devotion to the work by all concerned, and the spiritual atmosphere in which it had been carried on.

The opening day of the three-day dedication services, April 20, 1958, was the realization of the long-anticipated completion of this great project. Members from all the Pacific Islands were present, and about fifty from the States. Ted Cannon wrote that "an air of wonder hung over New Zealand this week, wonder that such a project as the New Zealand Temple, and the Church College, could be completed in such a spectacular way." The days preceding had seen many thousands of people, mostly non-members, who had waited in long lines, to view the interior of the temple. They were all amazed at what they saw. It was hard to realize the motive behind all this great effort, and enormous expense, which a Church, and its individual members, so willingly contributed toward world progress.

The explanation was given by President McKay, said Ted Cannon, in that the Church accepts the mandate given by the Savior to his Apostles, "Go ye into all the world and preach the Gospel to every creature." That commission has been re-imposed by the Lord to his prophets of this dispensation, and is accepted literally as one of their great missions in life. They are carrying out the mandate in every possible way, education through secular and spiritual development going hand in hand.

That is why the Church is willing to spend seven million dollars on the New Zealand College, and another million on the temple. That is why hundreds of members are willing to take work missions of one or two years, at enormous sacrifice, for the building programs. They do this for the pleasure of the service, looking forward to the time when they, and their children after them, will reap the benefits of the temple, schools, and chapels.

There were two sessions for each of the three days of

the dedication services. Talks were given by Apostles Stapley and Romney, and Elder Hinckley, and the officials who had taken part in the work of building and preparation. President McKay spoke at each of the sessions, and gave the dedicatory prayer. The sessions were most impressive, those present sensing the great importance of this momentous event in the history of the Church.

The prayer given by the President expressed gratitude that the descendants of Father Lehi were guided to these islands, to become associated with other leading and influential nations of the world. Thanks was expressed for the United States Constitution, which made possible the re-establishment of the Church of Christ upon the earth. "We are thankful also for the liberty existing in other free nations, especially in New Zealand, so that this great temple could be built," President McKay said. Blessings were invoked upon the British Government, that it might continue to cooperate with that of New Zealand in upholding that liberty.

Gratitude was expressed for the restoration of the Gospel through heavenly visitations, with the authority and power as they were present in days of the Savior and the Apostles. "We are also grateful for the restoration of the plan by which the hearts of the children are turned to the fathers," President McKay said, "and we pray that all may sense fully the spirit of Elijah, and utilize the temple for the purpose for which it has been built. We are thankful for the system revealed, by which, through the payment of tithes, this great work of salvation can be carried on. The need for carrying the Gospel message to the world must continue to be appreciated, and strength given to resist the influences in the world today which would undermine the divine mission of the Church."

Thus was completed the great project which had marked another mile-stone in the progress of the Church. President McKay had completed another great missionary service, and even though advanced in years, had impressed the entire Church and the world with his vigor and strength in this strenuous activity.

There was yet another satisfying service to be completed before leaving New Zealand, that of dedicating the college which was now already in use. The general public of New Zealand took part in this function, and was represented by the Prime Minister, the Right Honorable Walter Nash, who gave an address in which he expressed the appreciation of the nation for this service to his people. Other New Zealand notables who attended were L. F. Enspr, superintendent of Auckland Schools, Dame Hilda Ross, member of parliament for New Zealand, Francis H. Russell, United States Ambassador to New Zealand, and George F. Fennemore, United States Consul.

On the college campus are twenty buildings and twenty residences. The school opened with 350 students, aged thirteen to eighteen. Most were Church members, the majority being Maoris. The school has the largest auditorium, organ, and gymnasium, and the most modern class-room equipment in New Zealand. The courses include agriculture, homemaking, commerce, fine arts, education, and engineering. The teachers are mostly Americans.

Generous tribute was paid by the President to the many Church officials who had worked so hard and so faithfully over the years on these great projects, which had now been completed. No clear estimate could be placed on the hours of study and planning in the preparatory stages of development. The actual work, the labor and supervision, entailed endless application and devotion over many years. No more devoted effort could be given to any project for education and spiritual uplift, than had been shown by those engaged in the development and completion of the New Zealand college and temple. Through all the final stages of the building, the presence and influence of Elder Matthew Cowley seemed to be felt by all the workers. He had spent so many years with them, offering encouragement and help toward this very end, that most of them felt his actual participation in the completion of the work. Appreciation was also expressed for the great service of those who had filled work missions, without whom this work could not have been completed.

The efforts of the President in New Zealand were now completed, and the little party left for home. There was another interesting event on the homeward trip, however, that of the dedication of the beautiful chapel at Suva, Fiji Islands. Here, it will be remembered, a little group of members had been kept together, and active, over many years by Elder C. G. Smith, who was employed at Suva. Their efforts had been so noteworthy that it had been decided to help them with a meeting place.

On arrival at Suva, preparations had been completed for the services. First there was entertainment and an elaborate feast, such as can be provided only in the Pacific Islands. The chapel, itself, was described by Mrs. McKay as "one of the most beautiful Church edifices I have yet seen." The labor mission had functioned here as it had in New Zealand, and with surprising effects. Coral rock had been gathered and placed in cement in a most effective way. "The windows are layers of glass, each of which can be opened by the touch of a finger, and the wood is from the marvelous New Zealand trees. All around the windows are plateaus of green, green and red, and red leaves, so wonderful that flowers are not needed. But roses and other flowers are there too." Elder Smith had made a veritable paradise of the surrounding grounds, with wonderful plants and flowers, transplanted from various gardens on the island.

The President and Mrs. McKay went fasting to the dedication services, on May 4, 1958. The Governor, Sir

Ronald Gawey and Lady Gawey, with a party of four, the Mayor, Dr. A. D. Leys and Mrs. Leys, the Colonial Secretary, Mr. P. D. McDonald, and Mr. Maurice Scoot, attended, and were greeted by the congregation arising and standing until they were seated. This courtesy had already been extended to President McKay and his party when they entered. The little choir had been organized only recently but gave beautiful music for the service.

Talks were given by President Mendenhall and Elder Tingey, and then President McKay spoke to the subject, *Men's Hearts Can Be Changed.* The newspapers reported the address, which can be summarized very briefly. He said he had much pride in the building of this chapel, and in the devotion of the members here. The Mormon Church is dedicated, he said, to the changing of men's lives. Human nature does change, and it can be changed now as it has been in the past, and will be in the future, until the world is drowned in its own blood.

The world today has the power to whisper words through space. But what are they to whisper? The Church is answering that question by building chapels all over the world, except in Russia, and some day we will be there, because the Russian people will want to hear the word of God. That is why thousands of dollars are spent on this chapel, and on others like it throughout the world, President McKay said.

There was much interest manifested by the press in the dedication proceedings. Several reporters were present. One reporter was especially interested, since he and his wife, a teacher, had been having some talks with the missionaries. He asked about the missionary program, and the President related the story of a sailor as typical of the interest in missionary work. This young sailor had contacted the missionaries in the islands, and was impressed with their devotion to the extent that he wrote to his mother that he intended to send his checks to her, to be deposited to his credit, and to be used for a mission when his service was ended. In the event he did not return, the money was to be given to one who deserved to go on a mission, but who did not have the means to go. The boy did not return, and the mother used the money as the boy had advised. The man and wife were much impressed, and, with tears in their eyes, expressed their gratitude for the hour's talk the President had given them.

The long ride to Hawaii was tiring, but they had the usual enthusiastic welcome at Honolulu, and then motored to Laie to make a survey of the college, now nearing completion. The President then talked to two thousand students and their parents in the chapel. After an inspection of the college buildings and the temple, they returned to Honolulu.

The work now being completed, they left for Los Angeles and home, arriving without incident, and were welcomed by the usual devoted group of Church officials, family, and friends.

Chapter 21

The London Temple

The second temple to be dedicated by President David O. McKay in 1958 was the imposing structure at Newchapel Farm, Lingfield, England, some 26 miles south of London. This marked the fourth temple to be dedicated by President McKay as President of the Church.

Dedicatory services were conducted on Sunday, September 7, 1958, and continued through Tuesday, September 9, with two sessions held each day. As always, the dedicatory services were inspirational to all in attendance, and faith-promoting to the entire membership of the Church.

While he was in London for the dedication, President McKay also observed his 85th birthday, this occurring on September 8, 1958.

The London Temple, the second such edifice to be erected by the Church in Europe, stands on historic ground. The site was purchased by the Church from the Pears family in 1953, and is a 32-acre estate known as Newchapel Farm. The land was listed in the Domesday Book of William the

Conquerer. The oldest part of the large manor house on the property dates back to Elizabethan times.

Negotiations to purchase the site were begun under the direction of Elder Stayner Richards, president of the British Mission at the time. President McKay inspected the property in 1952 together with President A. Hamer Reiser, who had succeeded Elder Richards as mission president. President Reiser concluded the transaction for the Church in 1953.

After approving the purchase of the farm as a temple site, President McKay returned to the spot in 1953 to determine the exact location of the temple. As he arrived in England he confided to some of the brethren that he had some misgivings about the purchase of the land. But when he saw again the lovely, green landscape, the great manor house, and the beauty of the entire location, all doubt disappeared.

With Edward O. Anderson, temple architect, President McKay spent the greater part of a day walking about the grounds considering the most suitable spot for the sacred edifice. The location was finally decided, and a stake was driven to mark this new focal point of the ancient estate.

President McKay was particularly impressed with an ancient oak tree growing on the site. He was informed that the tree was at least 450 years old, and had been growing when Columbus discovered America. He gave specific instructions that the tree "be preserved."

Workmen at the site, following his instructions that the tree be retained, later named it the "David O. McKay Oak." A special plaque was inscribed and placed on the trunk of the tree as a tribute to the durability of the tree and comparing the life of President McKay to the strength of this oak.

At the time of the temple dedication, President McKay observed the plaque on the oak near the east walk of the temple, opposite the front door. He meditated over the beautiful inscription, and then modestly asked that his name be removed from the plaque, feeling that the inscription was a fitting tribute to the sturdy oak. The name of the tree, however, persists as an indication of esteem toward President McKay.

Several days after President McKay and Elder Anderson selected the exact location of the temple on the site, a meeting was scheduled to dedicate the site for its sacred purpose. President McKay presided at the open-air meeting held August 10, 1953. Some 100 members of the Church gathered to hear the address and prayer offered by President McKay.

From this beginning the preparations continued, and Elder Anderson and his staff began drawing plans, a task which required nearly two years. When plans were approved, the work on the structure was ready to begin.

While he was in England with the Tabernacle Choir prior to the Swiss Temple dedication, President McKay returned to the London Temple site and on August 27, 1955, officiated at the groundbreaking exercises. A crowd of 2,500, including choir members, stood in alternating showers and sunshine as President McKay spoke, and then turned the first spade full of earth marking the beginning of construction. Present with the President were Elder Richard L. Evans of the Council of the Twelve, Sir Thomas P. Bennett, head of the architectural firm in England selected by the Church to supervise the temple's construction, and President Reiser of the British Mission.

Elder Evans was selected by the First Presidency nearly two years later to preside at the cornerstone laying ceremonies held May 11, 1957. The walls of the temple had risen to the height of the first story, and the Portland limestone facing was in place. A cornerstone of the same material had been prepared, containing periodicals, clippings, the Standard Works of the Church, photographs, and other items of interest.

Over 1,000 persons braved the intermittent rains to witness Elder Evans place the cornerstone. Those in the congregation sang "God Save the Queen," "Praise To The Man," and "The Spirit of God Like A Fire Is Burning." A special duet, "Open The Gates of The Temple" was also performed.

During the ceremony, Sir Thomas Bennett, the architect, presented a special souvenir trowel to Elder Evans to deliver to President McKay. In an accompanying letter to Elder Evans he paid this tribute to President McKay:

> Would you say that I have the most lively memories of his gracious presence when this project was inaugurated about two years ago and say that no one could work with the Church without being impressed with the high esteem in which he is held by everyone who comes in contact with him. . . . We are sure that the project of this Church which your President launched is a great project which cannot help but have a great future in the Church itself.

In his remarks at the cornerstone laying, Elder Evans traced the history of the British Mission since its beginning in 1837, and also explained the purpose and sacred nature of the temple.

Progress on the construction was rapid following the laying of the cornerstone. By the end of 1957 work was well past the halfway mark. A solid concrete roof slab was poured and then covered with copper sheet. The needle point of the spire reached 160 feet from the ground and was weatherproofed with a sheath of copper.

By July, 1958, the end was in sight and plans were already underway for the dedication. The announcement was made that President McKay would preside at the ceremonies scheduled for September 7 through 9. All work, including the landscaping of the grounds, was to be completed before that date. The announcement was also made that Elder Selvoy J. Boyer and his wife had been appointed by the First Presidency to serve as president and matron of the temple.

Final touches on the building and grounds were completed during the first part of August, and thousands of Britons were allowed to see the interior beginning August 16. Temple and mission officials had thought some 50,000 people might visit the temple grounds, but they were hardly prepared for the nearly 80,000 who did come. Because of the large crowds the viewing dates had to be extended from August 30 to September 3. Crowds streamed onto the grounds in ever increasing numbers during the last week, and the guides had to stay on duty until after 10 p.m. each evening to accommodate them.

This interest caused one of the London newspapers, the *Daily Express*, to comment in one of its issues:

"Other churches in Great Britain would do well to take note of the response by the public created during the public viewing of the new London temple." The paper then pointed out that only one person in seven regularly attended church on Sunday in England.

Visitors to the temple saw some of England's loveliest grounds, as well as a movie on the temples of the Church, and they heard a message from President McKay on the purpose and meaning of temple work. This program was repeated 80 times a day.

Those who viewed the building noted that it was unsurpassed for the quality of materials and workmanship. It is perhaps unmatched in England in some of its features. It is not an especially large building, being just 160 by 85 feet. But the 160 foot high spire can be seen for several miles. The woodwork was done by one of the few firms in England still capable of doing high quality finishing. The teak and agba woods from Burma were the finest to be found in England, according to some authorities. The mosaic tiling from Italy, the completely automatic heating system and the copper-lead roof were features seldom found in Britain.

As to color scheme, the building was dominated by brown, beige, greens and gold in the rooms and furnishings. Lady Reading, first woman member of the House of Lords, was among those who visited the temple. She expressed a special fondness for the restful, simple color scheme. Her comment expressed the feeling of many who had seen the temple. "I feel the spirit of God there as I've never felt it before," she wrote. "I feel at peace with myself and I can't understand why."

General contractor for the construction was the firm of Kirk and Kirk of London.

As President McKay made plans to attend the dedication it became apparent that Sister McKay would be unable to accompany him. Her doctors advised against the trip, and so, heeding their counsel, she remained at home. This was his first trip as President of the Church without Sister McKay at his side.

President McKay and his party left the Salt Lake airport at 8:30 a.m. on Tuesday, September 2, and after a brief stop-over in Chicago proceeded to New York City where they spent the night at the Plaza Hotel. Their departure from New York was Wednesday, September 3, at 4 p.m., and they arrived in London Thursday morning, September 4. They were taken by private car to Grosvenor House. As soon as he arrived at the hotel President McKay sent messages of their safe arrival to Sister McKay and to members of the First Presidency.

A special press conference had been arranged during the afternoon by Elder Richard L. Evans. The conference was attended by 20 newspaper reporters, as well as the motion picture crew of the British Broadcasting Company with their recorders. Elder Evans reported that the interviews were handled "skillfully and considerately" by President McKay.

A reporter in the London *News-Chronicle* factually described the temple, and then said of President McKay:

> He has a leonine head, silver hair, and a broad, sunburned face that give him a certain resemblance to Mr. Ben-Gurion. This is perhaps appropriate, since his duties in Salt Lake City require him to fulfill the role of the post, established by Brigham Young, the man who led the great trek west.

The article was accompanied by a photograph of President McKay alighting from the plane upon his arrival in London and being greeted by members of the Church.

The Times of London used a one column picture of President McKay and stated that he would discuss many administrative matters of the Church while in Great Britain. They also published this comment:

> President McKay said he is confident that eventually everybody will come to believe in Christianity; Communists, Fascists, and all others will be forced to see its truth.

On Friday, September 5, President McKay visited the temple site and reviewed final arrangements for the dedication. That evening he returned to London and enjoyed a birthday dinner with his sister, Mrs. Joseph R. Morrell, and her daughter, Jeannette Morrell, professor of English at Brigham Young University in Provo, Utah.

On Saturday, September 6 President McKay held a special meeting with missionaries and mission presidents at 50 Prince's Gate in London. Other general authorities of the Church present for the dedicatory services also attended this meeting. The missionaries and mission presidents gave reports and bore testimonies in an inspirational session.

Saturday evening President McKay was the guest of Col. Harold Person, U. S. Air Force, manager of the Air Force offices in England. Following dinner they attended a performance of "My Fair Lady" at Drury Lane Theater. President McKay expressed his enjoyment of the performance, but said it would have been better if Sister McKay had been there to enjoy it with him.

The first of the dedicatory sessions was held Sunday morning, September 7. In attendance with President McKay were more general authorities of the Church than had been in England since 1840 when eight members of the Council of the Twelve came there as missionaries. With President McKay were President Joseph Fielding Smith of the Council of the Twelve, Elders Henry D. Moyle, Richard L. Evans, and Hugh B. Brown of the Council of the Twelve, Elders ElRay L. Christiansen and Gordon B. Hinckley, Assistants to the Council of the Twelve, and Bishop Thorpe B. Isaacson of the Presiding Bishopric.

General auxiliary officers present included President Belle S. Spafford, general president of the Relief Society, and Sister Emily H. Bennett, first counselor in the general presidency of the Young Women's Mutual Improvement Association.

"This is a great day for members of the Church," President McKay declared in his remarks before offering the dedicatory prayer. He noted that it marked a new era of the Church's growth in Great Britain. Speaking of the temple itself, President McKay said "It is important not only to the members here, but also to tens of thousands of others who have left these islands and now recall in sacred memory their ancestry for whom work will now be done."

Other speakers at the first session Sunday morning included President Clifton G. M. Kerr, president of the British Mission; Edward O. Anderson, temple architect; President Joseph Fielding Smith; and A. Hamer Reiser, former British Mission president. Music was furnished by choirs from the Sheffield and Manchester districts. The solo number, "Bless This House," which has become traditional at temple dedications, was sung by Miss Ardyth Twitchell, a missionary in England.

At the services only 600 persons could be accommodated in the main temple auditorium where the speakers could be seen. An additional 1,400 were crowded into the other rooms of the building where they heard the proceedings over a public address system. In all, some 12,000 persons participated in the services during the six dedicatory services through Tuesday, September 9. The Sunday morning session was reserved for members of the British Mission, with those of other missions receiving special seating in the additional sessions.

In his inspirational dedicatory prayer, President McKay made a fervent appeal for peace. A portion of the prayer follows:

> On the occasion of the dedication of this, the fourteenth Temple, may we first express overwhelming gratitude just to be alive in this great age of the world. We pause this morning to open our hearts to Thee for this special privilege. No other time in world history has been so wonderful—no other age wherein Thy secret powers have been more within human control; in no other era hast Thy purposes been nearer human comprehension. Help us, O Lord, truly to live!
>
> Next to life we express gratitude for the gift of Free Agency. When Thou didst create man, Thou placed within him part of

Thine Omnipotence and bade him choose for himself. Liberty and Conscience thus become a sacred part of human nature. Freedom not only to think, but to speak and to act is a God-given privilege.

Thou didst inspire thy servant President Brigham Young to say "Every man's independence is sacred to him—it is a portion of that same Deity that rules in the heavens. There is not a being made upon the face of the earth who is made in the image of God, who stands erect and is organized as God is, that should be deprived of the free exercise of his agency so far as he does not infringe upon others' rights save by good advice and a good example."

Personal liberty is the paramount essential to human dignity and human happiness.

Down through the ages men have been free to accept or to reject Thy Righteous plan. History records how many have yielded to the enticements of the flesh, and how few, comparatively speaking, have followed the path of Light and Truth that leads to happiness and Eternal Life.

But Thy Mercy, Thy Wisdom, Thy Love are infinite; and in dispensations past Thou hast pleaded, as Thou dost now plead, through chosen and authoritatively appointed servants, for Thy erring children to heed the Gospel message and come to Thee. Holy Temples are a means of extending Thy loving mercy to Thy children even beyond the grave.

When in the Middle Ages the Church departed from Christ's teachings Thou didst inspire honest, upright men here in Great Britain to raise their voices against corrupt practices. Mingling with the denunciatory messages of Luther and Melanchthon in Germany, and Zwingli in Switzerland, were the voices of George Wishart and later John Knox of Scotland. We thank Thee that before the scorching flames silenced his tongue and reduced his body to ashes that Thou didst permit George Wishart to glimpse that "This realm shall be illuminated with the light of Christ's Evangel, as clearly as ever was any Realm since the days of the apostles. The house of God shall be builded in it; yea, it shall not lack the very copestone."

Much clearer was the inspiration given President Wilford Woodruff and President Joseph F. Smith, and other more recent Apostles, who stated prophetically that "Temples of God . . . will be erected in the divers countries of the earth," and that "Temples will appear all over the land of Joseph—North and South America—and also in Europe and elsewhere; and all the descendants of Shem, Ham, and Japheth, who received not the Gospel in the flesh, must be officiated for in the temples of God, before the Savior can present the kingdom to the Father, saying, 'It is finished.'"

We are grateful that in 1840 authorized messengers were sent to Great Britain to announce to the people of the British Isles that God had again spoken from the Heavens and reestablished in its purity and fullness the Gospel of Jesus Christ; that thousands accepted the message and subsequently emigrated to the headquarters of the Church.

We thank Thee that Thou, Great Elohim, and Jehovah, Thy Beloved Son, answered the fervent appeal of the lad Joseph Smith, and through subsequent administrations of angels, enabled and authorized him to organize The Church of Jesus Christ in its completeness with Apostles, Prophets, Pastors, Teachers, Evangelists, etc., as it was established in the days of the Savior and the Apostles in the Meridian of Times.

In keeping with the unwavering Truth that Thy Church must be established by divine authority, Thou didst send Heavenly Messengers to confer upon the Prophet Joseph Smith and others the Aaronic and Melchizedek Priesthood, and subsequently all the keys of the Priesthood ever held by Thy Prophets from Adam, the Ancient of Days, through Abraham and Moses, Malachi and Elijah, with authority to "turn the hearts of the fathers to the children and the hearts of the children to their fathers down to the latest generation." For this consistency, and completeness of restoration of authority, we express gratitude on this occasion and praise Thy holy name.

We express gratitude to Thee for the leaders of Thy Church from the Prophet Joseph Smith through the years to the present General Authorities—the First Presidency, the Council of the Twelve Apostles, the Assistants to the Twelve, the Patriarch to the Church, the First Council of Seventy, the Presiding Bishopric.

With humility and deep gratitude we acknowledge Thy nearness, Thy divine guidance and inspiration. Help us, we pray Thee, to become even more susceptible in our spiritual response to Thee.

We express gratitude for the right of free peoples to resort to the ballot, and for freedom to meet in legislative halls to consider problems and settle difficulties without fear or coercion of dictators, of secret police, or of slave camps. O Father, help people everywhere more clearly to realize that government exists for the protection of the individual, not the individual for the government.

Bless, we beseech Thee, Her Majesty, Queen Elizabeth the II, the Houses of Parliament, and all branches of government throughout her Majesty's Realm, that the high reputation of this great government for the proper and just enforcement of law may continue to be meritoriously maintained.

May the United States government with Great Britain, Her Dominions, and freedom-loving countries everywhere, including South American Republics, hold so sacredly the principles of self government, and give to their peoples such enjoyment of peace, tranquility, and opportunities for progress as will make communistic governments of dictatorship, of mock trials, of unjust imprisonment, of enforced tyranny, so universally reprehensible as to be discarded forever by liberty-loving peoples.

That peace may eventually prevail, Thou hast again restored in its fullness the Gospel, and established authoritatively The Church of Jesus Christ. Even so, there are millions who are being influenced by false ideologies which are disturbing the peace of mind, and distorting the thinking of honest men and women. O Lord, guide and protect thy Messengers in their efforts to convince honest people in all lands and climes that Jesus Christ is "the way, the Truth, and the Light," and that "there is none other name under heaven given among men whereby we must be saved."

Bless well-meaning men in all climes as they strive to hasten the day when men will renounce contention and strife, and desire to use the great nuclear discoveries of the present day not for war and destruction, but for peace and spiritual advancement.

To this end, we beseech Thee to influence leaders of nations that their minds may be averse to war, their hearts cleansed from prejudice, suspicion and hate, and filled with a desire for peace and good will.

While His body lay in the tomb Christ, Thy Beloved Son, preached to the spirits in prison who once were disobedient in the days of Noah, thus evidencing that those who have passed beyond the veil must also hear the word of God and obey the eternal principles of life and salvation.

Temples are built to Thy Holy Name as a means of uniting Thy people, living and dead, in bonds of faith, of peace, and of love throughout Eternity.

Help all, O Father, to realize more keenly and sincerely than ever before that only by obedience to eternal principles and ordinances of the Gospel of Jesus Christ may loved ones who died without baptism be permitted the glorious privilege of entrance into Thy Kingdom.

Increase our desire, therefore, to put forth even greater effort toward the consummation of Thy purposes.

On Monday, his 85th birthday, President McKay again delivered the dedicatory prayer at both sessions. He had requested that no special observance be made of the occasion, but the great love felt for him by members of the Church everywhere could not be withheld, and letters, telegrams, gifts, and other expressions of appreciation and gratitude poured in to London for him. That evening he was honored at a special birthday party at Claridge House, with a number of the general authorities and other dedication visitors present. His day was made complete when he talked later in the evening with Sister McKay in Salt Lake City by telephone and shared with her some of the spiritual experiences of the dedication.

On Tuesday President McKay again repeated the dedicatory services in the morning and afternoon, and then instructed the temple workers to prepare it for the sacred ordinances to be performed therein. The first two endowment sessions on Wednesday, September 10, were reserved for members of the British Mission, with other sessions conducted throughout the remainder of the week in accordance with the demand for them. The normal schedule of sessions resumed the following week after the many dedication visitors had returned home.

As the ordinance work began on Wednesday, President McKay expressed a desire to travel to Wales and visit the birthplace of his mother, Jennette Evans. Arrangements were made for his sister, Mrs. Morrell, and her daughter, Jeannette, to travel with the President, with President Reiser to drive the car.

The occasion proved to be an eventful one, and an account of the trip which President Reiser included in his diary is quoted here because of its interest.

"We're looking for Plas Helygen House, Clwyd Defgwr, Cefn Coed y Cimmer near Merthyr Tydfil, South Wales, can you help us?"

This is the question you will have to ask if you are ever in South Wales and want to see the birthplace of Jennette Evans, mother of President David O. McKay.

President McKay had been there five or six years before, and I had visited the home in 1952 with Boldwin Davies, a cousin to President McKay. Between the two of us we felt it would not be too difficult to find the old country place. But, it proved to be quite an adventure.

Enroute, President McKay asked me to point out Runnymede and Magna Carta Park. The fog lay so densely in the fields that these could only faintly be seen as we passed. Over the most direct route from London we went. At Hammersmith, what had been London's worst traffic bottleneck three years ago, is now an open, fast "dual carriage way" west to Staines. Hence we made Bagshot and Basingstoke and set off over Highway 30 and 303 for Andover.

However, just as we approached a pass under a railway bridge (¼ of a mile) near the Georges Inn (three miles from Andover) the gas supply failed.

The men at the hotel garage . . . to get the car to start and stay running, had pulled out the choke and not returned it and I had not noticed it.

I walked to Georges Inn and said to the young proprietor:

"I am out of petrol just the other side of the bridge down the road. Have you a telephone I might use to call the Automobile Association and see if they can rescue me?" He looked me straight in the eye and said in his lovely English:

"Awkward, isn't it?"

"It is indeed," I said.

"I have not a tellyphone, but if you will not let me down, I have a small bit in a can which I shall give you. Will you please return the can and make good the petrol you use? That's all I ask."

Over the tavern counter he handed me an Army gasoline container—five gallon capacity in which was possibly a half gallon. Down the road I ambled to my patient companions.

I found that the neck of the car's petrol tank was in too far and the spout of the can too short . . . that I could not pour from one to the other without risking the loss of too much of the precious fuel. So I improvised a funnel of a daily newspaper. Though I lost something by absorption to the newspaper, I emptied most of it into the car and after vigorous priming we were off again.

To our good fortune about a mile and a half down the road we came upon a petrol station set up anew near a farm field, open and ready for business. I told the operator my plight and need.

"I set this station here for the benefit of just such people as you," he said.

He filled the tanks and then found the battery cells empty of water but the oil was all right. After paying him we were off back to the good Samaritan, keeper of George's Inn, to return his can filled with petrol, then about again and on our way to Andover.

In a few minutes we arrived at Amesbury where we heard unfolded the fascinating story of the Stonehenge. One of the interesting details of the story was that (according to one legend) one of the Prescilly stones was brought from the hills of Wales by raft down the Bristol Channel. The route was along the English Channel and it was accidentally dropped into the river and there it still remains.

From there we went up to Salisbury Plain and the mystery in the distance.

The time we spent there was filled with the wonder at the mystery of the Stonehenge and its clear detail. Such questions as these ran through our minds:

How had the stones been upended and the lintels put into place? How had they been tongue and grooved and mortised and tenoned together? What was the significance of the sun dial features, the cross Wren carving, the Minoan daggers and the incinerary burials in the circumference?

But we could not stay too long if we wanted to get to Wales.

We were in Cardiff by 5:30 and found a double room at the Angel Hotel for the ladies but "no place at the Inn for us." We were taken in at Mrs. Peas Guest House at 51 Dispenser St. President McKay had a comfortable clean bed in the front parlor bedroom and I had a third floor quiet back room.

After a good night's rest we were off at 8 a.m. for Merthyr and Cefn Coed in search of the beloved birthplace.

We arrived in about an hour and began making inquiry for the location of Plas Helygen House, Clwyd Defagwr. A young police officer was at a loss to help us.

A young mother living in Blodwin and Thomas Davies little house "Y Bythen Bach, Ponty Chapel" (under the bridge, near the chapel) thought she had seen such a name on a house up "among the villas" in a completely different section of town than my sense of orientation told me.

Nevertheless, we explored that section to no avail.

An older man, keeping a petrol station up the Cefn Road on the way to town said:

"No, Clwyd, Clywd Defagwr is on the southwest hillside there near that new housing estate." So we went back to explore.

I asked President McKay to let me take them over the route I remembered Blodwin had taken us when we were there in 1952 and he was willing. Up the steep, narrow, rough and rutted hillside road I drove in the direction of the old houses on the hillside.

We came out by a group clinging to the road which leads to the new housing estate. Up this road we went to Mile End House. There, off to the left led another road to another cluster and there a second led to a row of four or five terraced houses, each with its front yard enclosed by fence, and gate.

The President said:

"Let's inquire here." We were at No. 69.

I looked around the front yard and into a small shelter in the front corner of the lot.

Inside the fence came an old lady who looked friendly at me as I asked for directions.

By this time President McKay had come into the yard. She turned to him and said:

"Oh, I know you."

It was Ann Morgan, a spinster who had been born in the house 76 years ago.

She assured President McKay that "This is the place."

Then she showed President McKay and Mrs. Morrell into the small six by nine bedroom in which the bed completely occupied the narrow end of the room.

They stood with arms around each other weeping their emotions at being in this beloved place.

President McKay returned to London Thursday evening for meetings with mission and temple officials and remained until Sunday, attending Church services during the day. He boarded a plane for New York Sunday evening and arrived without incident in Salt Lake City Monday, September 15, at 3:40 p.m., less than 29 hours after he started the trip across the Atlantic.

He was met at the airport by many of the general authorities, members of his family, and most importantly by

Sister McKay. Everyone present was touched by the warmness of their greeting after an absence of two weeks.

Immediately upon his return President McKay plunged into the details of preparing for the October general conference and the many other matters awaiting his attention, but with a sense of pride and humility in the great accomplishment of another temple in this dispensation.

Chapter 22

A Testimonial Dinner

A community tribute of appreciation and high esteem, without parallel in the history of Salt Lake City, or Utah, was paid to President David O. McKay on Monday evening, December 10, 1962 at the Hotel Utah.

More than 460 prominent men of Utah, the majority of them not members of The Church of Jesus Christ of Latter-day Saints, gathered on that evening to pay verbal, as well as tangible, tribute to one whom they called "a great man."

A committee of twenty, whose names read like a "Who's Who" of Utah business and industry, planned the elaborate dinner and entertaining program in President McKay's honor. Those on the committee, and their positions at that time, included, J. P. O'Keefe, chairman, general manager of the Utah Division, Kennecott Copper Corp.; John M. Wallace, treasurer, chairman of the board, Walker Bank and Trust Company; Eric C. Aaberg, vice president and general manager, Mountain States Telephone Company; Gus B. Aydelott, President, Denver & Rio Grande Railroad, Denver, Colorado; Gus P. Backman, secretary, Salt Lake Chamber of Commerce; Clarence Bamberger, Sr., chairman of the board, Bamberger Company; L. F. Black, division manager, Geneva Works, United States Steel Corp.; Frederick P. Champ, banker, Logan, Utah; Newell B. Dayton, chairman of the board, Tracy-Collins Bank & Trust Co.; John W. Gallivan, publisher, *The Salt Lake Tribune;* Robert G. Hemingway, president, Commercial Security Bank, Ogden; James E. Hogle, chairman of the board, Hogle Investment Company; John C. Kinnear, Jr., general manager, western mining division of Kennecott Copper Corporation; William T. Nightingale, chairman of the board, Mountain Fuel Supply Company; Edward M. Naughton, president, Utah Power & Light Company; Marion C. Nelson, president, Gillham Advertising Agency, Inc.; William J. O'Connor, president, Independent Coal & Coke Company; Walter L. Roche, resident manager, Merrill, Lynch, Pierce, Fenner & Smith; Joseph Rosenblatt, chairman of the board, Eimco Corporation; James M. Stacey; Kenneth J. Sullivan, president, Continental Bank & Trust Company; and Scharf S. Sumner, president, Western Savings & Loan Association.

The Lafayette Ballroom of the Hotel Utah was elaborately prepared for the occasion. The tables were decorated with a profusion of red roses and Scotch heather. Attractive souvenir programs prepared as a service by Gillham Advertising Agency were at each place setting. The significance of the occasion, and the appropriate tributes of the evening can best be understood by a study of this program which is reproduced in its entirety on the following pages. The cover and the frontispiece picture of President McKay were reproduced in full color, though they show here only in black and white. No further details of the program arrangements will be described here, since it can better be gained by reading the program itself.

Honoring
President David O. McKay

David O. McKay

THE McKAY COAT OF ARMS
(reproduced on front cover)

The clan Mackay derives from a branch of the Royal house of Moray, probably deriving its style *Mac-ic-Moargainn* from Morgund of Pluscarden, a prince of the house of Moray. The first historic Chief was Angus Du (1380-1429). He was assassinated, and the clan was ruled by his younger son, until the rightful heir obtained his release from captivity on the Bass Rock, 1437. The latter's son was Chief and led the clan in the cruel fight of Blair Tannic, Caithness. In 1628 Sir Donald Mackay of Strathnaver, Chief of the clan, was created Lord Reay, with the remainder of his heirs-male bearing the name and arms of Mackay.

The major portion of the estate was sold in the seventeenth century to pay the cost of maintaining and transporting 2000 men whom Lord Reay recruited for foreign service to assist the Protestant cause in the great Thirty Years' War. The earliest Gaelic charter extant was granted by Donald, Lord of the Isles, to Brian Vicar Mackay in 1408.

Chief: Lord Reay.
Patronymic: Morair Maghrath.
Clan Seat: House of Tongue, Sutherland.
Slogan: Bratach bhan mhic Aoidh.
Plant: Great Bulrush.
Memorials: Kirk of Tongue.
Pipe Music: (1) Mackay's White Banner. (2) Mackay's March.

To Honor

President David O. Mc Kay

AS HE BEGINS THE NINETIETH YEAR

OF HIS LIFE

HIS COMMUNITY FRIENDS

PRESENT THIS DINNER AND PROGRAM

ON

MONDAY EVENING, THE TENTH DAY OF DECEMBER

NINETEEN HUNDRED AND SIXTY-TWO

AT HALF AFTER SIX O'CLOCK

IN THE LAFAYETTE ROOM

OF THE HOTEL UTAH

IN SALT LAKE CITY

General Committee

J. P. O'KEEFE
Chairman

JOHN M. WALLACE
Treasurer

ERIC C. AABERG	JOHN C. KINNEAR, JR.
GUS B. AYDELOTT	WILLIAM T. NIGHTINGALE
CLARENCE BAMBERGER, SR.	EDWARD M. NAUGHTON
L. F. BLACK	WILLIAM J. O'CONNOR
FREDERICK P. CHAMP	WALTER L. ROCHE
NEWELL B. DAYTON	JOSEPH ROSENBLATT
JOHN W. GALLIVAN	JAMES M. STACEY
ROBERT G. HEMINGWAY	KENNETH J. SULLIVAN
JAMES E. HOGLE	SCHARF S. SUMNER

Menu

LOBSTER THERMIDOR EN COQUILLE

HEARTS UTAH CELERY   MIXED QUEEN OLIVES
SALTED ALMONDS

CLEAR GREEN TURTLE SOUP AMONTILLADO
CHEESE STRAWS

CHARCOAL BROILED FILET MIGNON, MAITRE D'HOTEL
CROWN OF MUSHROOM

POTATOES MACAIRE
ITALIAN GREEN BROCCOLI, MORNAY

POMPADOUR SALAD

ORANGE SURPRISE

BEVERAGE

Musical Program

Entrance ceremony of President McKay and escorts, with selections by
Salt Lake Scots, under direction of Dale J. Bain

National Anthem...*Soloist: Roy Samuelson*
Accompanied by Utah Symphony String Ensemble

Dinner Music...........................*Utah Symphony String Ensemble and Brass Choir*
Conductor: Dr. David A. Shand, Assistant Conductor
Utah Symphony Orchestra

Formal Musical Program *(following Dinner)*

A. Male Quartet (Men of Music).......................*"I Need Thee Every Hour"*
Glenn Johnson, Loile Bailey, Robert Holbrook, Malcolm E. Pike
Accompanist: Anna Bailey

B. Harp Trio
1. Deep River Interlude..*Grandjany*
2. Tango...*Carlos Salzedo*
3. Zephyrs...*Carlos Salzedo*
Harpists: Camille Lamoreaux, Shru-De-Li Smith, Helen Hogan

C. Medley of Scotch Folk Songs..*Jean Preston*
Accompanist: Paul Banham

Speaker's Program

Presiding...J. P. O'Keefe
President, Salt Lake City Chamber of Commerce

Invocation.....................The Right Reverend Monsignor Patrick A. Maguire
Our Lady of Lourdes Catholic Church

Followed by Dinner, Dinner Music and Formal Musical Program

Tribute...John M. Wallace
Chairman of the Board, Walker Bank & Trust Company

Presentation...Joseph Rosenblatt
President, The Eimco Corporation

Response...President David O. McKay

Benediction...Rabbi Sidney Strome
Temple B'Nai Israel

Portrait of a Great Man

The life span of David O. McKay, now in his ninetieth year, bridges the important era of Mountain West development from the days of his pioneer parents to the present.

His birth in Huntsville, Utah on September 8, 1873, was the occasion of rejoicing for a staunch, saintly Welsh immigrant mother, Jennette Evans McKay, and a stalwart, devoted Scottish father, David McKay. They were tillers of the soil with the courage and industry and frugality of true pioneers.

Into the life of David O. McKay was instilled the true characteristics upon which the great western community of America was builded. They have been manifest in the almost magic touch and magnetic personality of one who has been a moving factor in the development of the West, spiritually, socially, educationally, and industrially.

His world travels began with a call as a missionary for his Church in the footsteps of his father. He went to the British Isles in 1897 and served with distinction as President of the Scottish Conference. In 1921 he made a world-wide tour of missions of the Church, traveling more than 62,000 miles by land and sea. Missionary service called again in 1922 when he became President of the European Missions with headquarters in Liverpool, England. Subsequent travels have taken him into almost all parts of the world. As one of the greatest missionaries

At about the age of five

Old family home and President McKay's birthplace, Huntsville, Utah

of all time, he has traveled by land and sea approximately one million miles. The last trip abroad was in August of this year, when he traveled by jet plane to his father's native land of Scotland to organize a Stake of the Church.

Trained for a career in education, he began a teaching assignment in 1899 at the Weber Stake Academy, now Weber College, and in 1902, he became principal of this same institution. In educational circles, he has also been Church Commissioner of Education, 1919-1922; a member of the Church Board of Education, 1906-1919; and now is president of the Church Board of Education. In recognition of his distinctive contribution in the field of education, he is the recipient of four honorary doctorates from Utah's three major Universities, and from Temple University of Philadelphia, as well as awards from various educational institutions and civic organizations.

For his devotion to Scouting, and in consideration of his outstanding record of service to youth, he has been awarded the coveted Silver Buffalo and the Silver Beaver by the National Council of the Boy Scouts of America.

Governments of other nations have honored him, and buildings have been named to perpetuate his outstanding achievements.

The major service of David O. McKay has been as one of the General Authorities of the Church of Jesus Christ of Latter-day Saints. Called to the Apostleship in

As a member of the first University of Utah official football team, 1894. FRONT ROW— A. B. Sawyer, Fred J. Mayes, Captain Harry Kimball, Fred Earles and Seth Thomas. MIDDLE ROW — Ernest Van Cott, F. W. Reynolds, A. E. Hyde and Joseph W. Stringfellow. BACK ROW — Paul Kimball, David O. McKay, F. N. Poulsen, Bernard J. Stewart, I. E. Willey, Theodore Nystrom

17 years of age, 1890

LEFT — Principal of Weber Academy, Ogden, Utah, in 1901, the year he married Emma Ray Riggs. CENTER — In 1897, as president and valedictorian of his class when he graduated from University of Utah, with sister, Mrs. Jeanette Morrell. RIGHT — As a missionary. President of Scottish Conference, Glasgow, Scotland, August 8, 1897 to August 24, 1899.

April, 1906, he has served well over half a century as a spiritual leader. In October, 1934, he was brought into the First Presidency as a counselor and continued in this position until he was sustained to the position of President and Prophet in April, 1951.

Members of his faith everywhere honor him as their great spiritual leader, and there are other thousands who join with them in our community and in Western America in honoring him for his service to the people. The sincerity of his character, and the masterful addresses given by

When chosen member of the First Presidency by President Heber J. Grant, 1934.

When chosen President of the Church of Jesus Christ of Latter-day Saints, April, 1951.

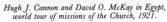

Hugh J. Cannon and David O. McKay in Egypt, world tour of missions of the Church, 1921.

President McKay at airport in Melbourne, Australia, February, 1955.

him in many public meetings containing words of inspiring counsel, instruction, admonition and advice, applicable not only to members of his Church, but also to freedom-loving men and women everywhere, have won for him a place of esteem and respect. He is a spirited citizen, always alert to the welfare of our community. This civic consciousness has been often demonstrated, and is fittingly memorialized in the recently dedicated Pioneer Memorial Theatre, and in the preservation of the Pioneer City Hall. Neither project would have materialized without the energetic leadership and support of President McKay.

Ceremonial Welcome — Tuhikaramea, New Zealand, April 19, 1958. President McKay carrying Challenge Spear and Ceremonial Stick, is led by a Maori woman who strews leaves in path of distinguished guests.

President and Mrs. McKay arrive at airport in Sidney, Australia February 5, 1955, during their visit to the missions of the Church in the South Pacific, New Zealand and Australia.

Dr. John M. Schiff, president of Boy Scouts of America, presents silver buffalo award in Los Angeles, July 17, 1953.

President McKay speaking at dedication of Temple site at Newchapel, Surrey County, England, August 10, 1953.

This great man has an honored place in the community as an exemplary family man — as a husband and father. At his side with her sustaining influence has been his companion and sweetheart, Mrs. Emma Ray Riggs McKay, whom he married in January, 1901. They are the parents of seven children, including one who is deceased, who are carrying on the family tradition of good citizenship.

No more fitting tribute has been given to President McKay than that given by his world-wide missionary companion, Hugh J. Cannon, who said of him:

President and Mrs. McKay attending Chuckwagon Roundup at B.Y.U. September 18, 1953.

At Huntsville farm on birthday, September 8, 1961.

234

A Testimonial Dinner

50th wedding anniversary, January 2, 1951.

On President McKay's 89th birthday, Sept. 8, 1962

"David O. McKay, a man every line of whose face denotes firmness and courage, intensely serious when serious matters are being considered, as immovable as Gibraltar when principle is involved, but withal a kindly man and one whose heart is full of sympathy and human tenderness and an unfailing love for all mankind.

"In no degree sanctimonious and with a highly developed sense of humor, he still has a deep appreciation of sacred things; refined and intellectual, he is yet one of the common people; a vital, dynamic power for good wherever he goes, he is still as humble as the little child whom we must all resemble in order to enter the kingdom of heaven."

Speaking to 10,000 students at B.Y.U.
September 18, 1953.

President and Mrs. McKay leading the 24th of July
parade, Salt Lake City, July 24, 1957.

BROTHERS AND SISTERS — *Seated on the lawn at Huntsville family home are Mrs. Thomas B. Farr, left, President and Mrs. David O. McKay and Mrs. Joseph R. Morrell. Standing are Dr. and Mrs. Joel Ricks, Dr. and Mrs. George R. Hill and Dr. Morrell. The four daughters and one son of David McKay met with their families and families of Thomas E. and William M. McKay on July 24 for a family reunion — 1958.*

IMMEDIATE FAMILY, CHILDREN AND GRANDCHILDREN — *birthday party at Lawrence McKay's following return from London Temple dedication, September 17, 1958. BACK ROW — left to right: Alice McKay, Dr. Llewellyn R. McKay, Soila Piekainen (exchange student), David Ashton, Mildred McKay, Marianne McKay, David McKay, David Lawrence McKay, Robert R. McKay, Frances Ellen McKay, Dr. Edward R. McKay, John McKay, Lottie McKay, Emma Rae Ashton, Conway Ashton. SECOND ROW — Vivien McKay, baby, Rebecca McKay, Emma Louise Ashton, Roger Ashton, Suzanne McKay, Emma Ray McKay, President David O. McKay, Lou Jean Blood, Joyce McKay. Two children in foreground — Mark McKay, Edward McKay.*

Favorite Poems Oft-Quoted by David O. McKay

ADDRESS TO THE UNCO GUID

Then gentl, scan your brother Man,
　Still gentler sister Woman;
Tho' they may gang a kennin wrang,
　To step aside is human:
One point must still be greatly dark,
　The moving *Why* they do it;
And just as lamely can ye mark,
　How far perhaps they rue it.

Who made the heart, 'tis *He* alone
　Decidedly can try us,
He knows each chord its various tone,
　Each spring its various bias:
Then at the balance let's be mute,
　We never can adjust it;
What's *done* we partly may compute,
　But know not what's *resisted*.
　　　　　　　　　—Robert Burns

Oh wad some power the giftie gie us,
To see oursel's as ithers see us.
It wad frae monie a blunder free us.
　　　　　　　　　—Robert Burns

*Giving lesson to a Scout, Los Angeles,
California, July, 1953.*

*President McKay is welcomed by the Council of
Presidents of Uruguay, at Montevideo,
Uruguay, January 27, 1954.*

Then let us pray that come it may,
   As come it will for a' that,
That sense and worth o'er a' the earth,
   May bear the gree, and a' that:
      For a' that, and a' that,
         It's comin yet for a' that,
   That man to man, the world o'er
   Shall brithers be for a' that.
                  —Robert Burns

The mother, in her office, holds the key
Of the soul; and she it is who stamps the coin
Of character, and makes the being who would be a savage
But for her gentle cares, a Christian man.
Then crown her Queen o' the world.
      —from on Old Play — taken from Forty Thousands quotations

To make a happy fireside clime
   To weans and wife,
That's the true pathos and sublime
   O' human life.
      —Robert Burns (from Epistle to Dr. Blacklock, stanza 9)

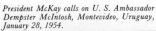

President McKay with Prime Minister of New Zealand, Hon. Walter Nash, at dedication of Church College of New Zealand, April, 1958.

President McKay calls on U. S. Ambassador Dempster McIntosh, Montevideo, Uruguay, January 28, 1954.

A *Testimonial Dinner*

Time for reflection — at Huntsville home, October 12, 1957.

O Brother Man! fold to thy heart thy brother;
Where pity dwells, the peace of God is there;
To worship rightly is to love each other,
Each smile a hymn, each kindly deed a prayer.

Follow with reverent steps the great example
Of Him whose holy work was 'doing good';
So shall the wide earth seem our Father's temple,
Each loving life a psalm of gratitude.

Then shall all shackles fall; the stormy clanger
Of wild music o'er the earth shall cease;
Love shall tread out the baleful fire of anger,
And in its ashes plant the tree of peace!
                    —*John Greenleaf Whittier*

Statements by David O. McKay

"Man's chief concern in life should not be the acquiring of gold, or of fame, or of material possessions. It should not be development of physical powers, nor of intellectual strength, but his aim, the highest in life, should be the development of a Christ-like character."

"The world needs men, men of character, God-fearing men."

"In the well-ordered home we may experience on earth a taste of heaven."

"The true purpose in life is perfection of humanity through individual effort, under the guidance of God's inspiration. Real life is response to the best about us."

"The Gospel brings peace; it is the one source of satisfaction in all the world."

"The finest thing for young people and everybody is to live the Gospel."

"Young people do not seem to realize that the religious life is the happy life. Doing for others, making others happy, and living the Gospel of Jesus Christ is the really happy life for everybody to live."

"I believe with others that government, institutions, and organizations exist primarily for the purpose of securing to the individual his rights, his happiness, and proper development of his character. When organizations fail to accomplish this purpose, their usefulness ends."

"The worth of man is a good measuring rod by which we may judge the rightfulness or the wrongfulness of a policy or principle, whether in government, in business, or in social activities."

"Our founding fathers, despite some natural fears, clearly regarded the promulgation of the Constitution of the United States as their greatest triumph."

"In these days of uncertainty and unrest, liberty-loving peoples' greatest responsibility and paramount duty is to preserve and proclaim the freedom of the individual, his relationship to Deity, and the necessity of obedience to the principles of the Gospel of Jesus Christ — only thus will mankind find peace and happiness."

"Our country's greatest asset is its manhood, upon which depends not only the survival of the individual freedom vouchsafed by the Constitution and Bill of Rights, and all other ideals for which the founders of the Republic fought and died, but the survival of the best that we cherish in present-day civilization."

"The noblest purpose of the public schools as a function of the government should be to teach loyalty and obedience to the laws of the country."

"The most potent influence in training youth to cherish life, to have increased Respect for human kind, to keep their Word of Honor, to love Justice, is the life and personality of the teacher."

"The real tragedy in America is not that we have permitted the Bible to slip out of our schools, but that we have so openly neglected to teach it in either the home or the Church."

"Never before was there such need of revitalizing the teaching of faith and repentance on the part of parents. Never before in the history of our country was the State in greater need of young men and young women who cherish the higher life in preference to the sordid, the selfish, and the obscene."

"Teach the boys that it is chastity during youth that gives vigor, strength, and virility of manhood. Teach the girls that chastity is the crown of beautiful womanhood."

"Force and compulsion will never establish the ideal society. This can come only by a transformation within the individual soul — A life redeemed from sin and brought in harmony with the divine will. Instead of selfishness, men must be willing to dedicate their ability, their possessions, their lives if necessary, their fortunes, and their sacred honor for the alleviation of the ills of mankind. Hate must be supplanted by sympathy and forbearance. Peace and true prosperity can come only by conforming our lives to the law of Love, the law of the principles of the Gospel of Jesus Christ."

*At April, 1962 Conference of the Church of Jesus Christ of Latter-day Saints,
Salt Lake City*

A Favorite Quotation

"There is a destiny which makes us brothers,
None lives to self alone;
All that we send into the lives of others,
Comes back into our own."

—*Edwin Markham*

After those attending had assembled in the ballroom, President and Mrs. McKay were escorted into the dining room by the Salt Lake Bagpipe Band. The audience stood while the President and his wife were escorted to their places at the head table by Henry R. Aloia, manager of Hotel Utah.

Chairman O'Keefe, noting that many congratulatory messages and telegrams had been received by the committee for President McKay, said he chose to read only one, that being a telegram from President John F. Kennedy. The text of this message follows:

> I am pleased to join the business and community leaders of Salt Lake City in extending sincere congratulations to President David O. McKay as you are honored this evening at the beginning of your ninetieth year. I am happy, too, to commend you for your long and devoted service to God, to your state, and your country. The bond of Christian brotherhood which has marked your religious pronouncements has helped to tie our people to those of other nations in a deeper spirit of Christian faith. May your influence for good continue to be felt by the members of your Church both here and in far off lands, and by others who admire and respect you. With all good wishes.
>
> John F. Kennedy.

Following the dinner, special music and the formal program, Mr. Wallace was then introduced to pay a tribute to President McKay. He said:

> Seldom in a lifetime does one have the privilege of publicly paying tribute to a universally beloved and admired leader as President David O. McKay, and I deeply appreciate the honor. To clasp his hand, to look into his eyes, to feel the warmth and inspiration of his presence, is an experience to be remembered. The unforgettableness of this man, his influence on people, his sincere love for all mankind, and his complete devotion to his church throughout his eighty-nine years, have endowed him with a remarkable capacity for leadership.

He is one of our greatest and most successful of missionaries. He has circled the earth, visited the farthest corners, traveling on foot, by horse and buggy, and by jet airliner covering over one million miles to present his convictions and the great strength of his personality to people everywhere on the globe. Through the magic of radio and television, his face and voice are known throughout the world. Millions have come to know the warmth, the strength, the humor, and the moving power of his presentations. Who among us can measure the contributions of this man, which fan out across the peoples of the earth like a geometrical progression from one generation to another? Who appropriately can evaluate for this individual who has amassed great fortune and statures in spiritual values, except perhaps to say that his life exemplifies the words of the Master, who, as he sat around the table with the Twelve for the last time, said to them:

'If any man desire to be first, the same shall be last of all, and servant of all; and whosoever will be chief among you, let him be your servant even as the Son of Man came, not to be ministered unto, but to minister, and to give his life a ransom for many.'

Notwithstanding his position of great responsibility and importance in his church, President McKay has always kept the common touch. Perfectly at home with the great and renowned, or with the lowliest, his deep sympathy for people, and his understanding heart, have opened channels of communication and influence to inspire and motivate thousands, especially the young people. These attributes have endeared him to everyone with whom he has come in contact.

The oldest son of a family of ten children, he followed the horse-drawn plow with his father in the fields when only a youngster. His roots were planted deep in the soil. His love for every growing thing has increased with the years, and still abides, typified by his love for his horse, Sonny Boy. His home in Huntsville is a citadel of courage and devotion to ideals. From example and precept of his Scottish father, Bishop David McKay, a convert to the Church of Jesus Christ of Latter-day Saints, and abiding faith of his Welsh mother, Jennette Evans McKay, he learned early in life to honor and respect his parents, and each member of the household. Performance of religious duties and daily life were carefully synchronized. Little wonder that he carried from that home the inspiration, the strength, and the devotion that have characterized his life.

In his heart he has a natural love for learning, which impelled him to study throughout his life. He attended Weber Stake Academy in Ogden, and later the University of Utah, where he was right tackle on the football team, was extremely popular with the student body, and was valedictorian of his class. About this time he became acquainted with Emma Ray Riggs, who later became his bonnie bride in the first marriage ceremony performed in the Salt Lake Temple in the twentieth century. They have enjoyed a wonderful life together for over 61 years, and have seven children, six of whom are living, which is refreshing to see in this day and age.

President McKay dearly would have loved to spend his life as a teacher, and a good one he would have been. He was offered a teaching position in Salt Lake County after graduation, but at the same time he received a call to go on a mission to Great Britain, which he accepted, and there he began his career as a dynamic, enthusiastic, and highly persuasive missionary. No assignment was too difficult, no other activity as important to him, and his great capacity for leadership soon was recognized as he moved through countless church positions, culminated in his being sustained unanimously by the membership as President on April 9, 1951. Under his leadership some of the most phenomenal growth and development in the history of the church has occurred. The church has adopted a so-called "international policy" which has been accompanied by great building programs for beautiful chapels, temples, and schools around the world. The widely published Welfare Program has been highly successful. Great energy and study have been given to a youth program in an effort to guide and encourage the youth in high ideals and sound endeavors.

In January, 1960, President McKay initiated a series of far-reaching fireside discussions, when he spoke by means of special radio hook-up to over 214,000 young people from the Atlantic to the Pacific, and from Canada to Mexico, on the subject of "Courtship and Marriage." Just recently plans have been put in operation to broadcast by short wave radio around the globe. President McKay called it more than a step forward—rather "a bound into space," to touch around the world.

In every way the church has been aggressive and resourceful under the leadership of President McKay. He has brought about a tremendous, ever increasing momentum, which portends great advancement over future decades. I can appreciate what joy and gratification that brings to his heart, for this is his life—this is his life's purpose. I quote from another Christian leader who lived about the year 1650:

"I abide lovingly united to God's will—and this is my whole business."

I wish it were possible, in some way, to convey to you the breadth of his experience, the extent to which he devotes all his amazing energy in service to his fellowmen. I have been privileged to review part of the biography of his life, prepared so meticulously by his secretary, Miss Clare Middlemiss. It is evident that no situation or location would be unusual for him. You might find him at the leper colony at Suva, talking to a woman he had met there on a visit 14 years previously; perhaps at the Hathaway Cottage in Stratford-on-Avon; maybe conducting a service at Johannesburg, South Africa. You might hear of his attending the King's Kava Ceremony at Apia, Samoa, or climbing the eighteen flights of steps at the great, inspiring statue of Christ at Corcovado—maybe laying the corner stone at the first Mormon Church edifice in South America at Montevideo, Uruguay—perhaps at the inspiring 12th century cathedral at Strasburg, France—or feeling the inspiration, but also the sorrow, of the landscape at the Holy Land.

You could hear of him at home enjoying the company of the employees at the Church Office Building at their Christmas party, speaking words of appreciation and encouragement. It is just possible you might find him riding his horse on the old home farm in Huntsville, where nostalgic memories warm his soul. This is the man we honor—well known and loved around the world by great scientists, civic leaders, religious leaders, and ordinary folks who work and struggle, as well as little children. To be so widely accepted and loved—to be so powerful and respected, and yet so humble and approachable—this would be achievement and honor for any man.

His name appears on the covers of books and numerous writings. It appears on testimonials and documents of high esteem—it appears on beautiful buildings around the world—it even appears on a masterpiece of nature, a magnificent 350 year old oak tree near London. But the record that will speak most for him is a changing, moving, cascading one, written in the hearts and deeds of thousands he has touched, and their posterity yet to be.

It is physically impossible, within the time limitations, to portray an adequate picture. Perhaps what we lack in completeness we can make up in simple, straightforward sincerity, when, uanimously, we say to him that he has our admiration and deep respect for all the richness and goodness that he has brought into the world. This charming Scottish-Welsh citizen of the world has earned and won our hearts completely. Appreciation from men of good will everywhere, regardless of creed, color, or race, goes out to you, President McKay, for the inspiration, the spiritual encouragement, and the messages of enduring faith and hope, which you so tirelessly proclaim to all people.

In summary, we have written these reflections of this great leadership, a part of which were expressed some years ago:

"I stood apart from a man of men
And beyond in timeless space
His works have fashioned a monument
That weathering years will not efface.

I stood apart from a servant of Him
Who sits on that Great White Throne
His monument is a spire of grace
Built from God's work alone.

I stood apart from a long life of toil
In the garden of peace sublime,
Through dark skies his faith spells the promise
Of God's peace on earth in our time."

Joseph Rosenblatt, president of the Eimco Corporation, then responded with the following tribute and presentation:

You know, I wish it had been possible for each of you to have had the view from my seat tonight. We are inclined in this day and age to be a little sophisticated and to think that the important emotions, which after all are so vital in controlling our character, should not be talked about. But I know that if you had sat with me, and you had been able to see this wonderful human being hold his wife's hand, if you had been able to see his sons, members of his family sitting there, and to have sensed that tremendous, wonderful flow of understanding, of affection that was there—I know that you would have felt with me that on this night God is indeed in his heaven, and there is peace in the land.

You know, I am particularly grateful to Mrs. McKay for having graced our meeting tonight, and this event, for I can go home now and tell my own wife that she need not be embarrassed if in all my ardor I reach over publicly to hold her hand, for I can say that it is now right and proper, and I do so by authority of the President's wife.

I am sure that all will recognize—President McKay and our head-table guests, and all of you who have listened—it is not an easy task to follow John Wallace. The only thing that can be said, President McKay, is that we will make it a well-rounded tribute, for as John quoted the New Testament, I promise to quote the Old.

I suppose in every man's life there comes a time when he is called upon for memorable action. Sometimes it is for the good, sometimes it is distasteful. And then the once in a lifetime epochal action when there is memorable challenge, and great responsibility, where really the effort is so beyond one's anticipated ability as to leave one impotent and overcome with such a deep sense of humility as to make the needed thoughts and words indeed hard to come by.

You know, gentlemen, as I have sat here participating in this memorable event, I could not help but wonder about my standing here and thinking about it with both much pride and much gratitude—You know my selection as the one privileged to make the presentation to President McKay was pure happenstance. I deserted what I think is my usual conservative reticence and spoke up when I should have listened. The next thing I knew, the long arm of your committee said, "You will follow John Wallace, and you will make the presentation."

Permit me to say without egotism, and only with much

humility and much gratitude, there is important significance that the one who is neither Gentile nor Mormon, should have been so selected, possibly significant for several reasons: One that it was prompted, I feel, by the inspiration of the all-encompassing and pervading humanitarianism of this beloved man whom we honor this evening, for it fosters and encourages the intuition of enlightened thought and action by free men in the environment and climate of our perfect democracy; and Second, that the one so selected traces his own lineage through the long generations to David of the Bible, and is thereby of the people of the Book.

Therefore, for these few words that I am privileged to speak to President McKay I pick two texts from the Bible, which I believe have full measure of meaning and understanding as one thinks of David O. McKay. The one text is from Job which you will recall reads: "The righteous also shall hold on his way, and he that hath clean hands shall be stronger and stronger." And second from the prophet Micah: "It has been told thee, Oh man, what is good and what the Lord doth require of thee, only to do justly, to love mercy, to walk humbly with thy God." Do you know of anyone who has listened to or lived this exhortation with greater faith or purpose than David O. McKay?

This is indeed an epochal and exciting occasion, gentlemen, for in our assemblage here, and in our action as we have gathered to pay honor and respect to this great leader, we are doing that which gives voice and action to the rights of free men under the blessed American way of life, that represents the most perfect democracy that God has permitted man to create.

We pay honor to David O. McKay, not that his theology is akin to ours, but really rather that it is not, for I think that we know him best as the ideal of what we look for in the great American. It is throughout the world that this has given inspiration to that which is America. In his every being and deed we see in him the genius for freedom under law, the conviction that democracy is the highest expression of a dignified social order. We see every day his talent for harmonizing diversities and the inspired leadership which brings and secures enrichment from varied cultural sources as he has brought them together as we have seen from every people, from every land, indeed to every generation.

And yet really, we have gathered not so much to pay honor to David O. McKay, for he has had honors heaped upon him greater than we can offer. We have gathered here that we might have opportunity to give full expression to the respect, to the affection, indeed the love and gratitude we have for him. We are here to loudly and clearly say that we as citizens of this community are the benefactors of the good that lies in this man's heart. We are the beneficiaries of his mind that sees more clearly, not that which divides men, but rather that which unites them.

I hope you will agree with me that the small gift which is but the symbol of our sincerity fits so well and simply in paying our tribute. Our gift to President McKay is an organ to be installed in the chapel which has been built in Merthyr Tydfil, Wales, to honor his mother, Jennette Evans McKay.

This is the plaque engraved for this occasion and reads:

"Presented to President David O. McKay by hundreds of his friends and business associates with their deepest respect and warmest affection, in recognition of his qualities of leadership and in appreciation of his outstanding community achievements, at a testimonial dinner and tribute, at the Hotel Utah, Salt Lake City, Monday evening, December 10th, 1962, and in memory of his beloved mother, Jennette Evans McKay, born in Plas Helygen, Merthyr-Tydfil, Glamorganshire, South Wales, wherein The Church of Jesus Christ of Latter-day Saints chapel is now being erected, this plaque and organ are to be placed, with the compliments of those in attendance on this historic occasion."

In doing this, President McKay, we try to give our understanding and our support to the importance not only to your ancestry which has contributed so largely to your accomplishments, but as well to the leadership that you give to us all in guiding us in sympathy to other times, to other places, to other customs, to understand that they are part and parcel of what makes our life here today an inspired opportunity.

In presenting this gift we hereby give our understanding to the warmth and to the purity of your character, inspired as it has been from every sense of virtue and of truth and of right, knowing that it must come from each generation and each area, and knowing as you have taught us that it must be passed on with ever-increasing influence and effectiveness. Gentlemen, will you please arise, and President and Mrs. McKay will you please stand."

(Ovation.)

And will you join me all to say the prayer that we ask is that the sounds of this organ will always inspire those who will hear it to follow in the footsteps of Jennette Evans McKay and her son, to bring their influence for good to the peoples of the world, to spread constantly the understanding of the need of faith and the love of God in righteous peace and happiness for all time.

We ask that the Lord will let his countenance shine upon thee and be gracious unto thee.

May he lift up his countenance upon thee and give thee peace, and may the blessings always be with thee and with thy people.

Chapter 23

A Dedication at Merthyr Tydfil

When August 25, 1963 was decided upon as the dedication date of the new chapel at Merthyr Tydfil, Wales, many doubted that the plan could be carried out. However, they underestimated the devotion of a united, dedicated people. Men, women, and younger people from the entire area joined in a supreme effort to have everything in readiness so that President David O. McKay could officiate at the dedication.

President McKay had visited the site on March 2, 1961 on the occasion of the groundbreaking. At that time a memorial plaque was placed on the nearby four-room cottage where his mother, Jennette Evans McKay had been born.

After the impressive groundbreaking services, with warm expressions of love and gratitude, a chorus of young people sang to the Prophet:

> We'll keep a welcome on the hillsides,
> We'll keep a welcome on the vales,
> This land of song will still be surging,
> When you come back to Wales.

This land of song will still be singing
With a love that never fails,
We'll kiss away each hour of herith, °
When you come back to Wales.

° (Longing)

President McKay was so touched by the sentiment of the song that he promised those present that he would return to Wales for the dedication of the chapel.

As the building neared completion in the summer of 1963, and assurance was given that President McKay would come for the dedication, the devoted building supervisors and Church builder missionaries exerted every effort to reach their objective.

Up to this time there had been four Church builders working on the chapel. This number was now increased to ten, and this gave an impetus to the work. Since the chapel would be used for district meetings and activities, as well as for the Merthyr Tydfil meetings, branch presidents of the Welsh District pledged full support toward completion of the building. Each member in the district soon learned that this full support meant a lot of hard work, but such was given by scores of businessmen, farmers, professional men, and those in all walks of life.

Of the 30,000 hours of donated labor on the building, 22,000 came from the Church builders, and 8,000 were given by local members. Probably the greatest record was set on Whitsin Monday when more than 220 men, women, and young people from the entire district put in over 1,600 hours of work on that one day. The donated hours for the week totaled 2,650.

Pride in the building, and enthusiasm for its completion, spread beyond the membership of the Church. The mayor of the city and other officials expressed their interest and good will. On one occasion the women of another church called and said, "When you are ready to clean the windows of your new chapel, let us know, because we should like to do that for you." And they did it!

Sir Thomas Bennett was the architect, and his devotion was evident throughout the entire construction of the building. It was with this kind of support, and the united efforts of the entire district that the chapel went from the footing stage to its completion in less than eight months. It is no wonder they termed it "the miracle at Merthyr Tydfil."

President McKay had asked that there be no announcement of his arrival in London on August 23, as the plane was due to land at night, and he was anxious to get as much rest as possible before the appointment of the following day. In spite of their desire to carry out his request, a crowd, including photographers and reporters, gathered at the airport. Each was given a gracious greeting, characteristic of the President under any circumstances. He was accompanied by his son, Dr. Edward R. McKay, and by the executive secretary of the Salt Lake Chamber of Commerce, Mr. Gus P. Backman and Mrs. Backman.

The following day, August 24, the President and his party were taken to the railroad station and placed in a private car, half lounge and half diner, to be taken to Cardiff, Wales. Upon their arrival, they were given comfortable rooms at the Royal Hotel. At 6:30 that evening, President Mark E. Petersen of the West European Mission and Mrs. Petersen were hosts at a delicious dinner for the London party, including President and Mrs. Marion D. Hanks, of the British Mission. The next morning at 8 o'clock cars called at the hotel for the drive to Merthyr Tydfil, where an inspection of the chapel was made before the service commenced.

The building covers an area of 15,660 square feet, and has fourteen teaching areas. The chapel seats 350, and the cultural hall 1,050. There is parking space for ninety-four cars. The foundation and floors are of concrete, the walls consist of facing brick and Norwegian white quartz spar rendering. The roof is made of green natural slate, and the tower of fiber glass with triangular pylon, gold-leafed, rising fifty-six feet above the ground. The site itself covers two and a half acres, and is situated on an eminence twenty feet above the road, overlooking the city of Merthyr Tydfil.

On Friday and Saturday preceding the dedication, the building had been open for public viewing and organ recitals had been given by Dr. Robert Cundick, organist for the London Hyde Park Chapel. Sunday morning every one of the fourteen hundred seats was occupied, with the first five reserved rows filled with city officials and special guests. Seated on the rostrum were two Lord Mayors of Merthyr Tydfil, the Honorable Charles Edward Webb, who attended the service of unveiling the memorial plaque on the cottage where President McKay's mother was born, and the ground-breaking ceremonies in 1961, and also the present Lord Mayor. Also on the rostrum were district presidents from Glasgow, Edinburgh, Ireland, and many other surrounding districts, and their wives.

Under the direction of President Petersen, a special edition of the *Millennial Star,* in honor of President McKay's ninetieth birthday, was published, and a copy was placed on each seat in the vast assembly hall.

At 9:45 on Sunday morning there was a short organ recital by Dr. Cundick, after which Mr. Backman, representing the more than six hundred business men who presented the organ and plaque to go with it to President McKay at a dinner given in his honor the previous December, now made the formal presentation to the President and the people of Merthyr Tydfil, in honor of Jennette Evans McKay. President McKay formally accepted the gift in honor of his mother, and asked Mr. Backman to convey to his friends his gratitude and the assurance that the installation of the beautiful organ and the plaque exceeded all expectations.

The dedicatory service commenced at 10:30, and was conducted by Branch President Ralph Pulman, a fourth-generation member of the Church, who remembered the growth of this branch from its small inception during his childhood. Though a wealthy property owner now, he was among the faithful members who, in rough clothing, worked early and late to complete the chapel.

After the playing of beautiful organ music, and two inspiring solos by Beti Jones and Annette Richardson Dinwoody, and a short address of thanksgiving by J. F. Dunyan, district president, an M. I. A. chorus sang a Welsh hymn, "Cal Lau." Then President McKay arose to give the dedicatory address and prayer. As he stood before that vast audience there was such an eloquent silence filled with love and respect that can best be described by the words of the poet Longfellow, in his *Evangeline*: "The whole air and the woods and the waves seemed silent to listen."

After expressing gratitude for the love and generosity expressed in gifts of certificates and pictures associated with his mother and her relatives here in Wales, he gave the following quotation from Carlyle: "How a thing grows in the human memory, when love worship and all that lies in the human heart is there to encourage it."

Then he drew from his own memory, the visit with Sir Thomas Bennett on March 2, 1961, for the unveiling of the plaque on his mother's birthplace, and for the ground-breaking ceremonies on the spot where this chapel now stands. He referred to the young people's singing of the song, "We'll keep a welcome on the hillsides . . ." He mentioned the concert given by the Tabernacle Choir in Cardiff in 1955, and one given by the International Chorus of the Relief Society Singing Mothers in Cardiff on March 2, 1961. He spoke with love of the group of friends who had presented the organ in honor of his mother. He expressed heartfelt gratitude for the services of the church building supervisors, and those in charge of the work throughout Europe who have assisted in this project in Merthyr Tydfil.

He explained that in the British Mission there are forty-six chapels under construction now, and thirty-six to be started before the end of this year, a total of eighty-five buildings for 1963. Sincere appreciation was expressed for members of the branch who had contributed twenty percent of the cost of this building; to the men, women, and children who have sacrificed time and means for its completion. Such sacrifice in this life is in contrast with the selfish, mean, and the sordid, which are prompting the nations to grapple with each other for selfish motives. "Let us preach the Gospel of peace, of self-control, love and harmony. God help us to attain the ideal of loving our neighbors as ourselves," he said.

At the close of the beautiful dedicatory prayer, there were few dry eyes in the audience of friends, members, and visitors. The Relief Society Singing Mothers sang "We Dedicate This House to Thee," and the benediction was offered by Lynn Davis.

Chapter 24

Ninetieth Birthday Celebration

The ninetieth year of President David O. McKay's life was filled with a series of celebrations and tributes to a truly great man. It seemed that the observances were a culmination of all the birthday celebrations which he had enjoyed over the years, including the early ones in Huntsville with the traditional dime, button, and tiny ring between layers of a birthday cake.

The series of tributes began with the significant dinner and gift of an organ by businessmen described in Chapter 22, and continued with the dedication of the chapel and organ at Merthyr-Tydfil, Wales, as noted in Chapter 23. On that occasion a special tribute was the issue of *The Millennial Star* produced under the title, "President David O. McKay's 90th Birthday Issue."

Two other celebrations worthy of mention include a tribute by the general authorities of the Church, and a family and community observance in Huntsville on the date of the 90th anniversary, September 8, 1963, which was a Sunday.

The observance at the Church Office Building, held a few days prior to the birthday anniversary, began with the receipt of letters, cards, telegrams, cablegrams, beautiful flowers, gifts, and messages from many parts of the world. President McKay was overwhelmed with the many tributes offered, and realizing that he could not acknowledge them all personally, said in a statement in *The Church News,* "These messages of love have helped to make my 90th birthday a memorable occasion. I take this opportunity to extend sincere appreciation and blessing to hundreds of friends everywhere who sent them."

The entire force of Church office workers, and as many of the authorities as were on hand, assembled to express birthday wishes and to have refreshments prepared by the secretaries, under the capable direction of Miss Clare Middlemiss, the President's faithful secretary of many years.

That evening in the Empire Ballroom of Hotel Utah, the general authorities gave a banquet in the President's honor. There were nearly one hundred present, including thirty-one of the thirty-eight general authorities, their wives, members of President McKay's immediate family, his four sisters and their husbands, and widows of former general authorities.

There was a heart-warming sense of love, fellowship, and inspiration as President and Sister McKay entered the room and were escorted to the place of honor at the head table. There were many smiles of happiness and delight from the President as he enjoyed a program of vocal selections of some of his favorite music. An unexpected part of the program was an appearance by the Osmond Brothers singing group from Ogden.

Elder Harold B. Lee of the Council of the Twelve acted as master of ceremonies. He said in part that it was difficult to represent everyone present in doing honor to President McKay, and to try to give him and his family a glimpse of

259

the exalted place he held in the affections of those associated with him in the councils of the Church. Elder Lee emphasized the example set by President McKay in rising above the ugliness of the world.

"If I were an artist," Elder Lee said, "and had to paint a picture of a prophet, I could find no better example to stand for all the prophets, past and present, than President David O. McKay."

Elder Lee then presented to President McKay a silver tray bearing a replica of the Salt Lake Temple, and including engraved signatures of each of the general authorities. Elder Lee explained that the engraving of the temple on the tray was indicative of the fact that more temples have been completed under President McKay's administration than any other president in this dispensation.

In his response, President McKay expressed appreciation for the lovely tray, and then said ". . . beautiful as it is, it will not be the reminder of your love and devotion that your presence at this testimonial has meant. That is engraved on our hearts forever."

The invocation at the special dinner was offered by President Joseph Fielding Smith of the Council of the Twelve, and Elder Spencer W. Kimball, also of the Council of the Twelve, gave the benediction to end the memorable day.

On Sunday, September 8, President and Sister McKay traveled to Huntsville, the place of his birth and boyhood years. The bishop of the Huntsville Ward sent a messenger early in the morning to the McKay home asking if it would be permissible for members of the Sunday School to come to the home and sing their birthday wishes to the Prophet.

President McKay sent back word that this would not be necessary since he planned to attend Sunday School at the Ward, and they could sing for him there if they desired.

President McKay with his four sisters: Mrs. Joseph R. (Jeanette) Morrell, Mrs. George R. (Elizabeth) Hill, Mrs. Joel E. (Katherine) Ricks, and Mrs. Thomas B. (Ann) Farr.

To the delight of everyone assembled at the Huntsville Ward chapel, President McKay was there to greet them and express his love for them. Among other counsel he gave to them, he said, "You may travel the world over, but you will never find real happiness and contentment until you lose yourself in the service of mankind."

These few words certainly reveal the key to his own happiness and contentment, for truly he is a man who has lost himself in such rewarding service. He is a man among men, a leader among leaders, a prophet among prophets, a true servant of God.

After enjoying the sweet spirit of the services in Huntsville, President and Sister McKay, along with their son and daughter-in-law, Mr. and Mrs. David Lawrence McKay, enjoyed a quiet, restful day at the "Old Home," and returned to Salt Lake on Monday.

Chapter 25

A Visit with President Johnson

On Saturday, January 25, 1964, at about 1:30 p.m., President David O. McKay received a long distance telephone call in his Hotel Utah apartment from the President of the United States, Lyndon Baines Johnson, who began the conversation with:

"President McKay, you will not remember me, but I visited you twice in Salt Lake City." President McKay quickly replied that he remembered him very well. Then President Johnson said: "President McKay, I need some strength and advice from you. Could you come to Washington for an hour's consultation with me—any time next week? Come at your convenience; I shall meet your time, President McKay."

During the fifteen minute conversation President McKay explained to President Johnson that he had been ill, but that he felt he would be well enough the next week to make such a trip, and would be honored to meet with him. President McKay then set the time of the meeting for Friday, January 31, 1964, at 1:30 p.m. President Johnson indicated this would be fine, and asked President McKay to confirm this

This flag, flying at the "Old Home' in Huntsville, flew over the nation's capitol during the inauguration of President Lyndon B. Johnson. It was presented by President Johnson to President David O. McKay as a token of esteem.

appointment with his secretary, and also let her know who would be accompanying him.

On Monday, January 27, David Lawrence McKay, at the request of his father, called the White House and told President Johnson's secretary that President McKay would leave Salt Lake City on Thursday morning, January 30. He said that he would accompany his father, along with President Nathan Eldon Tanner of the First Presidency. The secretary said that President Johnson had arranged for the meeting on Friday, but that the time had been set for 1:00 p.m.

In describing the trip President McKay later said:

"It was blustery as we arrived at the White House at about 1:00 p.m., January 31. We were received at the north west gate of the White House grounds, and after showing our identification, were taken into the annex offices, and from there into the Cabinet Room. Soon thereafter President Johnson came into the offices and said, 'Hello young men,' and he shook hands with us. He ushered us into his office where several pictures were taken, including Miss Connie Gerard from Evanston, Wyoming, and Miss Nancy Lou Larson of Salt Lake City, secretaries at the White House and both members of the Church."

After the pictures were taken and the secretaries had left, President Johnson explained to President McKay that he had called him on an impulse, and that he wanted his advice. He stated that President McKay had received him so kindly twice in Salt Lake City, and each time he had come away inspired. He said he would have come to visit President McKay if he could have done so, and greatly appreciated President McKay making the effort to come to Washington.

In answer to a comment from one of the party that he was surprised that the President knew enough about his secretaries to know their religion, President Johnson stated that both of these girls came early and worked late. He said they were devoted and industrious, and had high ideals. In fact, they acted like members of the Church. The President said he thought highly of members of the Church, and added, in fact, that he had never known a "mean" Mormon.

President Johnson then led President McKay and his party to the elevator leading to the second floor and to a circular room which he described as the former bedroom of Margaret Truman, and which Mrs. Kennedy had remodeled into a private dining room. Before that change it had been necessary for the White House family to take their meals down stairs in the formal dining room. The room was decorated with a large painting of Valley Forge.

The oval table was set, with place mats, for four. President Johnson sat at the head with President McKay at his right, President Tanner at his left, and David Lawrence McKay at the foot. President Johnson bowed his head, and offered the blessing of thanks for the food, and for the opportunity of their being together. Waiters served soup, which President Johnson described as "flavored water," but which was delicious vegetable soup. The next course consisted of crab thermidor over rice, with tomato aspic salad. The dessert was a banana pudding which he called "home made."

He told President McKay that events were crowding in on him: Cyprus, Viet Nam, the shooting of Americans over Berlin, Panama, etc. He felt that he needed help. When he was a boy he could rest his head on his mother's shoulder; now he needed another shoulder to rest on. He felt that we needed to strengthen the moral and spiritual fiber of the nation. He wanted advice from President McKay as to how this could be done. President McKay replied that he had read President Johnson's creed, that first of all he was a *free man*, second an *American*, third a *President*, and fourth a

Democrat, in that order; that he knew that the President was a man of honor. Then President McKay said: "Let your conscience be your guide. Let the people know that you are sincere, and they will follow you." President Johnson seemed impressed with this advice.

President Johnson said that his first contact with a prominent member of the L. D. S. Church was with Senator Reed Smoot, for whom he had a high regard. He became acquainted with him through Truman Young, who was the President's roommate about 1929. He went with Truman to hear Senator Smoot's address to the Senate, and noticed with what interest and deference the other senators listened to him. He spoke of Truman Young and of his work in the maritime offices in San Francisco at the present time. He expressed his pride in the Tabernacle Choir and hoped it would have an occasion to sing for him in Washington.

President McKay told of his experience at a luncheon with President Eisenhower. Being unaccustomed to White House protocol, he said he thought he had the responsibility, after being with President Eisenhower and others for three hours, to terminate the meeting. So, he suggested that they had been imposing long enough on the President. President Eisenhower said: "Now President McKay, this is my party. I will tell you when we will dismiss." He talked to them for another half hour and then said: "Now President McKay, we will arise."

During the meal President Johnson was interrupted several times by telephone calls. He had a telephone conveniently placed on the leg of the table nearest him. After they were through eating, President Johnson left to get Mrs. Johnson. She came into the room, and was beautiful and charming. She shook hands and visited with President McKay and the others. When President Johnson returned she told him there would be a White House tour of students on scholarships from the Hearst newspaper syndicate, and that she would handle the tour so it would not be necessary for him to speak. He said, however, he would try and speak to them.

The President then said he had requested Utah's senators to come and have their pictures taken with the group, and he was also trying to locate the Utah Congressmen. He said he thought very highly of Senator Wallace F. Bennett, who was a wizard in his work on the finance committee. He also expressed appreciation for Senator Frank E. Moss.

The two senators arrived and were served dessert. As they were finishing, Congressmen Sherman Lloyd and Laurence Burton arrived with Esther Peterson and Congressman Ralph Harding from Idaho. The President kissed Mrs. Peterson on the cheek, and when President McKay expressed marked surprise, Mrs. Peterson said, "President McKay, you have already kissed me; you kissed me when I was a little girl. Do you remember picking me up when I was nursing a broken arm, and carrying me into your living room in Ogden?" Mrs. Peterson was formerly Esther Eggertsen, a neighbor of President McKay.

Representative Lloyd told the President that he approved what he had done in economy measures, but his wife disapproved of his darkening of the White House. The President retorted that his mother had been very careful with money. She had always insisted on going around the house turning out the lights, and he got the habit from her. He noticed that she was the one who always had money under her pillow. He said he had inquired as to what the electric light bill was at the White House and found out that it was $4,800 per month. He had reduced this to $3,600 the first month, and would reduce it further, perhaps to $2,600. He saw no need for keeping lights burning all night in an empty office, lights burning in halls which were not used, and in all closets. He had insisted that the automatic switches be replaced by switches that can be pulled manually, and he insisted that they be pulled. He said that while $4,800 is nothing compared with fifteen billion dollars, still, unless people go around turning off lights they won't become economy conscious, and they are less likely to stress economy in other matters. He said when he became President there were thirty-six Cadillacs there. He cut this down to six, and gave the drivers of the others cheaper cars. This was not a great savings but it would make the drivers cost conscious.

Then he went into one of the larger fields. Secretary McNamara had shown him that there had been an increase in the national budget of five billion dollars annually. Mr. McNamara showed him how that could be stopped, and how there could be a saving in the defense effort. The President showed this to every member of his cabinet, and in a few days later each came back to him and stated that it would not be necessary to raise the budget as he had originally contemplated.

President Johnson then said laughingly, "Now I think we had better break up before President McKay dismisses us. I will take you around and show you the rooms on this floor." He took President McKay's arm and showed the group first where President Kennedy and President Lincoln had slept. In this room Mrs. Johnson was seated at a table writing. Further down the hall was the room in which Lincoln's bed and other furniture were placed. Still further on was the room in which statesmen slept while they were staying at the White House. He mentioned that there had been no one staying in that room since he had been President. He said he had a pair of pajamas that he would be glad to lend to President McKay if he wished to stay there. Across the hall was a room with a canopy bed in which Queen Elizabeth had slept.

President Johnson then guided the group down to the

first floor and to the swimming pool, which had been donated for President Roosevelt by children's dimes without expense to the government. It had since been redecorated by Ambassador Joseph Kennedy. One side of the room was covered by a mirror, so that the pool looks twice its regular size. The President stated that when he was not behind schedule, as he was today, he takes fifteen minutes before luncheon, and fifteen minutes before dinner and swims up and down the pool six times in water at ninety degrees.

The president then escorted the group out of the White House along an arcade from which he pointed out the rose gardens planted by Mrs. Kennedy. They then returned to the offices of the Annex, where he introduced them to Secretary McNamara who had been waiting for forty-five minutes. The President then shook hands and said goodbye.

President McKay then went through a battery of reporters who wanted to know what the conversation had been about. President McKay told them that they must get all that information from President Johnson. He did deny that a temple was about to be built in Washington.

President McKay, President Tanner, and David McKay, caught the 5 o'clock plane, but because of a delay in Chicago, they arrived in Salt Lake City at 11:45 p.m., which meant that President McKay had gone twenty-one hours without sleep.

The trip was strenuous but very successful. It was an historic event in the progress of the Church.

270

Chapter 26

The Oakland Temple

Some called it a "miracle," and others proclaimed it an example of pure faith. But whatever, there he was for all to marvel at. President David O. McKay, in his 92nd year, having suffered a severe illness only recently, was presiding at the dedicatory rites for the newest of the Church's temples at Oakland, California.

Even with all the beauty of the temple and the sacredness of the rites, the most often expressed feeling of the thousands in attendance was appreciation that the health and determination of President McKay permitted him to preside, offer the dedicatory prayer at all sessions, and give inspiring messages to those assembled.

President McKay had an ardent desire to be part of this occasion, since it was he some two decades ago who had inspected the site and had recommended purchase of the property as a future temple site.

The building now being dedicated would stand as a further monument to him as a builder of temples. Its dedication brought to five the temples which had been started and completed during his years as President. This represented more than one third of the 13 temples in use by the Church.

President McKay's interest in the Oakland Temple dated back to 1934 when he visited the site as one of the general authorities. It was on the basis of his original recommendation that the Church purchased the site in 1942. His next visit to the spot was in September, 1960, when he dedicated the East Bay Interstake Center on a portion of the property. At that time he was impressed by the urgency to proceed with the building of a temple on the site now known in the area as "temple hill."

Thus, on Monday, January 23, 1961, he made a dramatic visit to a special assembly of stake presidencies in the area who had met on call of the President. He flew from Salt Lake City that morning and in the meeting announced to the enthusiastic group that a decision had been made to erect a temple on the site. He presented a tentative design of the temple for approval.

In the meeting he recalled the prophecy of President Brigham Young cited earlier in connection with the Los Angeles Temple. He read to the group the following:

> On August 7, 1847, President Brigham Young made a prophecy contained in an epistle which he and Dr. Willard Richards had written to the Saints in California who had come around the Horn under the presidency of Samuel Brannan. This prediction was given toward the end of the letter—
> "And in the process of time, the shores of the Pacific may yet be overlooked from the Temple of the Lord."

President McKay also referred to the prophecy attributed to President George Albert Smith who had predicted in 1924, while looking eastward from his hotel in San Fran-

272

cisco, that a temple would one day surmount the East Bay Hills—one that would be visible as a beacon to ships as they entered the Golden Gate from the far-flung nations of the earth.

After making these references, President McKay said: "So, we feel that the time has come when these prophecies should be fulfilled."

Following the meeting, President McKay returned to Salt Lake City that afternoon, leaving behind an organization of dedicated leaders to raise a minimum of $500,000 in contributions toward construction of the new temple.

A revised design for the temple was prepared by Harold W. Burton, Church architect, and detailed drawings were completed and ready for the site dedication and ground-breaking on Saturday, May 26, 1962. President McKay again participated in these services, which saw some 7,000 persons in attendance. This was the largest group of Latter-day Saints yet to assemble in Northern California. President McKay offered the dedicatory prayer for the site, and also turned the first shovel of soil to signal the beginning of construction.

On Saturday, May 25, 1963, just a year after the ground was broken, the cornerstone was placed in appropriate ceremonies. President Joseph Fielding Smith of the Council of the Twelve officiated at these special services. Music was furnished by the Salt Lake Tabernacle Choir which had made special concert appearances during the week at Los Angeles and San Francisco. Elder Richard L. Evans of the Council of the Twelve, commentator with the choir, also assisted President Smith at the cornerstone rites.

From this point the majestic temple structure began to take shape and the work was pushed ahead as those in the area successfully raised more than $650,000 toward the construction.

As the work neared completion the First Presidency announced the appointment in January, 1964 of President Delbert F. Wright to be president of the new temple, with his wife as matron. Later the counselors in the presidency were added, these being Bernhard Herman Schettler of San Francisco, and Robert Lee Kenner of Berkeley.

Much of the success of the work was attributed to the temple district committee under the leadership of President O. Leslie Stone, president of the Oakland-Berkeley Stake. Those appointed in 1961 to serve with him on the temple committee were President David O. Haight, Palo Alto Stake, vice chairman; Pres. Carrol Smith, Klamath Stake, and President Dallas Tueller, Fresno Stake. Paul E. Warnick was named executive secretary.

Some changes occurred in the committee with the calls of President Haight to serve as president of the Scottish Mission, and President Smith as mission president in Canada. President James Price Ronnow of Reno Stake was added to the committee, and also President Wright after the announcement of his appointment as temple president.

Another appointment announced prior to the dedication was that of Paul Summerhays, counselor in the Oakland-Berkeley stake presidency, as director of the Oakland Temple Bureau of Information, with Sister Summerhays also assisting in this work.

During August of 1964 President McKay made a surprise visit to the area to inspect the work on the temple. He announced that dedicatory services would be held on Tuesday, Wednesday, and Thursday, November 17, 18 and 19, 1964. As he met with the temple district leaders and assembled stake presidencies on this occasion, he said: "I am thrilled to be here. My soul was uplifted last night as I gazed on this beautiful temple with its magnificent lighting.

It bears testimony to your fine endeavors, and I say God bless you for it."

Before the dedication date arrived President McKay became ill and many felt it would be impossible for him to participate in the services. But his faith and determination made it possible, through the blessings of the Lord, for him to attend and participate actively in all of the sessions.

In attendance with him at the dedication were all of the general authorities and their wives who were available to attend, along with many of the general auxiliary officers of the Church. These officials flew to Oakland on Monday, November 16, and returned Thursday afternoon following the final dedicatory session.

As the first session began, President McKay, the general authorities and their wives, and stake presidents and other Church officials of the area were seated in the beautiful gold-hued Celestial Room of the temple. From here the services were carried by closed circuit television to other rooms of the temple and to the adjacent East Bay Interstake Center. A congregation in excess of 6,000 witnessed the ceremonies.

President Stone conducted the first services, under the direction of President McKay, and also spoke briefly. Other speakers at the first session included President Joseph Fielding Smith, and President Wright, the temple president. Sister Jessie Evans Smith, wife of President Smith and a long-time member of the Salt Lake Tabernacle Choir, sang as a solo "Bless This House," with special words for the occasion. This song was repeated by other soloists in the other sessions. During the six sessions, special choirs were formed from the 40 stakes in the temple district to provide the dedicatory music. The sacred "Hosanna Shout" was a feature of each service following the dedicatory prayer, as well as the singing of the "Hosanna Anthem."

During the six sessions, President McKay spoke and offered the dedicatory prayer at each of the sessions. He was assisted in the direction of the services by his two counselors, President Hugh B. Brown and President N. Eldon Tanner. They also addressed the various services during the three days, as did others of the general authorities present.

In his remarks prior to the first session of the dedicatory services, President McKay spoke feelingly of his appreciation for the temple and of the responsibilities of those who enter therein. Rising to supreme spiritual heights, the beloved Church leader pleaded for love and kindness on the part of those who enter the temple. A portion of his remarks follows:

> One great purpose carried out by those who come into the Temple is the sealing of man and wife in the sacred bonds of matrimony. That purpose is based upon the fact that man and woman truly love each other. That means that a couple coming to the altar should be sure that there is love in each heart. It would be a terrible thing to be bound for eternity to one whom you do not love, but it is a glorious thing to be sealed for Time and Eternity to one whom you do love.
>
> Let us ever remember that love is the divinest attribute of the human soul. God himself is love. Our hearts are really one with Him in that eternal home, and so when a couple kneels at the altar and receives the privilege and blessing of that eternal sealing, one should be sure that love is binding those two hearts that will now be bound by the Holy Power of the Priesthood for time and all Eternity. Associated with that should be the realization that love must be fed; otherwise that binding, that sealing power, that covenant which is made, may not last forever. Love must be nourished; love can be starved to death just as literally as the body can be starved without daily sustenance. There is no one great protestation that anybody can make that will be sufficient to keep that love alive always. There are certain obligations taken by those who make covenants at the altar and those obligations must be manifest after they go out of the Temple. One is *Kindness*. There should be no unkindness manifest in the homes occupied by couples who leave the House of God.

In one of the epistles that Paul wrote, there are some statements now known throughout the Christian world as the Psalm of Love, the first of which is: "Love suffereth long and is kind." The word "suffereth" includes patience, tolerance, and consideration. We can visualize homes in The Church of Jesus Christ of Latter-day Saints in the great majority of which there is kindness on both parts because there is love there—a binding love which will not be separated by death. Love suffereth long and is always kind and gentle.

Men of the Church should remember, and women of the Church should realize that kindness will foster love, and that it should be a reciprocal act. There are men of courtesy, men who think of and give special thought to their wives, and wives who consider their husbands. Paul, in that same epistle, says, "Love seeketh not her own," but the welfare and happiness of others. And another line in that same epistle says, "Love believeth all things." If that love is fed daily and monthly and yearly throughout a lifetime, the husband's attention will not be drawn to somebody else, because there is trust in that binding power of the Priesthood, neither will there be attraction or indulgence in any other way, because love trusts, "believeth all things," and there must be foundation and cause for that trust the husband has in the wife, and the trust which the wife has in her husband.

Mormonism, the principal element of it, is the application of religion to daily life. That is what you members have done in participating in the erecting of this edifice; what the Church has done, bringing into the homes of the membership of the Church those elements which will make for happiness and peace here and now, and that is just what it will do. Our young people should be taught to choose mates who will feed, nourish, perpetuate that bond which brings them to the altar here in this Temple—*Love.* If your spirit lives after death, as it does, then that attribute of love will persist also, just as sympathy, just as reverence, and every other virtue that you have will persist.

In his remarks President McKay also spoke convincingly of the immortality of the soul, and the importance of the temple in opening the door of salvation and exaltation to the millions who have died without baptism. "I should think then," President McKay said, "that these people should have an opportunity to hear that same gospel and come through the door of baptism as you and I had to come through that door. It is not an impossible mission to our Father in Heaven, and this Temple ordinance work is one means of accomplishing it—one means of opening the door."

In concluding his impressive address, President McKay stated:

> What a glorious work the members in this Oakland Temple District have done in participating in the erection of this Holy House! They have accomplished it by giving of themselves, by living above the animal plane; by rising to that spiritual plane in which we can lose ourselves for the good of others. With all my soul, I say, God bless you for what you have done!
>
> Let me leave this thought with you this morning. Those who now take advantage of the House of God take upon themselves obligations when they kneel at the altar and each couple becomes man and wife. Furthermore, this obligation reaches out telling the world that there is no death. We do live after death strikes us; it is but a passing from one of Father's houses into another—into other rooms more glorious.
>
> God bless you! God help us to comprehend the significance and breadth, the expansiveness, the eternal nature of the Restored Gospel of Jesus Christ, I pray in the name of Jesus Christ, Amen.

His dedicatory prayer was a powerful appeal for the influence of the gospel to extend into the lives of men everywhere. He also prayed for the growth and advancement of genealogical and temple work.

In an especially spiritual part of the prayer he prayed for strength in his position as President of the Church.

"Bless with health and wisdom Thy servant whom Thou has called to lead Thy Church in this day," President McKay said. "Continue to reveal to him Thy mind and will as it pertains to the growth and advancement of Thy work among the children of men. Bless abundantly his counselors. May the First Presidency be united by the Spirit and Power of God in all their labors, and in every thought, word, and act may they glorify Thy Name. Here in this Holy House, with humility and deep gratitude, we acknowledge Thy divine guidance and inspiration. Help us to magnify our callings, and to preach to all the world the freedom which the Gospel gives. For Truth is Freedom, and gives the right to worship, to work, the right to serve. Help us never to lose sight of these blessings."

The dedicatory services seemed to infuse new vitality into President McKay and the spiritual experiences of the three days at Oakland were felt long afterwards as he continued to improve in health and continue his strong leadership of the Church.

Chapter 27

The David O. McKay Hospital

On Friday, April 22, 1966, President David O. McKay met with hundreds of Weber County business, civic, and Church leaders on a twenty-eight-acre site at 3950 Harrison Boulevard, Ogden, where groundbreaking services were held for an eight-level, 350-bed hospital which would bear his name.

President Albert L. Bott, chairman of the Hospital Development Committee, conducted the impressive service marking the beginning of construction. Special music was furnished by the Weber State College L.D.S. Institute male chorus and choir, singing "Your Land and My Land," "Thanks Be To God," and "The Prophet," a song written especially for President McKay.

The welcoming address was delivered by President Bott, who is also president of the Mt. Ogden Stake. He expressed gratitude for the presence of President McKay on this important occasion for Weber County. He was followed by Bart Wolthuis, mayor of Ogden, who said: "This will be not only a building of steel and stone, but it will have also character and personality because it bears the name of David O. McKay. We extend our appreciation to him and to the other general authorities for presenting to us the realization of a dream."

It was noted that of the estimated $10,000,000 cost of the hospital, some $8,000,000 was to be financed by the Church, and the remaining $2,000,000 was to be raised by the communities to be served by the hospital, including the counties of Weber, Davis, Morgan, and Box Elder.

Another speaker was Elder William J. Critchlow, Jr., Assistant to the Council of the Twelve, and a former stake president in Ogden, as well as a member of the Thomas D. Dee L.D.S. Hospital board of trustees. He said, in part: "This hospital facility is another milestone in the cultural development of the community under the leadership of President McKay, and may it serve as a monument to him."

Bishop John H. Vandenberg, Presiding Bishop of the Church and president of the Dee L.D.S. Hospital board of trustees, related how President McKay had urged them to go forward with construction of the new hospital. Then, turning to President McKay, he said, "Your life so exemplifies the teachings of the Lord—love, kindness, compassion, and leadership—that I know of no other man whom this hospital could be named for but you."

During the hour-long groundbreaking ceremonies the sun shone through the clouds as if to cast a spotlight on the occasion.

At the groundbreaking, President McKay pulled a switch that signaled the start of construction. He said, laughingly, "That was the easiest hole I ever dug." He also thanked the people of Weber and surrounding counties for beginning the hospital, which was to become a part of the L.D.S. Hospital System, and for thinking enough of him to so perpetuate his name. In answer to previous speakers who had voiced the hope that he would be with them for the hospital's dedication, he smiled broadly and said, "Don't worry. I'll be with you."

President McKay fulfilled his promise July 9, 1969, when he attended the dedicatory services of the $11.5 million hospital which bears his name. Accompanied by Sister McKay, their daughter, Emma Rae Ashton, and their son, David Lawrence, he sat in his car near the front entrance of the hospital and listened to the opening ceremonies, which concluded with Administrator Kenneth E. Knapp presenting the key to the hospital's front door to him and a sheaf of red roses to Sister McKay.

Lawrence read a message from his father, in which President McKay stated:

> I am grateful to the Lord that he has granted me the great privilege of being present with you this afternoon. A few weeks ago, I was thrilled to go through this building to be shown what is not only one of the most beautiful hospitals existing, but also one designed to be the latest word in efficiency in the care of the physically ill.
>
> My emotions are deeply stirred, as I share with you a feeling of humility and pride for our membership in a church that so magnificently supports an institution such as this, which will relieve suffering and pain, and restore new life and hope to the many thousands who will pass through these doors in the years to come.
>
> I know the Lord has blessed the people so that they were able to contribute to this worthy cause, and that he will continue to bless them for their generosity and love of mankind. I am also mindful and grateful for the tithing from the people of the Church that is always sacredly and carefully used to build such buildings as these to help and bless the people.
>
> We express our gratitude to the Great Healer above who has enlightened men so that we are able to provide the most up-to-date facilities known to modern medicine, so that we are able, with the help of skilled medical men, to carry on his work among the children of men.

Presiding Bishop Vandenberg, in his brief remarks, declared, "Through persistence and cooperation we now have this beautiful new hospital. It stands as a monument for man's willingness to serve mankind." He said that President McKay epitomizes service to God and man, and it is fitting that the structure has been named for him. "Your efforts have elevated you. Service always lifts. You may be proud of this hospital."

Other speakers at the service included Mayor Wolthuis and Dr. Joe Amano, president of the McKay-Dee Hospital staff. Prayers were offered by the Rev. Donald R. Steiner, president of the Ogden Ministerial Association, and President Bott. The Ogden L.D.S. Institute Chorale, directed by Ladd R. Cropper, sang several numbers.

The new hospital is truly, as Bishop Vandenberg stated, "a monument for man's willingness to serve mankind." Built of white facing, the imposing eight-story structure looks out over the valley to the west and faces the mountains to the east. The finest and most modern features are incorporated in the operating rooms, patient areas, outpatient clinics, and services facilities.

The interior decor is enhanced with beautiful works of art, including a large portrait of President McKay, painted by prominent Utah artist Ev Thorpe. The painting was shown to the Prophet when he toured the hospital on May 16, some seven weeks before the dedicatory services. At that time, one of the family members accompanying him commented, "I have never seen a portrait that so typically captures father's expression as this one does."

As they were about to leave the hospital, one of the family members suggested that President McKay again look at the picture, and she pointed out that the small boy and the man standing in the foreground were President McKay and his father. Tears of appreciation came to the eyes of the

Prophet as he viewed the work and beauty of this painting and the beautiful new edifice built and named in his honor.

Chapter 28

Love for Little Children

As thousands of children and young people can attest, President McKay was never too busy or in too great a hurry to stop and clasp an outstretched hand and to say a word of greeting. What this contact has meant in their lives is cherished as one of their finest experiences.

On a visit to his own ward in Salt Lake City he said: "I love to attend Sunday School and to be in the presence of children; to listen to their singing and speaking in praise of the Redeemer. It is music to hear little children speak the name of Jesus. There come to me the words of the Savior, 'Suffer little children to come unto me, and forbid them not; for of such is the Kingdom of God.'" (Mark 10:14) On another occason he made this remark:

"The Gospel teaches that each individual is a child of our Father in Heaven. Each one is precious in his sight. You are baptized as individuals, not as a group, and the Father is interested in your salvation and in the happiness of each boy and girl in the whole world."

When students in a humanities class at Brigham Young University
were asked to prepare a theme on someone who had influenced their
appreciation of the arts, Kent Goodliffe chose to prepare this
sketch of President McKay as the one who had most influenced
him. The young artist seems to have captured the smile so typical
of President McKay, and of which a *Deseret News* editorial
said ". . . has stirred thousands into better lives and firmer characters."

286

His own grandchildren and great-grandchildren adored him and looked forward to every opportunity afforded them to be in his presence. Individual stories of their experiences, and those of other children, will probably never be written, but they are inscribed indelibly in their lives and characters.

During the summer of 1963, at the old home in Huntsville, President McKay was in the garden with other members of his family, when a young couple with two small daughters came through the garden gate and apologized for intruding, but explained that the children refused to pass without seeing the President. The father had the smaller one in his arms, and as President McKay put out his hand to her, she fairly leaped into his arms, and threw her own little arms around his neck as she confided, "I pray for you every night."

An interesting story is told by Mrs. Helen Spencer Williams, a granddaughter of President Brigham Young, and with her permission, the following is given as she wrote it:

Robin Williams, aged 13, had been asking to attend a general conference since she was nine. She wanted to actually see and hear President McKay. Her parents kept assuring her that she would have a much better view of him on television. Nevertheless she kept insisting that she wanted to see him in person and that she might even get a chance to shake his hand if she were there. "I live right here in the same city with him, but I've never really seen him or spoken to him, and if I don't go to conference maybe I never will."

As the fall conference of 1962 drew near she again importuned her father to take her to the Tabernacle on Sunday morning. He consented. She wanted to be there early enough to see President McKay arrive and to be assured of a seat near enough to the front so she could watch him and hear him.

Robin and her father arrived at the Temple Grounds before 6 a.m. The grounds and doorways of the Tabernacle were crowded with people all endeavoring to go inside. It was an exciting and wonderful moment for Robin—one she had long awaited. Now the time had come for her to see President McKay and attend her first general conference.

Soon a gentleman's voice was heard. "All those who are from foreign lands and who are attending conference for the first time may enter." Then, "All who are over 80, next all stake presidencies, all bishops—any who are in wheelchairs may go in, and you will find places reserved for you." Hundreds of people filed past Robin into the Tabernacle. At last he announced that there were no more seats available and those who remained would find places in the overflow meetings.

Disappointedly, Robin and her father went back to their car. As they drove toward home, Robin spoke, "Daddy, don't be upset, it was just as it should be—I'll have other chances to see President McKay and maybe those who were allowed in the Tabernacle ahead of us never will." So once again Robin watched President McKay on television, but it did not satisfy her longing and desire to see him in person or to be near him when he spoke.

Then there was little Dale Buehner, aged 7. From the time he was old enough to pray aloud, he had been asking his Heavenly Father to please let him meet President McKay. Dale was one of five children but the one who seemed to be deeply serious and spiritual. Again and again his expressed desires to his mother were answered by, "Dale, dear, President McKay is so busy he can't meet every little boy, but I'm sure that some day your chance will come—just be patient."

Then one night after he had said his prayers, he looked at his mother and said, "Mother, you know you are going to wait too long to take me to see President McKay, either he will die or I will, and we will never get to know each other. Please take me!"

She knew then that she must endeavor to have her little boy meet the prophet if it meant so much to him.

The stories about Robin and Dale were told to Miss Clare Middlemiss, President McKay's devoted secretary. When she told President McKay about the two children, he told her to make arrangements to have the children meet him at his office the following Monday morning at 7 a.m. Then the very day before the appointment there appeared in the paper a notice that Sister McKay had been seriously injured and that President

McKay had not left her bedside. Of course it would be impossible for him to keep the early appointment with Robin and Dale—so it seemed.

But, at 6:00 a.m. Miss Middlemiss called to say that President McKay had just telephoned her to say he would not disappoint the children, but would meet them at the appointed hour, 7:00 a.m. as he had promised.

Dale and his mother, Robin and her father were waiting with Miss Middlemiss when the President came into the office.

It was a dramatic and wonderful moment when the beloved, white-haired, handsome President appeared and greeted them with his sweet smile and friendly handshake.

They all went into his private office, where he had them sit while he talked with them. Then he showed them some of the precious gifts, documents, letters and pictures from persons all over the world. Articles from leaders of countries and industries, as well as remembrances from members of the Church from the far corners of the earth. He offered them candy and shared with them his laughter, his humor and his beautiful spirit. He had them sit in his chair. Then he took them by the hand and as he did so, he touched their hearts and their lives. He had taken time from the sick bed of his wife, from his magnitude of responsibilities to let little children come to him. Their dreams and hopes had been realized.

As Robin and her father rode home, they were very quiet. The father's eyes were filled with tears. Just as they neared home Robin said, "I've always thought of the men in the Bible and the Book of Mormon as Prophets—but not until today when President McKay took my hand in his did I realize that he, too, is a Prophet of God."

Dale and his mother rode home in silence. Then his mother asked, "Dale, what are you thinking about?" And he answered, "I'm just thinking how good I feel inside."

These two children cherish this experience. In talking with them they both express the feeling that this experience on that early Monday morning will never be forgotten and that they were privileged and blessed by being in the presence of the Prophet and the President of the Church.

President McKay kept his appointment with two little children under difficult circumstances. His sweetness, interest and spirit during their meeting brings understanding to the Savior's admonition: "Suffer the little children to come unto me, and forbid them not for of such is the Kingdom of Heaven."

They will ever be grateful to President McKay and to Clare Middlemiss for making their visit possible.

The V.I.P. Blair Strings, composed of 22 children, ages five to eleven years of age, performed for President and Sister McKay on December 19, 1969.

Chapter 29

Kindness to Animals

One of the characteristics that marked the life of President David O. McKay was his love of animals. From his early youth he loved and cared for a variety of pets, and throughout his life he maintained a particular fondness for horses.

One of his earliest pets was a large, black Newfoundland dog named "Toss." The dog was a favorite of all the family, and would trot along side any family member who invited him for a walk. For several years a trusted and loved housekeeper worked for the McKays. Her home was some distance away, and when she would go there in the evenings she would call Toss and the two would go side by side until she reached her mother's cottage. As she entered the home the faithful dog would lie down outside until she appeared for the return journey. Then, no matter how dark the night, she felt as safe as though she were accompanied by a police escort.

One evening young David O. went to the old rock schoolhouse for a rehearsal, and when it was over and the crowd came out, Toss appeared out of the darkness and was at his master's side for the trip home. One of the boys said tauntingly, "I suppose you think that dog would protect you if anyone attacked you!" To this he replied, "Do you want to test him?" There was a chorus of "Sure, let's see if he is any good!" The boy was told to attack as though he meant real harm, and as he did so, David O. called, "Toss!" and the dog jumped upon the intruder, instantly ready to protect his master. No one in the crowd ever doubted Toss again.

There was a soft mat on the south porch, in front of the dining room door, which was claimed by Toss as his particular resting place, and members of the family, instead of disturbing him, merely stepped over him when entering that room. One day a friend came to call and was being ushered in by some of the children who knew him well. As he neared the door he gave Toss a kick, which was resented by the dog as well as by the children. Toss expressed his resentment by showing his teeth and growling, and the man entered the house with one bound, and without the courtesy of knocking.

Almost a year later the same man returned, and as he turned the corner of the house, Toss jumped toward him, and if one of the boys had not been there, the friend would have fared badly. After the visit was over, mother said, "I wonder why Toss growled so at that man when he came; it is so unlike him to greet anyone in that way!"

David replied, "He had a perfect right to growl at him, because he was kicked by that man once."

Toss, the faithful watch-dog, lived as a beloved member of the family for many years, and there was deep mourning when he died of "causes incident to age."

The boys always had ponies, and they were expected to care for them personally, so they would never become the responsibility of the one whose duty it was to attend the work horses and the carriage team. It was sometimes a temptation to shirk this responsibility, especially when there was a swimming party or a baseball game on.

The boys knew, however, that unless "Mingo" and the "little gray mare" were kept clean, and properly fed and watered, there would be no riding when they were ready to join their friends in that sport. Their personal care and kindness won for them the love of their ponies.

When David and his brother, Thomas, asked if they might have pigeons, their request was granted, providing they would make houses for them, attach them to the gable of the large barn, and then take proper care of them. The boys of the neighborhood were interested in the preparations, and everyone was delighted when the first pair of pigeons was purchased and placed in the new house, which was made so attractive, with a well filled food box at the door that there was never a question about their remaining.

As the pigeons increased in numbers, new houses were made until the boys boasted of quite a large flock. Each one was an individual pet, and many of them were named. There were "Sandy," "Whitey," "Spot," "Brownie," and many others, all loved and counted daily as they came down to be fed with the chickens gathered on the grass in front of the granary.

One day a hawk flew over and caught one of the pets in his claws and flew off toward the meadow below the barn yard. David immediately jumped on his pony, and brandishing a long stick, soon overtook the hawk with the pigeon which was a heavy load for the attacker. Believing that if he kept the thief from settling in the willows which surrounded the open field, he could rescue his pet. He circled the meadow, shouting from the running pony, until the hawk finally dropped his prey. Unfortunately the pigeon was dead. He was brought back and given a proper burial, complete with headstone and flowers, with the children of the neighborhood as mourners.

When the boys asked if they might add rabbits to their growing number of pets, the same requirements were made by the parents, and acceded to by the children. This time, however, Father McKay added his skill to the building of the hutches, and when the first one was completed, a pair of pink-eyed bunnies was purchased. As the rabbits multiplied, more hutches were built, until there seemed to be white bunnies everywhere around the barn yard. When someone suggested that rabbits made delicious stew and pie, David was horrified. These pets were always well cared for, and the number was depleted only occasionally when a pair was given as a present to some of their friends.

One rainy day Bishop McKay returned from the Dry Hollow farm bringing a wet baby magpie that had fallen from its nest high up in a cottonwood tree. The tiny bird was wrapped in a flannel cloth and placed near the stove until it was perfectly dry, when it was fed and soon became quite at home with the children.

David made a cage out of a crate, tacking wire netting across the front, and making a slide door on the side through which food and water could be placed inside. He named this pet Jack, and became devoted to him.

One day a friend suggested, "You will have to split his tongue if you want to teach him to talk." David was shocked and replied, "I wouldn't think of hurting Jack that way if he never learned to talk."

Through kindness and much repetition, the bird learned to speak quite plainly, and became the wonder of the neighborhood. He was allowed out of the cage and felt free to go in and out of the house. He even ventured as far as the barnyard, always coming back to his cage in the evening.

On one of these excursions he was following David, when the wind closed the barn door on his leg, fracturing it. David immediately became surgeon, binding the limb with splints, and the bird hopped on one foot until the other healed. The leg was not quite straight, however, and later became a means of identification.

A number of wild magpies often lighted among the chickens and pigeons at feeding time and claimed their share of the grain that was scattered generously by the boys. At first Jack remained on the high board fence and watched these strangers, but his curiosity led him closer to their chattering, and soon he became quite friendly with them. David realized that his pet was making new friends, but felt secure in the thought that Jack always returned to his cage in the evening. As winter approached, the birds prepared to leave and to his chagrin, Jack left with them.

Early in the spring the magpies returned to share the food of their domestic friends, and David recognized his pet by the crooked leg. Excitedly he called, "Hello Jack," and the bird cocked his little head and replied, "Hello Jack." He flew away, however, when there was an attempt to catch him.

Jack was replaced by another baby bird, and the lonely cage became again the center of interest and love. The second Jack was allowed the freedom of the large lot surrounding the house, but was not encouraged to join the pigeons and chickens at the barn yard. He lived to be much older than his predecessor, and was a constant source of joy.

President McKay's love for horses was proverbial. The gray team, Kate and Puss, the spanking sorrels, Prince and Charlie, were more than farm animals—they were friends and were treated as such. He was always known as a fast rider

President David O. McKay on his favorite horse, "Sonny Boy."

and driver, but when the horses were returned to their stalls, they were always rubbed down, blanketed and fed properly, and in return for this consideration, they gave their best in responsive service.

During his entire life President McKay was never without horses. One of the most beloved was his horse "Sonny Boy," who gave many years of pleasure and delight to the President. He was often pictured with or on "Sonny Boy" and took excellent care of him, as he did with all his horses.

Typical of this care is an example related by the family. When it became difficult for President McKay to see that the colts were trained and broken, arrangements were made to take them to the best trainer available. When a young horse was being sent some distance, one of the President's sons asked, "Why send him so far when there is a good man this side of Centerville?"

President McKay replied promptly, "He uses the whip too freely and I don't want my horses mistreated. They can be trained with kindness much more effectively."

When his horses were in the large pasture and he entered the gate and called, they all came trotting up to him and stood perfectly still to be bridled or saddled. When his grandchildren were there they waited eagerly for their turns to ride on "Papa Dade's" prize horses.

Several years ago someone broke into the farm and stole the President's best saddles from the saddle house. One of these was a hand-carved Mexican saddle, and was prized very highly by President McKay. When the unfortunate incident became known, a group of stake presidents in Weber and Davis counties presented him with the best saddle available, so that he could still enjoy riding his horses while in Huntsville. Care was taken that this new saddle was kept in a safe place. Other saddles were later purchased to replace the ones that were stolen, and these were kept in the saddle house, but under lock and key. One day, during hot weather when members of the family were at the home in Huntsville, two of President McKay's sisters were out for a drive and decided to check on things at the farm. They found the door to the saddle house locked, but one of the windows open. They immediately corrected what they felt was a bit of carelessness, and went on their way with a feeling of satisfaction that another theft had been averted.

That afternoon President McKay drove up to keep an appointment at Huntsville, with barely enough time to return to Salt Lake City for a later engagement. Upon being told of the open window, he said, "I left that window open purposely because there is a bird's nest inside, and that is the only entrance the parent birds have to carry food to their babies. I think I shall just have time to run over."

When the sisters said they would correct the mistake, he insisted on doing it, saying, "I must pick up a halter that needs repairing, anyway." When he returned to the house after the two-mile drive, he said in his gracious way, "It was just as I expected—one little bird was outside trying to get in, and the mother was inside attempting to get out."

His kindness to everyone and to everything gave him a benign demeanor that was one of his great characteristics. It made him more like the One who "marks the sparrow's fall."

Chapter 30

Through the Years

The growth of The Church of Jesus Christ of Latter-day Saints was phenomenal during the years that David O. McKay served as its President. It came in every program and endeavor of the Church, and resulted in a friendly appreciation by the thinking people of the world.

This period was marked with an active program of temple construction, and eight temples were built or announced during his administration. More than 3,750 Church buildings were constructed throughout the world, including more than 2,000 ward and branch chapels. In addition to major building programs at Brigham Young University, 69 new school buildings were constructed, including elementary schools and high schools in many islands of the South Seas and in Central America, South America, and Mexico. The David O. McKay Hospital in Ogden, Utah, was completed, and construction was begun on the new Church Administration Building, which when it is completed in 1972 will become the tallest structure in the Mountain West.

The number of missions more than doubled, to a total

President David O. McKay and his beloved companion, Emma Ray Riggs McKay in a photograph taken on their 65th wedding anniversary, January 2, 1966.

of 88, and the full-time missionary force grew from about 2,000 to more than 12,000. Membership of the Church in 1951 was 1,111,000; in 1970 it has climbed to nearly three million. Today more than 175,000 students are enrolled in the seminary and institute programs, and enrollment of Brigham Young University has quadrupled—from 5,000 in 1951 to more than 20,000 in 1970.

Priesthood correlation was broadened under President McKay's direction, with the introduction of an organized program of family home evenings; new emphasis on home teaching; and the appointments of Regional Representatives of the Council of the Twelve.

During much of his career as a general authority, Miss Clare Middlemiss was his faithful secretary. In 1966 she prepared this appraisal of the work of President McKay since he became Church President in 1951:

> In gathering and preserving in scrap books and diaries a vast store of clippings, speeches, editorials, special letters, and notes, concerning the activities of President McKay, I have been profoundly impressed with the magnitude of the work accomplished, and the services rendered by him. These records show that he has had personal visits from more than 1,500 distinguished men and women from all over the world. Among these have been four presidents of the United States, Harry S Truman, Dwight D. Eisenhower, John F. Kennedy, and Lyndon B. Johnson. This is in addition to thousands of Church officials and laymen whom he has met.
>
> President McKay has delivered 1,443 major addresses since his appointment to the First Presidency of the Church. He has attended and spoken at hundreds of funerals. Numerous Church edifices, temples, seminary buildings, and civic structures have been dedicated by him.
>
> During this period, 1,000 or more couples have had the honor of being united in marriage by him in the House of the Lord. This does not include the thousands of unrecorded acts of kindness performed by him.
>
> Throughout all this unselfish service individual members

of the Church have not been neglected. Thousands have been recipients of his counsel, advice, and administrations. His understanding of the human heart and his incomparable tenderness, have drawn people close to him, and his deep interest and concern in their welfare have won for him the loyalty, love, and respect of many thousands of the members of the Church.

Since this volume is not the complete biography of President McKay, and includes only some of the highlights in the life of this great man, it seems proper to include a listing of some of the significant events in his life. Even this list is not complete, though it does include some eventful dates that have not been described in his book.

September 8, 1873, David O. McKay born in Huntsville, Weber County.

December 14, 1885, ordained a Deacon in the Aaronic Priesthood.

July 17, 1887, received his patriarchal blessing from Patriarch John Smith.

January 19, 1891, ordained a Teacher in the Aaronic Priesthood.

August 4, 1893, ordained a Priest in the Aaronic Priesthood.

September, 1894, entered the University of Utah.

June 9, 1897, graduated from the University of Utah, and delivered the class oration.

July, 1897, received a call to serve as a missionary in Great Britain.

December 4, 1898, appointed president of the Scottish Conference.

August, 1899, completed his mission and sailed home.

September 20, 1900, appointed second assistant in the Weber Stake Sunday School superintendency.

January 2, 1901, married Emma Ray Riggs in the Salt Lake Temple.

April 17, 1902, appointed principal of the Weber Stake
Academy.
April 8, 1906, sustained as a member of the Council of the
Twelve.
April 9, 1906, ordained an Apostle by President Joseph F.
Smith.
October 6, 1906, sustained as second assistant in the general
superintendency of the Deseret Sunday School Union.
April, 1909, appointed as first assistant in the general super-
intendency of the Deseret Sunday School Union.
November 27, 1918, appointed general superintendent of the
Deseret Sunday School Union.
May 9, 1919, appointed Commissioner of Education for the
Church.
December 4, 1920, departed for a world tour with Elder
Hugh J. Cannon.
July 2, 1921, appointed to the Board of Regents of the Uni-
versity of Utah.
June 22, 1922, awarded an honorary Master of Arts degree
from Brigham Young University.
September 14, 1922, appointed as president of the European
Mission by the First Presidency.
November 17, 1922, left Montreal, Canada, to preside over
the European Mission.
December 6, 1924, left England to return home after presiding
in the European Mission.
May 28, 1931, elected president of the Weber College Alumni
Association.
May 30, 1931, delivered the commencement address at Weber
College.
February 18, 1932, appointed chairman of the Utah Council
for Child Health and Protection after attending the
White House Conference on Child Welfare.

October 6, 1934, appointed as second counselor in the First Presidency to President Heber J. Grant.

October 31, 1934, released as general superintendent of the Deseret Sunday School Union.

June 10, 1935, delivered the baccalaureate sermon to graduates of the University of Utah.

1938-1947, chairman of the Utah Centennial Commission.

May 3, 1940, appointed a member of the Board of Trustees of the Utah State Agricultural College (now Utah State University).

October 19, 1940, laid the cornerstone of the Idaho Falls Temple.

August 17, 1941, dedicated the Oahu Stake Tabernacle in Hawaii.

1942, served as chairman of the Utah State Advisory Council of the American Red Cross.

May 21, 1945, sustained as second counselor to President George Albert Smith.

June 2, 1950, received an honorary Doctor of Laws degree from Utah State Agricultural College.

January 2, 1951, observed his golden wedding anniversary with Sister McKay at their home in Salt Lake City.

April 9, 1951, sustained as President of The Church of Jesus Christ of Latter-day Saints.

April 16, 1951, appointed president of the Board of Trustees of Brigham Young University.

April 16, 1951, appointed senior editor of *The Improvement Era*.

June 4, 1951, received an honorary Doctor of Humanities degree from Brigham Young University.

June 9, 1951, received an honorary Doctor of Letters degree from the University of Utah.

June 14, 1951, received an honorary Doctor of Letters degree from Temple University, Philadelphia, Pennsylvania.

October 14, 1951, appointed honorary chairman of the Boy Scouts of America relationship committee for the Church.

June 13, 1953, received the honorary Master M Man Award.

July 17, 1953, received the Silver Buffalo award from the Committee on Awards for distinguished service to the National Boy Scouts of America.

September 10, 1954, received honorary membership in the International College of Surgeons at Chicago, Illinois.

November 29, 1954, received the Cross of the Commander of the Royal Order of the Phoenix, a Greek award.

December 14, 1954, dedicated the David O. McKay Building on the Brigham Young University Campus.

November 20, 1955, received the Golden Medal of the Greek Archdiocese of North and South America, a Greek church Award.

January 20, 1956, received a Silver Beaver Award from the Great Salt Lake Council of the Boy Scouts of America.

May 15, 1956, given honorary membership in the Blue Key National Honor Fraternity.

July 29, 1957, given honorary membership in the National Council, Boy Scouts of America.

June 12, 1959, given All-Church YMMIA Trophy.

December 10, 1962, honored by the business and civic leaders of Salt Lake City.

February 22, 1964, received the "U" Blanket, University of Utah Athletic Award.

February 26, 1965, the first David O. McKay Honor Day was established in Ogden before an audience of three thousand people in the Tabernacle, honoring him as a world leader in education, freedom, and humanity.

June 5, 1965, he received an honorary Doctor of Humanities degree from Weber State College. This was the first year that Weber State had been authorized to award honorary degrees, and President McKay was the recipient of the first one to be awarded.

December 6, 1965, became a member of the Weber County Hall of Fame.

January 2, 1966, with Sister McKay, noted his sixty-fifth wedding anniversary.

April 22, 1966, participated in the groundbreaking services for the new David O. McKay Hospital in Ogden, Utah.

May 15, 1966, was honored by student leaders and faculty members of the University of Utah in a special tribute in the Tabernacle.

June, 1966, received the 1966 Freedom Award from Utah Young Americans for Freedom, "in grateful tribute to his life-long dedication to the ideal of freedom under God."

December 16, 1967, became the longest-lived general authority in this dispensation; previous holder of this distinction was Charles Penrose, who lived 93 years, three months, and eight days.

March 18, 1968, received the Exemplary Manhood Award from Brigham Young University, as the "man who has best exemplified manhood to this generation." March 19 was designated at BYU as David O. McKay Day.

September 8, 1968, observed his ninety-fifth birthday. A special program on his life, "Portrait of a Prophet," was broadcast simultaneously on KSL-TV and KSL-Radio.

November 5, 1968, equalled the record of the longest service as a general authority, held by Heber J. Grant: 62 years and 210 days.

December 3, 1968, received the "Distinguished American" award from the National Football Foundation and Hall of Fame.

May 8, 1969, was paid a courtesy visit by Spiro T. Agnew, Vice-President of the United States.

July 9, 1969, attended the dedicatory services for the new David O. McKay Hospital in Ogden, Utah.

July 24, 1969, became honorary president of the Royal Scots Pipe Band, and rode in his automobile in the Days of '47 Parade, with the band marching behind.

September 8, 1969, noted his ninety-sixth birthday, which was highlighted by the groundbreaking ceremony for the Ogden Temple.

December 6, 1969, marked the eighty-first anniversary of his first call to service in the Church. On December 6, 1888, at age 15, he was chosen as second counselor in the presidency of the deacon's quorum of the Huntsville Ward.

January 18, 1970, died in his Hotel Utah apartment of congestive heart failure. He was 96 years old.

January 22, 1970, was buried in the Salt Lake City Cemetery, following a funeral service in the Salt Lake Tabernacle.

This significant chronology of honors and accomplishment in the life of one man could not begin to measure his true greatness. His whole life was testimony of this.

In an essay on "Self Culture," William E. Channing says of greatness in men: "The greatest man is he who chooses the right with invincible resolution, who resists the sorest temptations from within and without, who bears the heaviest burdens cheerfully, who is calmest in the storms, and most fearless under menace and frowns, whose reliance on truth, virtue, and God is most unfaltering."

Bessie Stanley has said: "He has achieved success who has gained the respect of intelligent men, and the love of little children; who has filled his niche and accomplished his task; who has left the world better than he found it; who has never lacked appreciation of earth's beauties, or failed to express it; whose life has been an inspiration, and whose memory is a benediction."

Measured by any standard, President David O. McKay proved by his daily life and accomplishments that he achieved success, that he was one of the great men of his time, and a true and beloved Prophet of God.

Chapter 31

The Death of a Prophet

If ever a man of modern history left his world better for having lived in it, that man was David Oman McKay.

"Wherever he passed, men lifted their heads with more hope and courage. Wherever his voice was heard, there followed greater kindness among men, greater tolerance, greater love. Wherever his influence was felt, man and God became closer in purpose and action."

Thus did the *Deseret News* pay tribute to President David O. McKay in a special edition on January 19, 1970, the day following his death.

On January 18, 1970, the beloved prophet, seer, and revelator died peacefully at his Hotel Utah apartment of congestive heart failure. At his bedside were his sweetheart of 69 years, Emma Ray, and five of their six children.

As news spread around the world, hundreds of letters, telegrams, and other expressions of love and sympathy began arriving. Heads of nations and average citizens, Latter-day Saints and nonmembers alike, mourned the passing of a widely

As President McKay's funeral cortege begins to form
at the Church Office Building, long lines of mourners still
waiting to pay their respects extend around the block.

loved and respected leader. Special resolutions were passed
in the Senate of the United States, as well as state legislatures
and other governmental bodies. All united in expressing their
deepest feelings of sorrow at his passing, as well as in gratitude for the example, inspiration, strength, and influence of
his life.

Beginning Tuesday afternoon, January 20, and continuing through Thursday morning, January 22, President Mc-
Kay's body lay in state in the foyer of the Church Office
Building. The bronze casket was surrounded by huge banks
of beautiful floral tributes. Tens of thousands of mourners,

who included small children as well as elderly persons, civic leaders, and members of other faiths, came to pay their respects to the President of the Church. At times the line of mourners stretched three-deep completely around the block, despite occasional rain. Often, as the mourners reached the steps of the Church Office Building, the strains of "We Thank Thee, O God, for a Prophet" were heard, sung by young people who had, in many cases, never known another prophet in the Church.

On Thursday morning, January 22, the doors to the Church Office Building were closed while family members and general authorities paid their last respects. Then, at 11:30 a.m., the funeral procession, led by a police escort,

General authorities, special guests, and Tabernacle Choir stand as casket is placed in front of Tabernacle.

Sister McKay, surrounded by members of the McKay family, at the funeral.

moved slowly to Temple Square. The pallbearers—grandsons and great-grandsons of President McKay—followed the hearse. Behind them were members of the Council of the Twelve, who were honorary pallbearers.

In the Tabernacle, the funeral service at noon was conducted by Elder Hugh B. Brown, first counselor to President McKay. The invocation was offered by Elder Alvin R. Dyer, a counselor to President McKay. The Tabernacle Choir provided the music, which included three favorite hymns of the Prophet: "I Need Thee Every Hour," "Crossing the Bar," and "I Know That My Redeemer Lives."

President Joseph Fielding Smith, who had served in the First Presidency with President McKay and was to succeed

After funeral, cortege leaves Temple Square.

him as tenth President of the Church, paid the following tribute to the man with whom he had associated in the presiding councils of the Church for 60 years:

> He was a true servant of our Lord—one who walked uprightly before his Maker; one who loved his fellowmen; one who loved life and rejoiced in the privilege of service that was his; one who served with an eye single to the glory of God. . . .
>
> I thank God for the life and ministry of this great man. He was a soul set apart, a great spirit who came here to preside in Israel. He did his work well and has just returned clean and perfected to the realms of light and joyous reunion.
>
> If ever there was a man to whom these words of scriptural benediction might well be said, it was President McKay:

313

Family members gather around the gravesite, as President Hugh B. Brown conducts brief service.

"Come, ye blessed of my Father, inherit the kingdom prepared for you from the foundation of the world" (Matt. 25:34), for ye did all things well that were entrusted unto thy care.

President Brown, in addition to conducting the services, paid tribute to President McKay. He stated:

"Here and there, and now and then, God makes a giant among men." President McKay was a symbol of moral strength to the people of many nations. His life was an inspiration, his memory a benediction.

He was a man who was tall in character as well as physically. He stood out, head and shoulders, above the crowd—a measuring standard for manhood. He was known for his largeness of spirit and the grace with which he lived. . . .

314

When a great man dies, for years the light he leaves behind him lies on the paths of men. The love, the teachings, the life of President McKay have been an inspiration and a proud influence for good in the world.

President N. Eldon Tanner, second counselor in the First Presidency, told of personal experiences he had had with President McKay that had lifted his spirit and given him renewed faith. He summarized his feelings in these words:

> He has spent his whole life in the service of his Lord and Savior and of his fellowmen. It has been a signal honor, privilege, and blessing and a most rewarding experience for me to have been called by the prophet as one of his counselors, and for six glorious years to sit in council with him, to feel his great spirit, and to have been taught and inspired by the Lord's anointed. I have continually prayed and shall continue to pray and strive to be worthy of this rare and wonderful opportunity and blessing, which is beyond compare.

The concluding speaker was Elder Harold B. Lee, of the Council of the Twelve, who said:

> To you, his beloved family: You bear one of the greatest family names that has ever been among all the children of men on this earth. Teach your children and your children's children to the last generation to honor that name and never defile it, that the name of the McKay family might be perpetuated through all time.
>
> And to the Church: Cherish his memory, you Church members, by living in your youth, in your marriage, in your homes, as nearly to the perfection that he has demonstrated. He has been called home. New leadership will carry on, not to take his place—no one can take his place—but merely to fill the vacancy caused by his passing. If we look to the leadership that God will place and will follow thereafter as we have followed President McKay, all will be right with the world; and in the words of some, "stick with the old ship," the kingdom of God, and trust in Almighty God, and he will bring us safely through.

Elder Richard L. Evans of the Council of the Twelve offers prayer at the gravesite.

Following the benediction by Elder Ezra Taft Benson of the Council of the Twelve, the funeral cortege formed again and proceeded slowly up South Temple to the Salt Lake City Cemetery. There, in a peaceful hillside setting overlooking the Salt Lake Valley, Elder Richard L. Evans of the Council of the Twelve offered the prayer, and a double quartet from the Tabernacle Choir sang "Abide with Me." Then the body of President David O. McKay was laid to rest beside the grave of a son, Royle, who died in infancy.

How does one summarize the life of David O. McKay? Perhaps the words of the *Deseret News* editorial express the feelings of those who knew him well as well as those of the millions who did not know him personally but who felt his influence and radiance:

Like the end of a beautiful day or the close of a great symphony, the passing of President McKay leaves a quiet sadness. Not to see again his quick, boyish grin as he tells an anecdote straight from his Scottish ancestry; not to hear his warm, compelling counsel for love at home and integrity in dealing with one's fellowmen; not to hear his stirring testimony of the Lord Jesus Christ; not to feel with a burning surety that here is a living prophet of the living God—this loss is hard to bear.

President McKay spent his life in the aura of an inspiring influence. That influence was the word of God.

It shaped the lives of his ancestors. It filled his childhood home where goodly parents presided under its influence. It rested upon and sanctified his marriage. It helped him build and bless his own family. It ennobled his service during more than six decades as a General Authority. . . .

President McKay is gone in body, and we will feel the loss. But his influence remains; it will always remain, spreading constantly outward in both space and time, blessing and uplifting men whenever they seek the truth.

Postscript:

Emma Ray Riggs McKay, sweetheart and wife of David O. McKay for 69 years, passed away on Saturday, November 14, 1970, just ten months after her husband's death. Funeral services were conducted in the Assembly Hall on Temple Square by members of the First Presidency on Wednesday, November 18. She was buried in the hillside lot of the Salt Lake City Cemetery beside her beloved husband and companion.

Index

Index

Index

Manu Forti